THE **GREAT LEADER** AND THE **FIGHTER PILOT**

ALSO BY BLAINE HARDEN

Africa: Dispatches from a Fragile Continent

A River Lost: The Life and Death of the Columbia

Escape from Camp 14: One Man's Remarkable Odyssey from North Korea to Freedom in the West

THE GREAT LEADER

AND FIGHTER THE PILOT

THE TRUE STORY OF THE TYRANT WHO CREATED NORTH KOREA AND THE YOUNG LIEUTENANT WHO STOLE HIS WAY TO FREEDOM

Blaine Harden

VIKING

VIKING
Published by the Penguin Group
Penguin Group (USA) LLC
375 Hudson Street
New York, New York 10014

USA | Canada | UK | Ireland | Australia | New Zealand | India | South Africa | China
penguin.com
A Penguin Random House Company

First published by Viking Penguin, a member of Penguin Group (USA) LLC, 2015

Excerpt on page vii from *Freedom from Fear and Other Writings* by Aung San Suu Kyi (Penguin Books)

Photograph credits
Courtesy of Kenneth Rowe: Insert pages 1 (top, bottom), 3 (top, bottom), 4 (top), 11 (top), 12 (top, bottom), 13 (top), 14 (top, bottom); courtesy of the Korean Friendship Association (KFA), www.korea-dpr.com: pages 2 (top, bottom), 4 (bottom), 5 (top, bottom left and right), 15 (top); National Archives, photo no. 111-SC-306875: page 6 (top); National Archives, photo no. 26-G-3584: page 6 (bottom); U.S. Air Force Photo: pages 7 (top, bottom), 9 (top, bottom), 10 (top, bottom), 11 (bottom); © 2014, *The Washington Post*. Reprinted with permission: page 8 (top); *San Francisco Chronicle*/Polaris: page 8 (bottom); U.S. Department of State Photo—Herbert J. Meyle: page 13 (bottom); photo handout from the Korean Central News Agency/AFP Photo/KCNA via KNS: page 15 (bottom); photo by Blaine Harden: page 16

ISBN 978-0-670-01657-0
ISBN 978-0-525-42890-9 (Export Edition)

Printed in the United States of America
10 9 8 7 6 5 4 3 2 1

Set in Warnock Pro with Knockout
Design and Map Illustrations by Daniel Lagin

For Jessica, Lucinda, and Arno

Under the most crushing state machinery courage rises up.

Aung San Suu Kyi

CONTENTS

PART III
FLIGHT

THE **GREAT LEADER** AND THE **FIGHTER PILOT**

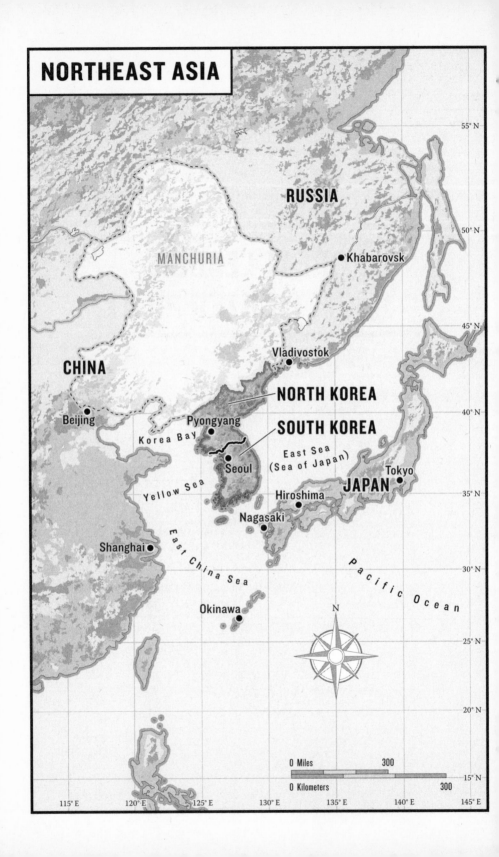

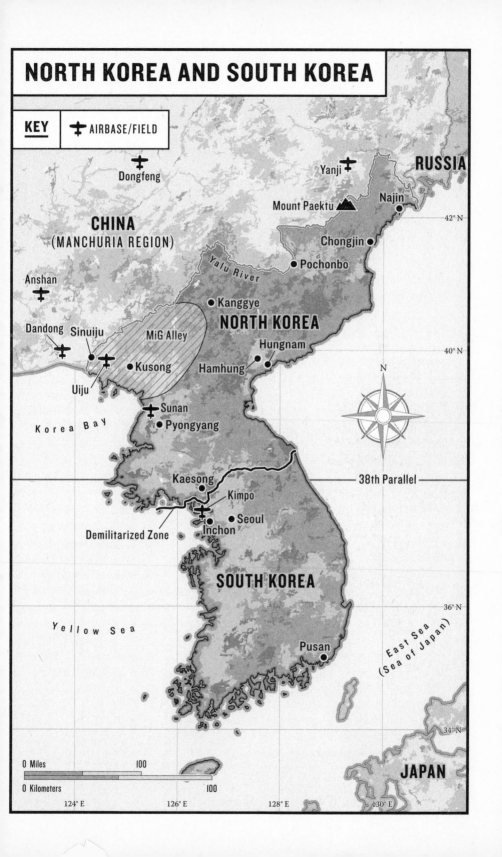

NORTH KOREA AND SOUTH KOREA

KEY ✈ AIRBASE/FIELD

✈ Dongfeng

✈ Yanji

RUSSIA

Mount Paektu ▲ Najin

CHINA
(MANCHURIA REGION)

42° N

Chongjin ●

Yalu River

● Pochonbo

Anshan
✈

● Kanggye

NORTH KOREA

Dandong Sinuiju
✈
✈

MiG Alley

Hungnam

40° N

● Kusong

Hamhung ●

Uiju

✈ Sunan

K o r e a   B a y

● Pyongyang

Kaesong ●

N

● Kimpo

38th Parallel

Demilitarized Zone

✈
Inchon ● ● Seoul

SOUTH KOREA

36° N

Y e l l o w   S e a

Pusan ●

E a s t   S e a
(S e a   o f   J a p a n)

34° N

0 Miles   100

0 Kilometers   100

124° E   126° E   128° E   130° E

JAPAN

INTRODUCTION
Players and Game

I

The man who would become the Great Leader stood on an indoor mountain of chemical fertilizer. Snow-white, stone hard, and two stories high,
the mound of ammonium sulfate was eye candy for the masses, a symbol
of the good life on offer from Comrade Kim Il Sung. Without fertilizer,
people in North Korea go hungry, and some starve. It is true now, and it
was true on February 22, 1948, when Kim had men cut the fertilizer flat
on top, rig up a sound system, and conscript an audience. Three rings of
soldiers, each armed with a Soviet-made submachine gun, protected the
man atop the huge pile of fertilizer.

The stage was socialist realism writ large, as straightforward as it was
brutal: Support Kim Il Sung and eat. Challenge him, and his men will
sort you out, using guns and muscle from the Soviet Union.

Kim was thirty-five years old that day, but he looked younger, with
smooth cheeks, short black hair, and a snug-fitting Mao suit. He had been
back on the Korean Peninsula for just two and a half years, having spent
much of his life fighting the Japanese in Northeast China. He had not yet
purged, jailed, exiled, or executed all his political rivals. It would be

another year before he had the gall to call himself the Great Leader and another decade before he would package himself as "the sun of mankind and the greatest man who has ever appeared in the world."

But he was getting there. His control of the police and the army was absolute. State-owned newspapers and radio applauded his every move. His paunch was expanding with his power.

As Moscow's chosen one—he had caught the eye of advisers close to Premier Joseph Stalin—Kim was rushing to rebuild and revolutionize a society traumatized by four decades of Japanese colonial domination. Following a Soviet script, factories were nationalized and labor unions created. The eight-hour workday became law. A mass literacy campaign taught millions of subsistence farmers and their families to read. New laws limited child labor and guaranteed women equal pay for equal work. Kim's government seized and redistributed farmland from wealthy landlords.

Peasant farmers liked what they saw and grew more food. In cities, the poor and the young also seemed to be buying what Kim was selling. But the wealthy, the landed, and the well educated were frightened. About two million of them fled south, where, in a similarly new nation called South Korea, bullying politicians were preaching capitalism while being advised, armed, and bankrolled by the United States.

The Americans and the Soviets divided the Korean Peninsula in the anxious final days of World War II. On August 11, 1945, two American colonels working after midnight in Washington used a small National Geographic map to draw an arbitrary line across the peninsula. It tracked the thirty-eighth parallel, a border with no connection to Korea's history, politics, or geographic features. The east-west line gave two-thirds of the peninsula's population to South Korea, along with most of the arable land. President Harry S. Truman believed it was a good solution. Surprisingly, so did Stalin, and the deal was done. In theory, over the next five years, the wartime allies would work on their respective sides of the border to reunite Korea's thirty million people. Unification would supposedly occur after they moved beyond the hysteria of war and developed democratic institutions.

But they did not calm down, and democracy was stillborn. The leaders who emerged, Kim in the North and Syngman Rhee in the South, were aggressive, egocentric nationalists. Each wanted to reunite Korea on his own uncompromising terms. Each wanted to rule it all, with weapons, money, and ideological window dressing from his superpower patron.

Because of the mass exodus from the North, there was far more social cohesion and political stability in Kim's realm than in Rhee's, where striking workers and farmers clashed constantly with American-armed police. An American intelligence report concluded, "Younger people throughout North Korea, especially between the ages of fifteen and twenty-one, are beginning to believe in the Communist government."

To build on that belief, Kim traveled to rice farms and teachers' colleges, irrigation projects and dance schools. Most often, he visited factories, where he charmed workers, listened to local complaints, and gave "on-the-spot guidance" as state media took his picture.

That is what he was doing on the fertilizer mountain: sweet-talking, inspiring, and intimidating a crowd of ten thousand cheering supporters, most of them young. His speech was the main event for his visit to Hungnam, an industrial city on North Korea's east coast, where the Japanese had built several modern factories, including Chosen Nitrogenous Fertilizers, the largest fertilizer works in the Far East. Soviet soldiers had liberated the place in the late summer of 1945 as the defeated Japanese scurried away. Kim's government nationalized it and repaired machinery the Japanese had tried to destroy. Fertilizer was brought back into production—glorious news in a mountainous nation of subsistence farmers, tired soil, and chronic food shortages.

"Our workers are now mass-producing fertilizer essential for the peasants," Kim said as he began his speech. Besides fertilizer, he said, the "extremely creative enthusiasm" of Korean technicians was increasing pig-iron production and repairing hydroelectric dams. "All this proves that we can build a prosperous, independent, and sovereign state by ourselves."

But a "happy society" required much more. Kim said a "genuine people's government" must destroy the "enslavement policies" of the

"American imperialists and their stooges" and take control of the entire Korean Peninsula. He was hinting, not very subtly, at a military invasion of the South, which he was already planning.

On a secret trip to Moscow just before he launched that invasion, Kim assured Stalin that Koreans in the South would joyfully support a Communist invasion and the Americans would slink away in fear.

"The Americans," he said, "will not risk a big war."

II

No Kum Sok was there that day.

He was sixteen years old and a student at Hungnam First High School, which had closed at midday in honor of Kim's visit, as had the city's factories. Ordered by teachers and foremen, students and workers queued up outside the fertilizer plant, where soldiers frisked them for guns and explosives. Two years earlier, someone at a rally had tossed a hand grenade at Kim. Thanks to a Soviet minder who grabbed it out of midair (and was severely wounded), Kim was not hurt. Since then, though, security had tightened.

After soldiers searched him, No entered a cavernous warehouse more than three stories high and longer than three football fields. Afternoon light drizzled down through greasy skylights. With four classmates, No climbed a ladder to a steel balcony. He watched from there as Kim—surrounded by attendants who carried his photograph and led the crowd in chants about his genius—marched into the warehouse and climbed the mound of fertilizer.

Kim radiated a raw animal magnetism and had a broad fatherly smile. The boy had never seen or heard anyone like him. The leader's voice was strong, his language plain and powerful. To No, Kim seemed somehow larger than other human beings, although photographs and contemporary descriptions show that he was not all that large, about five feet seven inches. Workers in the factory were spellbound as Kim praised them for being the "prime movers of modern society." No hung on every word.

Kim's rise to power had changed the very words the boy could speak, read, and write. When Japan ruled the peninsula, the Korean language was banned; everyone was supposed to speak Japanese. It was the only language No could fluently read and write. After Kim and the Soviets took over, Japanese was banned; speaking it was seditious. Russian replaced English as a foreign language in middle school. Baseball, the game No's father had played and loved, was condemned as a decadent waste of time. A new law banned any meeting of more than five persons without official permission. A teacher told No's class that freedom of religion would, of course, be protected under Kim's rule. But the teacher also said there would be state-enforced limits: devout Christians, if they behaved like "superstitious fools," would not be allowed to hold jobs in the military or in the professions. The boy, whose churchgoing father had attended a missionary school, got the message. He stopped going to church. He also stopped listening to the Voice of America on the radio, fearing what he might learn and inadvertently say to teachers and class-mates.

The rise of Kim Il Sung delighted several of No's relatives. His paternal grandfather called him a "genius." Yoo Ki Un, his maternal uncle, decorated the living room and bedrooms of his Hungnam home with photographs of Kim and Stalin. Uncle Yoo, who worked as a supervi-sor in a machine-assembly plant, tolerated no criticism of his leader.

To keep the peace with Uncle Yoo, to prevent his school friends from snitching on him, and to give himself a future in the new North Korea, No decided to pretend to be a "No. 1 Communist." He began his act soon after seeing Kim's speech, and it would save his life.

He lied on his examination for admission to the North Korean Naval Academy. In answer to questions about his family background, he wrote that his recently dead father had been a socialist-leaning laborer who hated the Japanese and loved the Great Leader. The one truth in that statement was that his father was recently dead.

No's father had been a successful manager for a Japanese industrial conglomerate. The Noguchi Corporation had built nearly all the big fac-tories in Hungnam, including the one where Kim delivered his speech.

Thanks to his father's career with Noguchi, No grew up rich, as measured by Korean standards. His mother, Veronica, who grew up in a well-to-do Catholic family, owned a stylish fur coat. In the heat of the North Korean summer, the family traveled to a summer cottage in the mountains. Their soy sauce was top-drawer, Kikkoman, imported from Japan.

III

The Great Leader was staggeringly wrong about the Korean War. South Koreans never supported his invading army, and the United States did not slink away. Kim's invasion triggered a hugely destructive war with no victory, easy or otherwise, for any country involved.

Rival armies from North and South Korea, from China, and from a United Nations force dominated by the United States ranged back and forth across the Korean Peninsula for about a year before settling into a blood-soaked stalemate that lasted two more years. By the end, about 1.2 million soldiers had been killed, including more than 36,000 Americans. Territory was neither gained nor lost. There is still no official peace, only an armistice. While there were no winners, the war's biggest losers were probably the people who lived in North Korea when it began.

In an air campaign that the American public never paid much attention to, the U.S. Air Force massively and continuously bombed North Korea for three years, turning nearly every city, town, and village in the Pennsylvania-sized country into rubble.

"We were bombing with conventional weapons everything that moved in North Korea, every brick standing on top of another," said Dean Rusk, a key supporter of American involvement in the Korean War and later a secretary of state during the Vietnam War. A Soviet postwar study of American bomb damage in the North found that 85 percent of all structures in the country were destroyed. The air force ran out of targets to blow up and burn. While there are no numbers from the North Korean government for civilians killed, the official population of the country declined during the war by 1,311,000, or 14 percent. General Curtis LeMay, head of the Strategic Air Command during the Korean War, estimated the percentage of civilian deaths to be even higher. "Over a period of three years or so, we killed off—what—twenty percent of the population [1.9 million people]," he said.

LeMay urged his bosses, at the start of the war, to force an immediate surrender by using massive bombing to kill civilians quickly and in large numbers. But politicians in Washington found that to be "too horrible," LeMay said, so they used massive bombing to kill civilians slowly and in large numbers.

Kim's control of North Korea survived the destruction. He made himself the center—the fatherly leader of a revolutionary family—around which a traumatized society could unify, rebuild, and find direction.

Being wrong never seemed to hurt the Great Leader. When events contradicted his promises or challenged his policies, he invented a new reality and forced his people to accept it. In North Korea's version of history, war began when South Korea and the United States invaded the North. It ended with a heroic North Korean victory orchestrated by his brilliant generalship. The pivotal roles played in the war by the Soviet Union, which armed the North, and by China, which fought the Americans to a draw on the ground and saved Kim from his ineptitude as a military commander, were airbrushed away.

To make his fictions credible at home, Kim isolated North Korea from the outside world. It became a prison state, with the Great Leader as warden. He decided what inmates could know, where they could live, if they could travel. Hundreds of thousands of security agents spied on everyone, rewarding citizens when they informed on one another. People were sorted geographically based on his perception of their loyalty. Those judged to be "wrong thinkers" were sent to labor camps in the remote mountains, where hundreds of thousands of prisoners and their family members died. After more than half a century, these camps are still going strong. A United Nations commission of inquiry has found that guards in the camps commit "unspeakable atrocities" that "resemble the horrors" of Nazi Germany and constitute crimes against humanity.

By keeping North Koreans in a cage for half a century and feeding them lies, Kim succeeded in convincing them that he was indeed a wonderful human being—and that *his* No. 1 enemy, the United States, would forever be *their* enemy. Although he died of natural causes in 1994, Kim lives on among his people as their Eternal President.

For outsiders struggling to understand contemporary North Korea, Kim's pivotal importance also lives on. His rise to absolute power is the essential story that explains the government's belligerence, paranoia, and sustained mistreatment of its own people. The feudal, caste-bound social system that he invented is still in place.

Before dying, the Great Leader tried to make sure his creation would never die—and that his bloodline would always rule. He set up a Stalinist monarchy that crowned his eldest son, Kim Jong Il, as leader. When Kim Jong Il died in 2011, power passed to his third son, Kim Jong Un, who was just twenty-eight when he took command.

For all their fakery and falsified history, three generations of dictators named Kim have found—and continue to find—legitimacy from a true and ghastly story of the Korean War: the U.S. Air Force's bombing and napalming of the North. It was a propaganda gift to the Kim family that keeps on giving.

"[Our people] have strong anti-U.S. sentiments because they suffered great damage at the hands of the U.S. imperialists during the war," Kim Il Sung told American journalists in 1972. "Since the situation is tense, we cannot but continue stepping up preparations for war. We make no secret of this. Who can guarantee that the U.S. imperialists will not attack this country again? What is most important in our preparations is to educate all the people to hate U.S. imperialism."

Under Kim's son and grandson, that hatred has been reinforced daily, as the government works hard to keep the old war terrifyingly fresh. State media constantly remind North Koreans that their parents and grandparents were incinerated and dismembered by Americans. Schoolchildren are still trained to bayonet dummies of American soldiers. State media still lie about who invaded whom during the Korean War. Sixty years after the war ended, hundreds of thousands of North Koreans gathered in Pyongyang's May Day Stadium to celebrate their "victory." Outside the stadium on the day of the celebration, a book was on sale, titled *The U.S. Imperialists Started the Korean War.*

"It may seem strange to Americans when we hear that North Koreans are worried about an attack from the United States, but from their point of view it is not strange at all," said Kathryn Weathersby, a Korean War scholar. "It is still the 1950s in North Korea and the conflict with South Korea and the United States is still going on. People in the North feel backed into a corner and threatened. It is, of course, very useful for the Kim family to keep them afraid."

The U.S. bombing narrative—together with semi-fictional news reports about what the imperialists are up to now—has given the Kim dynasty what it desperately needs: justification for spending nearly all its resources on nuclear weapons, long-range ballistic missiles, and a huge military that conscripts every young North Korean.

As important, the perceived persistence of the American threat—and the Kim family's sacred duty to fight against it—is an all-purpose excuse for the country's long slide into isolation, poverty, and hunger. The family's argument goes like this: Sure, it's miserable living in North Korea, but don't blame us. Imagine how much worse it would be if we weren't protecting you from the American bastards. Never forget, their bombs killed Grandma.

IV

No Kum Sok carefully researched his role as a true believer in Communism. He convinced an instructor at the naval academy that he had the right ideological stuff to fight the Americans in the air. Soon after he joined the North Korean air force, he discovered he was better at flying than he was at regurgitating Communist platitudes. He certainly liked it more.

At nineteen, he became the youngest jet fighter pilot on either side of the Korean War. He flew more than a hundred combat missions in a Soviet-made MiG-15, a formidable killing machine for its time. On a remote runway during the war, he personally showed off one of these fighter jets to the Great Leader and his young son Kim Jong Il. As they inspected the aircraft, No gave serious thought to assassinating the elder Kim but never mustered the courage to pull his service pistol out of its holster.

Throughout the Korean War, MiGs tormented and shot down American bombers. They forced the Americans to bomb under cover of night. In thousands of encounters along the border between North Korea and China, MiGs faced off against American warplanes in the world's first all-jet dogfights. The U.S. Far East Command was so obsessed with MiGs that it offered a $100,000 reward (about $900,000 today) to the first enemy pilot who delivered one to an American air base.

In the cockpit of his MiG, No dressed like a World War I flying ace. He wore a leather flying jacket, leather gloves, puffy blue cotton pants, and tall leather riding boots. His flight helmet predated the jet age by at least three decades. It was made of leather and looked not unlike the one Snoopy wore in the *Peanuts* comic strip.

No's pretend persona as a Communist fanatic was sorely tested in jet-to-jet combat. He tried to seem gung ho in the eyes of his fellow pilots, yet he avoided close encounters with American fighter pilots. He quickly learned that they had better flying skills—and that they were feverishly competing with one another to kill pilots like him.

Back on the ground, No compensated for his caution in the sky by ramping up his Red fanaticism. He volunteered to give dramatic readings of Kim Il Sung's speeches. When North Korean pilots gathered for meetings of self-criticism, he denounced them for not showing enough love to the glorious leader. Having known pilots who were executed for perceived wrong thinking, he worried that someone would see through his act and order him shot.

No's performance ended on a sunny September morning in 1953. He climbed into a MiG-15 for what was supposed to be a routine combat-readiness mission.

He knew nothing of the much-publicized reward that the U.S. military had promised to any pilot who delivered a combat-ready

MiG. Nor could he have known that in Washington the new American president, Dwight D. Eisenhower, disapproved of paying cash for an enemy airplane. Ike viewed it as a bribe, beneath the dignity of the United States. He did not want a stolen MiG and did not want to pay taxpayer money to a Commie turncoat.

As he took off that morning, No did know that Kim Il Sung had created a new law authorizing his government to execute the family and friends of defectors.

North Korean ground control became suspicious when the MiG did not return on time. An impatient voice squawked over No's headphones, using coded language to ask, Where the hell are you?

He did not reply.

PART I

GUERRILLA AND RICH BOY

CHAPTER I

Beginnings

I

Kim Il Sung led a guerrilla raid on the night of June 4, 1937, that, in his words, "heralded the dawn of the liberation of Korea."

The attack on Pochonbo, a speck of a town on the Korean border, did nothing of the sort. It was a strategically insignificant pinprick. But it mightily annoyed the Japanese. Over the next three years, they crushed Kim's insurgency. By the end of 1940, his guerrillas were dead, in prison, or holed up in the Soviet Union.

Pochonbo, though, was a fine piece of personal branding. The Japanese elevated Kim Il Sung to their list of most wanted Red bandits. International newspapers reported the raid and his gallant leadership. Thanks to Pochonbo and a handful of other guerrilla strikes that stung the Japanese in the late 1930s, Kim became a household name among millions of Koreans who seethed under their Japanese colonial masters. To an ill-educated peasantry hungry for heroes, he became a legend. Stories spread about his wizardry: he fashioned bombs out of pinecones, walked across rivers on leaves, and could make himself invisible.

Kim treasured Pochonbo as his finest military moment. He and about two hundred partisans crossed the Yalu River on rafts from Manchuria, as northeastern China was then called, and sneaked into the Korean village.

"At 10 p.m. sharp, I raised my pistol high and pulled the trigger. Everything that I had ever wanted to say to my fellow countrymen back in the homeland for over ten years was packed into that one shot reverberating through the street that night. The gunshot, as our poets described, was both a greeting to our motherland and a challenge to the Japanese imperialist robbers whom we were about to punish."

The punishment that followed was real but limited. A post office, a police station, and a few other buildings were burned. A handful of Japanese policemen were killed or wounded. Kim and his men rounded up about ninety new guerrilla recruits and fled that night across the river to a hideout in Manchuria.

Before they left, Kim wrote, admiring townsfolk asked him to give a speech.

> Looking round the crowd, I found their eyes, as bright as stars, all focused on me.
>
> Taking off my cap and waving my uplifted arm, I made a speech stressing the idea of sure victory and resistance against Japan. I concluded with the words: "Brothers and sisters, let us meet again on the day of national liberation!"
>
> When I left the square in front of [the town hall], which was a mass of flames, my heart felt heavy and full of pain, as if pierced with a knife. We were all leaving a part of ourselves behind in the small border town as we marched away, and the hearts of those left behind wailed silently as they watched us go.

The legend of Kim Il Sung is part Robin Hood, part Harry Potter, and partly true. For many years, Kim's political adversaries—including South Korea and the United States—made little effort to sort out fact from fiction. A rumor spread in North and South Korea that the real Kim Il Sung was killed in Manchuria sometime after the Pochonbo raid and, with the assistance of the Soviet Union, was replaced by a much younger guerrilla leader. The fake Kim, rumor had it, was a Soviet stooge who became the Great Leader. A confidential American intelligence biography stated flatly in 1952 that Kim was an "imposter."

As rumors go, this one had extraordinary staying power. It gained credence because few Koreans knew what Kim looked like or that he was so young, just twenty-five when he led the raid on Pochonbo. Adding to the confusion, he changed his name, taking the nom de guerre Kim Il Sung (meaning "become the sun"), which other partisan fighters in Manchuria had used. The fake-Kim story was especially appealing to anti-Communists in South Korea, where for years it was a propaganda staple that undermined the legitimacy of North Korea.

The rumor also persisted because of Kim's character. He was a shameless self-promoter. All his life, he exaggerated his achievements to the point of absurdity. A key to understanding Kim is "his enormous self-regard," writes Bradley K. Martin, one of his biographers. "[He] developed very early a preference for the company of people who acknowledged him as a genius, hero, and great man."

The speech Kim claims to have delivered in Pochonbo is a case in point. As the village burned and his men killed and looted, did Kim really take time for grandiloquence in front of starstruck peasants? One of his longtime partisan comrades in Manchuria said the Pochonbo speech was fabricated, self-serving piffle: "Here he was busy running away. What type of mass speech could he give?"

Narcissism and nonsense notwithstanding, Kim Il Sung was not an impostor. Photographs and government records, along with Korean, Chinese, and Russian eyewitnesses, verify that the young guerrilla leader who led the raid on Pochonbo was the same young man (albeit slightly older and better nourished) who rose to power in North Korea.

He was born Kim Song Ju in a village near Pyongyang in 1912. His father was a teacher and practitioner of herbal medicine who was more educated and less poor than most Koreans of that time and place. His father attended Sungsil Middle School in Pyongyang, which was founded and run by American Presbyterian missionaries. The city then had the fastest-growing Christian community in East Asia and was sometimes described as the Jerusalem of the East. Kim's mother came from an educated, Christian family. In his memoirs, Kim acknowledges that both his parents attended church regularly, taking him and his two younger brothers along. His father taught him to play a pump organ in church.

But it was great-power maneuvering, not religion or missionary teaching, that shaped Kim's world, pushing him and his family into exile in Manchuria and transforming him, while still in middle school, into a Communist guerrilla leader who spoke excellent Chinese and was eager to fight Japan.

Imperial Japan established complete control of the Korean Peninsula in 1905, after defeating Russian naval forces and accepting a peace proposed by President Theodore Roosevelt, who won a Nobel Peace Prize for his trouble. The backstory of that deal was less than noble. It was a trade-off between rising colonial powers in Asia: Japan agreed not to interfere with America's occupation and exploitation of the Philippines, and the United States, despite a late-nineteenth-century treaty of "amity and commerce" with Korea, quietly accepted Japanese dominion over the Korean Peninsula.

In 1910, two years before Kim was born, Japan formally annexed Korea and began to force Koreans to accept Japanese culture as their own. This pushed hundreds of thousands of Koreans into Manchuria, which for a time was slightly less oppressed by the Japanese. In some parts of eastern Manchuria, Koreans outnumbered Chinese four to one. Kim's family moved there in 1920, when he was seven. That same year Japan sent troops to eastern Manchuria to root out Korean nationalist fighters. The Japanese killed about thirty-six hundred of them but in the process enraged the half million Koreans who had settled there. Manchuria became a fertile recruiting ground for the Chinese Communist Party.

Kim was fourteen when his father died. Three years later, he was expelled from middle school and sent to jail for nine months for joining a Communist youth group. After a long cold winter behind bars, he changed his name to Kim Il Sung and never returned to school. He had been radicalized. When Japan launched an all-out military conquest of

Manchuria in 1931, he joined the Moscow-backed Chinese Communist Party.

This is when his transcendent genius as a revolutionary theorist and military leader kicked in, according to his memoirs and the official history of North Korea. He created the Korean People's Army, taught Marxism to Korean children, and seized supreme command of an anti-Japanese war based in eastern Manchuria. "I believed that revolution in my country would emerge victorious only when it was undertaken on our own responsibility and by the efforts of our own people, and all the problems arising in the revolution must be solved independently and creatively," Kim wrote in his memoirs.

Yet it was all fiction. There never was a Korean People's Army in Manchuria. As a child expelled from middle school, Kim had not read Marx (which was unavailable to him in Chinese or Korean), and he almost certainly did not understand Marxism well enough to teach it to anyone. He fought the Japanese in Manchuria as a member of a Chinese insurgency. He was almost always under Chinese command. There was no separate group of Korean Communist partisans for him to join. Kim did not work independently to foment revolution.

The untruths were the work of Kim Il Sung and his legion of hagiographers, blowing self-serving smoke back through time. A vast tapestry of these state-sanctioned lies and distortions has obscured and diminished Kim's real achievements, according to his most respected biographer, the historian Dae-Sook Suh, whose careful sifting of evidence found that Kim's military exploits in Manchuria were impressive, particularly for someone so young.

"It is his persistence and obstinate will, characteristic of many successful revolutionaries, that deserve recognition," Suh writes. "What is most damaging to his record is his exaggerated claims."

II

In 1937, while Kim Il Sung was killing Japanese policemen and becoming a legend, No Kum Sok was a chubby-cheeked five-year-old riding a tricycle imported from Japan. A photograph taken that year shows him sitting on the tricycle wearing a thick wool coat with shiny buttons, a Japanese-style cap, short pants, kneesocks, and white shoes.

He was "upper-class," especially when compared with most Koreans living under the thumb of imperial Japan. Decades of colonial rule had transformed the peninsula into a well-run, rapidly industrializing, but profoundly inequitable police state. Four out of five Koreans held menial and unskilled jobs, mostly on tenant farms. Food production increased sharply in Korea under colonial occupation, but the availability of food in local markets did not. Most of it was shipped to Japan. The daily lives of twenty-four million Koreans were dominated by fewer than a million Japanese settlers, nearly all of whom made a comfortable living from white-collar jobs, managing factories, and running the colonial government. Most Japanese lived in well-lit urban neighborhoods. They had electricity, gas, drinkable tap water, and underground sewers; most Koreans had none of these services. In their homes, Japanese women relied on poorly paid Korean servants to clean and cook. On buses, the Japanese forced Koreans to give up their seats and routinely shouted racist insults at them in shops.

Japan tightened its colonial vise even more in 1937 as it went to war in southern China and began to milk its empire for raw materials, soldiers, prostitutes, and slave labor. The Japanese moved with particular ferocity in Korea, squeezing the national identity out of its subjects and trying to replace it with a "profound gratitude for the limitless benevolence of our Emperor." Shifting into what historians have characterized as "colonial totalitarianism," Japan attempted to "blot out an entire culture."

In the run-up to World War II, Koreans were forced to give up their language, their literature, their religious shrines, even their names. Children were punished if caught speaking Korean at school. As part of their "imperialization," hundreds of thousands of Korean men were conscripted as slave labor, and thousands of others were forced to "volunteer" to fight in Japan's overstretched military. Tens of thousands of Korean women were compelled to work as "comfort girls," servicing the sexual needs of Japan's military.

Along with cultural extermination, Japan's colonial policies in Korea insisted on growth and profits—for Japanese investors. To that end, imperial Japan exported heavy industry and state-of-the-art infrastructure to the peninsula, encouraging Japanese conglomerates to take advantage of cheap land, abundant mineral resources, and eager-to-please colonial officials. They built steel mills, chemical factories, fertilizer plants, and several large hydroelectric dams. To connect their plants to ports and to one another, the companies built the most developed network of railroads in Asia outside Japan. As a result, Korea entered the 1940s with the best-managed network of railways, roads, and ports in the developing world.

No Kum Sok was chubby because of his father's managerial job with the Noguchi Corporation. The Japanese conglomerate had built most of Korea's hydroelectric and chemical plants and linked them by rail.

The company was created and run by Jun Noguchi, a chemical engineer turned mogul. He was known as the "Entrepreneurial King of the Peninsula," and one of his admirers wrote that while "modern America was created by Columbus's discovery . . . modern Korea was created by Noguchi." His extraordinary success in Korea, however, owed as much to colonial manipulation as to capitalist acumen. He used the colonial government to obtain development rights to Korea's major rivers, where he built hydroelectric dams that powered his chemical plants. By 1942, Noguchi's company controlled a quarter of all the capital invested in Korea.

As much as Japanese companies discriminated against Koreans, they also needed local managers who could keep the trains of empire running on time. No's father, No Zae Hiub, did exactly that, managing rail lines that delivered construction materials to hydro plants. He found the job through a relative of his young wife, but he qualified for it because he had disciplined himself to have all the skills the Japanese wanted in a Korean.

No Zae Hiub was born in 1904, the year Japanese gunboats chased Russian ships from Korean ports. He came of age as colonial control tightened, winning awards at school for penmanship and calligraphy, skills highly valued in Japan. Alone among five brothers and two sisters in a poor family, he graduated from a middle school run by foreign missionaries. The Youngsang Middle School was founded by Presbyterians from Canada and was similar to the missionary school in Pyongyang that Kim Il Sung's father attended.

His teachers and his books made No Zae Hiub pro-Japanese and pro-American. So did baseball. He was the standout pitcher at middle school and, after going to work for Noguchi, played into his thirties as an all-star pitcher for a city league team. In a photograph, No Kum Sok, age three and wearing a pith helmet, sits on a blanket with his father, who is wearing his city league uniform and cap.

An American missionary introduced baseball to Korea, but it was Japan that rammed the game down Korea's throat. Baseball blossomed in Korean schools in the 1930s and 1940s as courses in Korean history, language, and literature disappeared. The highly structured, drill-focused Japanese way of playing baseball weaned young people from Korean traditions and prepared them for a regimented adult life under tyrannical colonial coaching.

No Zae Hiub embraced baseball and accepted Japanese rule as an inescapable fact of life. He bought his son a baseball glove and taught him to speak Japanese. In their house, he required No Kum Sok to speak Japanese a third of the time. If the boy mastered the language and excelled at school, his father told him, he could attend a top private university in Tokyo and become "a real Japanese."

The Noguchi Corporation treated No Kum Sok's father well and transferred him often. The boy lived in ten cities and towns throughout northern Korea before the age of seventeen. The company typically housed the family in a four-room bungalow with free electricity and easy access to subsidized luxuries in the company store. As an only child (an older sister died soon after his birth), No always had his own room, and his father made certain he had a desk for his studies, a radio, and a tall bookcase. The boy grew up with treats and possessions other Korean kids could only dream about—walnuts and colored pencils, toy airplanes and a live turtle, a phonograph, and more than a hundred Japanese and Korean vinyl records. His mother owned an American-made Singer sewing machine, a treasure none of the other Korean mothers had.

No's father often greeted him in the morning by saying "Good morning," and required the boy to respond with the same English words. Several of the Japanese books he bought for his son described the wonders of American life: affordable cars, big houses, abundant food, and large universities. Because No was drilled in Japanese at home, he spoke the language fluently when entering his first year at primary school. It was a crucial competitive advantage over other children, especially after 1940, when colonial authorities insisted on Japanese-only schooling. That year all Koreans were ordered to change their names to Japanese. No's name was Okamura Kyoshi, and he answered to it until 1945, when the Russians marched into Korea.

No's father believed Japan would win World War II—and so did his son, whose teachers told him that the emperor Hirohito was a living god. They explained to the boy that Korea did not actually exist; it was a part of Japan, and so was he. By 1944, when he was twelve and in his last year of elementary school, the brainwashing was complete. The boy previously known as No Kum Sok desperately wanted to help the Japanese fight back against the massive American fleet that was transporting marines and soldiers to attack Saipan in the Pacific. Tokyo advertised in Korea for young aviation cadets willing to serve their emperor and prove their patriotism by dying as kamikaze pilots.

No needed his father's permission before he could formally volunteer. The boy found him at home, sitting on a cushion in the living room. No asked his question while standing close to his father, expecting to be praised for bravery and love of Japan. But the moment his father understood the request, he erupted.

"You want to dive into an American warship?" he shouted. "Are you crazy?"

Smarting from embarrassment, the boy understood for the first time that there were limits to his father's embrace of Japan: he was a Korean pragmatist, not a Japanese patriot. The emperor was not worth dying for.

The boy's suicidal aspirations melted away. So did his conviction that Japan would win the war.

III

The Japanese put a bounty on Kim Il Sung's head, dispatched a posse to kill him, and made him the most wanted partisan leader in Manchuria. But they never caught up with him.

It was the Chinese Communists who nearly did him in. They arrested Kim as part of a witch hunt that went after ethnic Koreans in Manchuria. Although Kim survived, at least a thousand Korean partisan fighters and Korean civilians were tortured and killed in the 1930s on baseless charges that they collaborated with the Japanese colonial police. Chinese Communists killed Koreans for spilling rice while eating, sighing in public, or fleeing a Japanese prison rather than staying put for execution.

This obscure racist purge on the eastern fringes of Manchuria—called the Minsaengdan incident—nearly destroyed the common struggle of Chinese and Korean Communists against Japan. More enduringly, it seared paranoia into Kim's character. As a guerrilla leader and later as a dictator, he never forgot and rarely forgave anyone who crossed him. The tense relationship that North Korea has today with China—a mix of dependence and suspicion, cooperation and contempt—can be traced back to the rage that he felt as Chinese Communists tortured and killed his Korean comrades. Kim called it a "mad wind . . . [Koreans] were being slaughtered indiscriminately by [Chinese] with whom they had shared bread and board only yesterday."

The Minsaengdan (People's Livelihood Corps) was a small militia created by the Japanese police, supposedly to protect Korean civilians from bandits in eastern Manchuria. But Chinese partisans saw it as part of a massive Japanese effort to use Korean spies to destroy the Communist movement. For two and a half years, Chinese partisan leaders operated on the assumption that Koreans in eastern Manchuria were pro-Japanese. Because Koreans (including the parents of Kim Il Sung and hundreds of thousands of exiles from the Korean Peninsula) were in the majority in the region, there were a great many people to arrest, interrogate, torture, and kill.

The purge killed or scared off nearly all the senior guerrilla commanders in eastern Manchuria who were ethnic Korean. After his arrest in 1934, Kim escaped execution because he spoke Chinese well and had important friends in the Chinese Communist command. He was also perceived as being too young, at age twenty-two, to be a spy for the Japanese.

In his memoirs, Kim says that he confronted the Chinese Communists at a party meeting and persuaded them to end the purge.

"Comrades, stop gambling on people's destinies," he claims he told the Chinese. "The only way to redress the murder of thousands of martyrs on a false charge of involvement in the Minsaengdan is to stop this pointless murder and concentrate all our efforts on the struggle against the Japanese."

There is a dispute among scholars about whether Kim even attended that meeting. But historians agree that it was in the mid-1930s, as the Chinese Communists realized the purge was crippling their fight against the Japanese, that Kim became the preeminent Korean guerrilla leader. He seems to have been the last Korean leader left standing.

Kim then put together a new guerrilla unit, consisting of ethnic Koreans who had been arrested and held as traitors. At a Chinese guerrilla outpost called Mount Mann, he freed a hundred of them and burned their criminal files. "When the bundles of papers turned into flames, the men and women [who had been under suspicion for years] burst into tears. They understood me," Kim wrote.

By saving these fighters, Kim created a core of followers who would serve him for the rest of their lives—and help him create and manage North Korea. The Minsaengdan suspects—and twenty orphaned Korean children rescued at Mount Mann—came to see Kim as a "parental leader." They joined him to fight the Japanese in Manchuria and later followed him to North Korea, where they helped him run the country.

Four of the rescued orphans grew up to become directors of a North Korean school that taught generations of the North Korean elite how to worship the Great Leader and do his bidding.

After 1934, the anti-Japanese war in Manchuria gathered momentum. Working again with the Chinese, Kim led raids that secured his notoriety. In addition to the raid on Pochonbo, Kim's men famously lured a Japanese expeditionary force up a snow-covered hill where other guerrillas were camouflaged beneath white cloth. They reportedly killed or captured twenty-seven Japanese officers and soldiers.

The movement was built on "love and trust and unity," Kim claims in his memoirs. A spy for the Japanese, a woman named Chi Sun Ok who spent nearly a year with Kim and his fighters, reported that Kim was indeed an idealistic leader who, between attacks and retreats, preached endlessly to his men about international Communism and Korean nationalism.

But in the freezing Manchurian hinterlands, love and ideology did little to provision Kim's guerrillas. To feed and clothe them, he extorted protection money out of opium and ginseng farmers. He terrorized Chinese and Korean landowners, using blackmail, hostages, and murder. His men stormed into villages, press-ganged young men into service as soldiers, and demanded ransoms.

"If you do not bring [money, food, and clothing] by tomorrow noon," said one note delivered to a Manchurian village, "we will cut off ears of one of the kidnapped and will return him to your families, and if you do not comply within three days, we will cut off heads of the kidnapped and return them to you."

In Kim's politics, as in his daily struggles to find food, there was never a question of whether the ends justified the means. He had become a thug with a cause. But thuggery was not nearly enough. In Manchuria, the Japanese had too many troops and too much firepower. Few of the young men Kim forced to become fighters believed his lectures about Communist revolution or a Korea that would one day be free. Many deserted at the first opportunity. By the late 1930s, the guerrilla war was lost. Kim fled into the far east of the Soviet Union, seeking sanctuary near Vladivostok, where he was immediately arrested.

IV

When World War II ended, so did the cosseted childhood of No Kum Sok. In August 1945, Americans dropped atomic bombs on Hiroshima and Nagasaki, Japan surrendered, and Russian soldiers stormed into the newly invented North Korea.

No was thirteen and living with his parents in a Noguchi Corporation bungalow in Kanggye, a city near the Chinese border, as units of the Soviet Union's Twenty-fifth Army rolled in on trucks. It was an army of louts. "The immoral behavior of our men is horrible," a Soviet officer wrote. They had been conscripted into a Soviet army decimated by war in Europe. Some regarded Koreans as racially inferior conquered enemies. As the Japanese quickly surrendered or fled south, the young Russians, many of them illiterate sons of peasant farmers, settled in for several delirious weeks of pillaging, raping, and drinking.

No watched them loot stores in Kanggye, where they seemed to take a particular interest in wristwatches. Soldiers wore several on each arm, rarely bothering to set or wind them. They were crazy for anything alcoholic. No saw them drink antifreeze and vomit in the streets. He heard stories from his neighbors about Russians bursting into houses, where they raped mothers and daughters in front of their families. This became a routine practice across northern Korea. Terrorized women began dressing as men to escape assault in the streets. Soviet troops were sometimes disciplined for rape, via a firing squad, but it was relatively rare. Industrial-scale looting began, with soldiers loading timber, grain, machinery, and fertilizer on trains for transport back to the Soviet Union. Within two blocks of No's house, Russian troops set up one of these large operations inside a Japanese military depot with a dozen two-story, redbrick buildings stocked with boots, uniforms, medicines, rice, and underwear.

After the Russians arrived, No's family did not have enough money for food. They stopped eating meat. His father was still expected to manage the railroads, but he was barely paid. The Noguchi company store had been cleaned out. The Russians cut phone and mail service with Noguchi headquarters in Seoul, which was south of the thirty-eighth parallel in a new and suddenly foreign country ruled by the U.S. military. To eat, No's parents sold many of the possessions that had made the family upper-class: the Singer sewing machine, the phonograph, and all the records.

His parents warned him to stay clear of the Russians. But No spied on them as they swarmed around the Japanese military depot, noticing their eagerness to trade nearly anything for drink. They seemed to especially like *sool*, a Korean spirit made from rice. No's father kept a large bottle of it in the house. One morning, No poured some into a small bottle and brought it to the depot as a friendship offering for the Russians. The guard at the gate was dubious. He pushed the bottle to No's lips, forcing him to take a drink. Satisfied it was not poison, he escorted the boy to an inner courtyard, where No saw a dozen Russian sergeants sitting around a table, eating boiled chicken and black bread. They were delighted with the gift of rice spirits and returned the favor by giving the boy two pairs of Japanese leather boots, each pair worth a month's wages.

While No was inside the depot, he noticed that local Koreans were loading Soviet trucks with boots and other goods. He asked one of them how he had gotten the job. Line up before sunrise, he was told. The next morning, No was there, the youngest and smallest kid in line. He flexed his biceps for amused Russians and was among twenty Koreans chosen to help them steal Japanese goods. His pay was extraordinarily generous. For a day's work, the Russians gave No two more pairs of boots, a hundred pounds of rice, and a dozen pairs of socks. He and the other Koreans also helped themselves to all the underwear they could hide beneath their clothes and still manage to walk. The boy shuffled home wearing five undershirts and five pairs of undershorts. An unexpected bonus was lunch, No's first chance to eat Russian-style: butter, cheese, and salami. The next morning, he was back in line and again scored a big bag of rice and several years' worth of boots and underwear. On the third day, as word spread about the benefits of helping the Russians, the line of job applicants started forming at midnight. There was a near riot. Teenagers tried to climb the depot's wall. One of No's neighbors was shot in the leg and crippled.

By October 1945, lawlessness in Kanggye and the rest of northern Korea had been brought under control after Stalin himself ordered the commander of Soviet occupation forces to "strictly observe discipline, not offend the population, and conduct themselves properly." That order came too late to alter the views of No's parents, who saw the Russians as "barbarians" whose arrival had wrecked their lives. In the next two years, about two million Koreans abandoned their homes and possessions, heading south to the American zone, sometimes on foot, to escape Soviet occupation.

Worried about his pension, No's father risked a journey to Seoul. With half a dozen colleagues from his company, he traveled by train to the last station north of the thirty-eighth parallel and hired a guide to lead them south. In Seoul, the office of the Korean branch of Noguchi was empty. There would be no pension. No's father wandered around Seoul and, as he later told his son, was impressed by the American soldiers in the streets. They were clean, smartly dressed, and well behaved, especially in comparison to the Russians back in Kanggye. He bought his son an American-made toothbrush and a poster of South Korea's new leader, Syngman Rhee.

No's father liked what he saw in South Korea, but he was afraid to move his family there. He still had a company-provided house and a railroad job. He doubted he could find a job or a place to live in the South and worried that his family would go hungry in the South's chaotic, strike-crippled economy.

So they stayed on in Kanggye, where No attended middle school and, following his father's lead, became known as the most pro-American kid in his class. For a while, the Russians tolerated some freedom of expression in the school, in part because few teachers were trained in a Communist curriculum. No earned an A in English and latched onto his

Japanese-trained English teacher, who coached soccer and was vocally anti-Communist. The teacher was later fired and fled to South Korea, where he served in the army.

School soon began to change. No was required to join the Korean Democratic Youth League, a Communist group. Teachers tried to stamp out religion, requiring No to repeat, "There is no God, no mystery, no secrets of life. Everyone can know everything." In a political science course called "People," No's teacher said the United States was a poor country.

While the boy could accept that religion was a sham, he simply did not believe that America was poor. On that subject, he had authoritative counter-information. Picture books that he had committed to memory showed a California couple taking a Sunday-afternoon drive in a big automobile as their dog poked its nose out the car window and lapped at the cool breeze. The dog lived better than he did. Another book described a Japanese stowaway who jumped off a ship in America and became rich. In Kanggye, No had seen the houses of American missionaries. They were large and luxurious and had flush toilets, a rarity in Korea. No believed that the United States was paradise and his new teachers were liars. At thirteen, he began to dream about stealing away to America.

CHAPTER 2

Poodle and Pretender

I

In September 1945, Kim Il Sung returned to Korea, not as the famous liberator of his homeland, but as an unannounced nobody in the Soviet army. He was a lowly captain and wore a Soviet uniform.

Because he had a legend to protect, he was worried about how this would look to his countrymen. He also wanted his Soviet masters to give him and his partisan comrades a high-profile role in chasing the Japanese out of Korea.

"Commander, sir, please make it so that it appears as though the anti-Japanese partisans participated in the war of liberation," Kim reportedly begged Major General Nikolai Lebedev, the political commissar for the Soviet occupying forces.

Lebedev refused, and Kim was not allowed to join Soviet troops when they routed the Japanese and marched victoriously into Pyongyang. Kim might have been kept out on direct orders from Stalin, who did not want him getting credit for ending colonial rule and building a populist base independent of Soviet control.

So Kim did as he was told. He came home in the shadows.

Along with about sixty other Koreans, he tried to travel overland to Korea from the Soviet Union, but a bridge across the Yalu River had been blown up. So his party backtracked to Vladivostok, boarded a Soviet navy ship, the *Pugachev*, and landed one afternoon without ceremony in the port city of Wonsan. After finding lodging on the second floor of a restaurant, Kim and his men marked their first night in the fatherland with bowls of noodles, according to Yu Song Chol, a Soviet Korean officer who was traveling with Kim and would later become chief of operations in the North Korean army.

After eating his noodles, Kim told his men to maintain a low profile: Don't get drunk, cause trouble, or raise eyebrows. If they were asked about their mission, they should say they were an advance party planning the grand arrival of Kim Il Sung. He ordered them to say nothing about the "age, place of birth, or personal history" of Kim Il Sung. Yu was puzzled but later concluded that Kim "simply wanted to hide the truth of his shabby, humble return to Korea."

Years later, propagandists in North Korea concocted a more suitable narrative: "General Kim Il Sung returned home in triumph, leading the anti-Japanese fighters . . . The Korean people who welcomed their Leader found no proper words to express their happiness. Every town and village all over the country seemed to surround the General and dance with joy."

As Stalin's lieutenants worked to Sovietize the northern part of the Korean Peninsula, Kim's willingness to do as he was told—and his grassroots fame as a guerrilla leader—made him a Korean worth employing and exploiting. While the role of Soviet poodle was problematic for his image as a legendary Korean freedom fighter, it did a world of good for his health, his family, and his career.

Stalin's investment in Kim began in 1941 in the Soviet Far East, where he was briefly arrested after fleeing Manchuria to escape the Japanese. Quickly identifying Kim as someone who might prove valuable, the Soviet army fed, sheltered, educated, and indoctrinated him. For about two years, he was assigned to the Khabarovsk Infantry Officers School. Then he was sent to a military base in the woods about fifty miles northwest of Khabarovsk, where he was promoted to captain. There, he commanded the First Battalion of the Eighty-eighth Sniper Brigade, a multinational unit of six hundred soldiers created to gather intelligence on Japanese forces in Manchuria.

Kim, though, did not spend much time in the field. After years of hunger, cold, and stress as a guerrilla leader in Manchuria, he was in poor health. He was "lean and weak, and his mouth was always open, perhaps because he was suffering at the time from hypertrophic rhinitis [chronic nose infection]," according to Yu, then his army colleague.

During his half decade at the Soviet base, Kim's health improved, he gained weight, and he started a family. He married Kim Jong Suk, a partisan fighter seven years his junior who had joined his band of fighters in Manchuria as a sixteen-year-old kitchen helper. The Japanese later arrested her as a spy when she tried to buy food for the partisans. After her release, she followed Kim to the Soviet Union. She bore him two sons at the Soviet base, including Kim Jong Il, and was posthumously named a "revolutionary immortal" and a member, along with her husband and firstborn son, of North Korea's "holy trinity." (An official North Korean biography of Kim Jong Il later claimed he was born at a secret guerrilla camp on the slopes of Mount Paektu, the sacred mountain of Korean revolution. In Kim family mythology, this is where his father led the anti-Japanese revolution to victory.)

With the Soviets, Kim finally had time for political and military training. He worked hard to impress his Soviet superiors, who viewed him as a capable leader and strict disciplinarian intolerant of excessive drinking. At the military base, he was not the highest-ranking Korean, but he was the most influential.

After Kim's return to Korea, there was no plan to install him as a significant official in the new Soviet satellite state. "No one among us was thinking that Kim Il Sung would become the new leader of North Korea," recalled Yu.

Kim seized the initiative when he arrived in Pyongyang in the fall of 1945. Rather than become the city's police commander, which was the job the Soviets had chosen for him, he maneuvered to place his partisan friends in important security jobs. They soon dominated every police and military organization in the North, giving Kim a formidable and well-armed power base. To speed these appointments, Kim orchestrated boozy banquets for Russian generals, including Major General Lebedev, with Korean and Japanese prostitutes hired by Kim and his men.

The Soviets needed a local figurehead who had credibility with the Korean people, but Kim was not their first choice. Instead, they wanted Cho Man Sik, by far the best-known and most trusted political leader in northern Korea. A former school principal, he was sixty-two and a devout Presbyterian. Some called him the Korean Gandhi. Trained as a lawyer at an elite university in Japan, he became famous during the war by publicly disobeying Japan and refusing to change his name from Korean to Japanese. The Soviets met with Cho several times in the fall of 1945, negotiating with him about the shape of the new state. They offered him the presidency of North Korea, provided that they could pull strings in the background.

But Cho was not a Communist and hated the idea that a new nation in Korea would be under Soviet control. He was also proud and stubborn, insisting that he be treated as the most important person at meetings, which annoyed Soviet generals. Still, they felt they had to work with him, as Cho embodied every important tradition in Korean politics. He was wellborn, well educated, well respected, and an elder. One evening in late September, the Soviets invited Kim to help them persuade the old man to see reason. Their dinner at Club Hwabang, a pricey restaurant and brothel, failed to make any progress in turning Cho into a puppet. But Kim's presence suggested that the Soviets were beginning to hedge their bets.

The Soviets soon gave up on Cho, deciding that Kim better suited their needs. To make it official, tens of thousands of people gathered on October 22, 1945, on an athletic field in Pyongyang, where General Lebedev introduced Kim as a national hero and "outstanding guerrilla leader." Kim's speech—written in Russian by the political affairs section of the Soviet Twenty-fifth Army and translated into Korean—was clotted with Marxist jargon and incomprehensible to most Koreans who heard Kim stumble through it.

To help Kim look like a leader that day, a Soviet major lent him a blue suit that was a size too small. Kim had never worn a necktie, and a Soviet colonel helped him get it around his neck. Pinned on his lapel was a Soviet medal, the Red Banner of Combat.

In the audience, most Koreans knew (or thought they knew) a great deal about the legendary Kim Il Sung and his heroic exploits in Manchuria against the Japanese. They had heard fantastical stories about him for so many years that they quite naturally assumed he was an elderly fellow like Cho Man Sik: gray-haired, well dressed, distinguished, and eloquent.

The youth who stepped up to the rostrum, nervously clutching his speech, uncomfortable in his tight suit, was not at all what they expected.

"He looked like a callow young man, even younger than his actual age of thirty-three," wrote Yu. "I even heard one woman next to me comment, 'That is not him. What type of Kim Il Sung could that be?'"

Another witness, the personal secretary to Cho Man Sik, reported,

His complexion was slightly dark and he had a haircut like a Chinese waiter. His hair at the forehead was about an inch long, reminding one of a lightweight boxing champion. "He is a fake!" All of the people gathered upon the athletic field felt an electrifying sense of distrust, disappointment, discontent, and anger.

Oblivious to the sudden change in mass psychology, Kim Il Song continued in his monotonous, plain, and duck-like voice to praise the heroic struggle of the Red Army . . . He particularly praised and offered the most extravagant words of gratitude and glory to the Soviet Union and Marshal Stalin, that close friend of the oppressed peoples of the world. The people at this point had completely lost their respect and hope for General Kim Il Song. There was the problem of age, but there was also the content of the speech, which was so much like that of other Communists whose monotonous repetitions had worn the people out.

When the speech was over, the Soviets knew they had a problem. Kim's performance had backfired, enhancing the stature of Cho Man

Sik. But the decision had been made: Kim might have looked like a waiter in a bad suit, but he flattered Stalin in every speech. He found Korean *kisaeng* girls for Russian generals. He was worthy of being a Soviet puppet.

To sell their selection to the masses, the Soviets embarked on a major propaganda campaign that emphasized Kim's guerrilla credentials and authenticity. (After Cho Man Sik resigned in protest on February 4, 1946, from the chairmanship of a Soviet-created governing bureau, he was arrested and disappeared. He was probably shot just before or during the Korean War.)

The custodians of Kim's image would erase the embarrassment of his first appearance in Pyongyang. They rewrote the words and reimagined the Great Leader's coming-out speech. Photographs were retouched: Russian generals who stood behind Kim as he read his speech disappeared, as did the Red Banner of Combat pinned to his chest. Oil paintings were commissioned that showed Kim's triumphant return to Korea without Russians. People "could not take their enraptured eyes from [Kim's] gallant figure," wrote an official biographer. They "were dancing with joy and hugging each other." They cheered out of "boundless love and respect for their great leader."

II

No Kum Sok soon began to see a lot of General Kim Il Sung—and Stalin.

At school, on the street, in every newspaper—the young Korean leader and the old Soviet dictator were inescapable. The first wave of photographs, posters, and billboards showed Kim with a skinny face and wearing a Western-style coat and tie. In the months to come, as more posters flooded the cities, his face filled out. Kim shifted to a Mao suit and posed with workers and students. The newspapers were silent about his years in the Soviet Far East, his rank as a captain in the Soviet army, and the whereabouts of Cho Man Sik.

Like many Koreans, No and his father regarded Kim as a fake and a temporary placeholder. They believed the Korean Peninsula would unify under a democratically elected government, perhaps with the help of a respected elder like Cho Man Sik.

Instead, the intense propaganda praising Kim Il Sung became overwhelming. Phony or real, Kim was the Soviets' chosen leader. When the government released a song about Kim's legendary achievements, it became the most popular musical number in the North. All schoolchildren, including No, learned it by heart.

Who is the partisan whose deeds are unsurpassed?
Who is the patriot whose fame shall ever last?
Over Korea ever flourishing and free.
So dear to our hearts is our General's glorious name.
Our beloved General Kim Il Sung of undying fame.

No's father was diagnosed with stomach cancer in 1947. Surgeons operated in a Japanese-built hospital but told the family that cancer would soon return. No's mother and father decided to move to Hungnam, the coastal city near their families. No, then fifteen, traveled there ahead of his parents in the fall of 1947 to enroll in high school. His parents followed the next spring. For several months, No lived with his mother's sister and her husband, Uncle Yoo, who idolized Kim Il Sung.

No quickly realized that his uncle and aunt were poorer than his parents. They struggled to buy food for themselves and their four children. The boy tried not to eat too much or make his uncle angry. He hid his poster of Syngman Rhee, although his uncle found it and scolded him. When Uncle Yoo lectured him about the genius of Kim, No learned to nod agreeably.

Keeping Uncle Yoo happy could be helpful.

No discovered this when he tried—and failed—to enroll in high school. He had been an excellent middle school student in Kanggye, and he and his parents had hoped that his grades would smooth his admission into a new high school. But transferring between schools was difficult in North Korea, a holdover from the Japanese colonial era, when authorities wanted people to stay put. When No presented his transcript to the principal at Hungnam First High School, he was denied admission.

Three months later, Uncle Yoo had an idea. His nephew should impress the principal and the teachers with his insatiable hunger for learning. He should show up early every morning at the large room where teachers assembled before class. He should stand there all day, looking eager for knowledge. It worked. On the third day, the vice-principal called No to his desk and praised the boy's courage in pursuit of an education. No started high school the following morning. Uncle Yoo was delighted and seemed to have convinced himself that his nephew had become a "real Communist." Uncle Yoo told his nephew to report all anti-Communist behavior he saw at Hungnam High.

No did not become a snitch in school, but he sensed teachers would not tolerate an America-is-best attitude. He avoided Japanese or English words and began studying Russian. When Kim Il Sung unexpectedly visited Hungnam for the speech on top of the fertilizer mountain, the boy knew it was important to show enthusiasm. He had become an excellent liar.

Several weeks after the fertilizer speech, No's parents made their way to Hungnam. They could afford only a modest house of unpainted wood with four rooms and a sheet-metal roof. Money for food and clothing was scarce. His father's stomach cancer had returned, and he was too sick to work.

III

Kim Il Sung's competitive edge over rival politicians depended on Moscow, which supplied the guns and money that created and sustained North Korea. To nurture and strengthen that relationship, Kim constantly and effusively praised Stalin, calling him the Sun of Mankind and Glorious Leader of Worldwide Revolution. His flare for flattering higher-ups was matched by an instinctive feel for what was going on down below. When peasants were stirred up, he had a gift for turning their anger into his power.

Five weeks after his bumbling performance in Pyongyang, Kim

sensed opportunity in Sinuiju, a border city across the Yalu River from Manchuria. There, in the early afternoon of November 23, 1945, Soviet soldiers joined Korean Communist security forces in shooting to death a hundred students and wounding about seven hundred others. The Soviets called in aircraft to strafe crowds of young people. The mass killings halted the single largest anti-Communist protest in North Korea since the arrival of the Soviet army.

The trigger for the demonstration was the arrest of Principal Chu, the senior administrator at a local middle school. The Soviets had angered the principal, his teachers, and his students by cutting resources, reducing teachers, and controlling the content of classroom instruction. But there was much more to it than that. The boorish behavior of Soviet troops had infuriated the entire population of Sinuiju. As they had in Kanggye and across much of North Korea, Russian soldiers robbed stores and homes, busted up local brothels, and roistered around city streets, drunk, disorderly, and heavily armed. The coming of the Russians coincided with food shortages, price hikes, and rising hunger. Soldiers stole food to feed themselves, angering farmers and landlords. The sizable population of Christians was outraged because the Soviets called them part of a "bourgeois social stratum" and limited their influence in city affairs.

With help from Christian pastors, a thousand students from seven local schools surrounded Communist Party buildings. To get close, they cheered Stalin (a variation of the flattery game that Kim Il Sung played so well). Then they shouted, "Charge!" They scaled walls and began fistfights with Soviet and Korean security forces. Shooting broke out with handguns, rifles, and machine guns. Reports of the killings spread quickly, sparking demonstrations in several cities and catching Communist authorities off guard.

Suddenly the Soviet occupation forces needed damage control.

Three days after the shootings, a Soviet aircraft delivered Kim Il Sung to Sinuiju. He visited several schools, where he calmed people down by listening to their complaints and reminding them of his credentials as an anti-Japanese guerrilla and a Korean patriot.

"Shooting between our people is not only a disgrace to the nation but also a serious hindrance to nation-building," Kim told the students.

He told a citizens' assembly that "genuine Communists" could never have shot the young people, and he blamed "fake Communists" who had infiltrated the party. The cure for youthful discontent in Sinuiju and across the North, Kim said, was paying more attention to the masses and ridding the Communist Party of "rogues."

Sinuiju changed Kim, convincing him that he and all party leaders risked chaos if they did not keep an ear to the ground.

Within a few weeks, Kim began giving "on-the-spot guidance" at farms, factories, and mines, listening to complaints and instructing all government and party officials to do likewise. The word "Communist" was associated with the beastliness of Russian soldiers, so Kim either soft-pedaled or eliminated it. The Communist Youth League, the party's primary tool for organizing young people, became the Democratic Youth League. The Communist Party became the Workers' Party, and its membership was allowed to expand from 26,000 in late 1945 to 400,000 in the fall of 1946, drawing in new members from factories, unions, and women's organizations.

Kim also discovered new methods in Sinuiju for rooting out and crushing his rivals. He played the sympathetic populist who recognized the innocence and purity of his people. He did not blame students for criminality. Instead, he called them "naive" and "misled." He reserved his vitriol for "the influence of reactionary wirepullers behind the scenes." It was his first recorded discovery of offstage villains as the cause for whatever ailed North Korea. In years to come, Kim would find and purge tens of thousands of politicians, bureaucrats, and military officers, often without any evidence other than his word that they were reactionaries, splittists, factionalists, American spies, Christian traitors, or Japanese collaborators. Going after the purportedly pro-Japanese was an especially easy and efficient way of eliminating political competition. Nearly everyone in Korea had come of age under Japanese occupation, and nearly everyone had been forced to cooperate in some way with the colonial government. Kim could get rid of nearly anyone.

Kim came away from Sinuiju as a proven Soviet fixer and as a dem-agogue on the make. He listened to peasants and breathed life into their dreams of an independent, self-governed Korea. He also strengthened a state that ruled from the top down. He did not apologize to the parents whose children were shot in the face by Soviet and Korean security forces. Instead, he said that nation building demanded discipline and that everyone should follow his lead as a battle-tested freedom fighter. His government forcibly merged all organizations for the young into the Democratic Youth League. Kim made it clear that while his govern-ment would listen to the concerns of young people, it would not take orders from them. "Just as an army lacking iron discipline cannot win battles," he said, "so an undisciplined youth organization is up to no good."

The military began to draft young people, who were then drilled by Soviet occupation forces. About ten thousand soldiers a year were sent to Siberia for training. Some of the best and brightest young people in the North were chosen to serve in the Peace Preservation Officers' School, where they were subjected to mandatory "thought inspection" and self-criticism. One of these indoctrination academies took over a middle school in Sinuiju. Its three thousand students included many who had survived the mass killing of November 1945.

Sinuiju and nearby towns were soon singled out for vengeance. The Soviets moved in more soldiers. They searched train and bus passengers for weapons. Churches were destroyed and ministers executed. In nearby Uiju, according to American intelligence reports, a Methodist minister was ordered to pull an oxcart through town while wearing a sign that said, "National traitor." His church was burned.

Years after the demonstration, the North Korean government con-tinued to punish Sinuiju residents suspected of participating in the riot. In 1950, a student pilot taking MiG flight training suddenly disappeared. His fellow students were told that he had been involved in the Sinuiju protests.

The Sinuiju incident was a breakthrough for Kim. He learned how to demonize his political rivals and blame anything that went wrong inside

North Korea on foreign agitators. He listened to the masses as the state media celebrated his common touch. Then, in the name of nation building and self-reliance, he told everybody what to do.

IV

A few days after No Kum Sok turned seventeen, his father died of cancer. Without money for a funeral service, relatives dug a grave in a community cemetery and lowered him into the ground in an unpainted wooden box. With savings gone, No's mother became a street trader, buying soy sauce and bean cakes in stores and selling them to restaurants. Her life improved marginally when her son graduated from high school in the spring of 1948. His grades were good enough to win him a stipend to attend Hungnam Chemical and Engineering College, a technical school that trained workers for the fertilizer plant and other factories in town. The boy gave his mother the money, a few dollars a week.

After his father died, No tried not to show emotion. He grieved in private and continued thinking about how to escape the state his father had despised. Millions of Koreans had found their way by train or bus to the thirty-eighth parallel and walked into South Korea. But the border had become dangerous to cross, with soldiers on both sides and constant skirmishes. Rumors of an all-out North-South war grew with each passing month.

Next door in China, Communists were finally in charge. After nearly two decades, the Chinese civil war ended with victory for Mao Zedong, and a quarter of the world's population joined the Communist fold. Kim Il Sung celebrated the triumph and used it to whip up support for a unified Korean Peninsula under Communist rule. He moved the bulk of the North Korean People's Army to within a few miles of the thirty-eighth parallel. His army was flush with weapons, thanks to the Soviet Union, which in 1949 had withdrawn its troops after North and South Korea formalized the division of the peninsula. The Soviets left behind all the armaments used by the 120,000 men in their Twenty-fifth Army, plus all the weapons they had seized from the Japanese. The United States also withdrew its military from South Korea, except for a small group of advisers, and left behind its arms. But the balance of firepower tipped overwhelmingly in favor of the North, which also retained more than three thousand Soviet military advisers.

Along with every young male in North Korea, No was ordered to register for the draft. He despaired at the prospect of fighting for a government he loathed, but he tried not to let it show.

He projected Red enthusiasm at school and at mandatory meetings of the Democratic Youth League. There were two meetings a month at school, each lasting two hours. He feigned interest and struggled not to fall asleep. Every two months, there were higher-level Democratic Youth League meetings at city hall. Important Communists from Pyongyang delivered speeches about Marxism-Leninism. These talks were often longer, often delivered in Russian, and always more sleep inducing. Every family in Hungnam also had to send at least one member to twice-a-month meetings of the North Korean Workers' Party.

Forced feedings of Communist doctrine, together with rising anxiety about war, pushed No to consider new avenues of flight. One way out was Hungnam harbor, where foreign cargo ships dropped anchor. A former English teacher at Hungnam Chemical and Engineering College, who had lost his job when Russian courses replaced English, found work as an interpreter in the harbor. He boarded a foreign freighter, asked for asylum, and escaped to South Korea via Hong Kong, leaving behind his wife and two small children. The story of that escape was well known when No, in his first year at college, was sent down to the harbor to help unload ships. On board a Canadian freighter, he tried to use his limited English to ask for asylum. The Canadians were gruff and unwelcoming. Before he could make himself understood, he lost his nerve.

Yet war was coming, and No did not want to die in Kim's infantry. When he saw an announcement on the town bulletin board for an entrance examination to enter the naval academy, he applied. He believed, quite wrongly, as it turned out, that the navy would train and educate naval cadets for three years before sending them to war. He told his mother he would become an educated naval officer and take a gunboat to South Korea.

Nothing worked out as planned.

His first failure was the exam. To take it, he obtained a copy of his chemical college transcript from a physics professor and traveled by train to the nearby city of Hamhung. In an auditorium there, he completed a written test and an oral examination and underwent an exhaustive physical exam. Confident he had aced the tests, he waited outside with fifty others for results to be posted. Two hours passed before a naval officer emerged, tacked a list to a bulletin board, and walked away. No's name was not on it.

Riding home on the train, he wondered what he had done wrong. He was sure he had correctly answered nearly every question on the exam, and he was physically fit. Suddenly it hit him: he had been honest about his father. During the oral exam, he told an examiner that his late father had worked for a big Japanese company.

A few weeks later, No saw another announcement for the naval academy exam. This time he prepared a suitable pack of lies. Besides lying about his father's job, he lied about his mother's Catholicism and his own church attendance. For religion, he said, "None." He passed the exam, and no one, it seemed, noticed how radically his answers had changed from those he had given on the first exam.

Shortly after dawn on the last day of July 1949, No said good-bye to his mother and grandmother. His mother was sad, but his grandmother was angry. For days she had been demanding that his mother stop him. Her anxiety was prescient; she would never see her grandson again. She was killed, along with her granddaughter (No's cousin), in the summer of 1952 by an American bomb.

The journey to the naval academy began with an overnight train ride to Najin, a coastal town not far from the Russian port of Vladivostok. From the train station, No walked to the harbor, where he saw two strikingly beautiful Russian girls—both dressed in white uniforms—walking around on the docks. In a cold drizzle, he took a forty-minute boat ride to the naval academy, which had recently taken over a Japanese-built naval base hidden in the folds of towering coastal mountains. From land or water, the base was all but impossible to see until a boat landed at its docks. The campus consisted of fifteen run-down, two-story concrete buildings. There was also a mess hall, a theater, and a field for marching.

No joined a class of 150 cadets. They wore navy whites and navy blue caps, and marched with bolt-action, Russian-made rifles manufactured before the Bolshevik Revolution. But their starchy formal appearance was deceptive; they lived like inmates in a penal colony. The only food served at breakfast, lunch, and dinner was a bowl of rice and a bowl of watery beef-flavored soup. At the academy, No was never offered vegetables, fruit, eggs, or meat.

He had never had such wretched food and so little of it. Like all the cadets, he quickly lost weight. An exception to the rule of regimented malnutrition was kitchen duty. When it was No's turn to work in the kitchen, he gorged himself, often to the point of severe stomach cramps, vomiting, and diarrhea.

Discipline in the barracks was severe. The enforcer was Sergeant Wun Byong Koo, who was overweight, unreasonable, angry, and loud. Wun demanded that cadets be clean shaven, although the academy provided no razors. No learned how to yank his whiskers out with his fingernails. He got so good at it that he helped fellow cadets by yanking out their whiskers. He also fantasized about using his ancient Russian rifle to shoot Sergeant Wun.

Seven days a week, the sergeant's shouting awakened No before dawn for calisthenics. After splashing water on his face, he shouldered his old rifle and marched to the dining hall for breakfast, singing songs of the partisan revolution. He attended seven hours of classes a day for calculus, physics, chemistry, Russian, Soviet Communist Party history, meteorology, navigation, and weaponry. Then came an hour of gymnastics, including rings, high bar, and parallel bars. To pass, every cadet had to become proficient on each apparatus. On the parallel bars, for example, No needed to perfect sixteen moves. To build enough arm strength to survive gym class, he did a hundred push-ups a day. After gymnastics, cadets marched outdoors, goose-stepping with their rifles. After supper, they were allowed two hours a night for study. When lights went out in his barely heated barracks, No fell dead asleep on a straw mattress that had one blanket and one sheet but no pillow. Because the barracks did not have showers or hot water, cadets washed themselves from three common faucets. Once a month they were taken to a public bath in a nearby town, and once every fifteen days they changed underwear. Vacations and visitors were not allowed.

About a month after arriving at the secluded naval base, the cadets were ordered to move. They packed up immediately and relocated to Chongjin, another coastal city, about fifty miles south. The new base was in the hills outside the city and considerably smaller, with wooden buildings instead of concrete. But the workload, the discipline, and the privations were unchanged.

No and many other city-bred cadets were angered by the prison-like conditions. They talked about quitting and going home. One of them, Kim Man Suk, asked if he could resign. His request was denied, and he was told that if he asked again, he would be sent to prison. When the warning became common knowledge, No concluded the only way to survive the academy was to excel.

Not long after training began, cadets were called to a mandatory meeting in the base auditorium. The academy's commander, Admiral Kim Kuang Hiob, delivered a speech that terrified No.

"Comrades, I must warn you that because we have begun in such a hurry to start training, your individual biographies are not too complete," he said. "If you have anything to confess that you have not told us—if you are a churchgoer, if you have relatives in South Korea, or if your parents worked for the Japanese police or engaged in anti-Communist politics, tell us now.

"If you come to my office and admit it, it will be forgiven. But if we locate the falsehood ourselves, you will be severely punished."

Smelling a trap, No stayed silent. He had no intention of helping his commanders investigate his past.

A few weeks later, No ran into a naval officer who knew he had flunked his first attempt to enter the academy. Having given No his first oral examination, he also knew that the boy's father had worked for a Japanese company. The officer was chairman of the mathematics department at the academy, but No was not his student and until then had managed to avoid meeting him face-to-face.

"How did you get in here?" asked the officer, who was the only instructor at the academy who could link No's face to a failed entrance exam.

"I took the exams and passed, comrade officer," No said, before running off to try to blend into a crowd of cadets, all dressed in white.

In decades to come, a North Korean's social origin would be an indelible stain. Descendants of property owners, children of "traitors" who fled to South Korea, and relatives of those who collaborated under Japanese rule would all be classified as members of the "hostile class." They would be sent away from Pyongyang, consigned to jobs in mines or farms, and never allowed into universities or military academies that trained the future elite. In 1949, however, the caste system was just beginning to develop. War was coming. Record keeping was a mess. Liars leaked through.

For unknown reasons, the naval officer who knew about No's failed examination and his father's work history did not make an effort to hunt the boy down, expel him from the academy, and send him to prison. Unlike millions of North Koreans then and in generations to come, No did not have to pay for the sins of his father.

CHAPTER 3

Sweet-Talking Stalin

I

To go to war, Kim Il Sung needed a green light from Stalin. To get it, he invited Terentii Fomich Shtykov to lunch. Shtykov was the Soviet Union's ambassador to North Korea and the man to see. When Shtykov sent telegrams to the Kremlin, Stalin read them personally.

Back in Moscow, Shtykov was known as Mr. Korea. He had been the Soviet proconsul in Pyongyang from 1945 to 1948 and a conscientious midwife to the birth of Kim's government. The son of a poor farmer, he was an autodidact and a canny careerist under Stalin. Nikita Khrushchev described him as "brilliant." There was not a major event in the creation of North Korea that Shtykov did not influence. After the North established a nominally independent government in 1948, he was the obvious candidate to be the first ambassador.

Shtykov shared Kim's enthusiasm for invading South Korea. In several telegrams to Stalin in 1949, the ambassador exaggerated the risk that South Korea would, without any provocation, invade the North. He deliberately downplayed efforts by the United States to restrain the

South's army. Shtykov also supported Kim's belief that victory would be fast, easy, and cheap.

So when Kim invited Shtykov to lunch at the Ministry of Foreign Affairs on January 17, 1950, the Great Leader knew he would be preaching to a convert. Still, as the lunch began, Kim flattered and groveled, expressing his "love and gratitude" to Stalin for liberating Korea from the Japanese. After everyone had eaten and a Chinese trade representative left the room, Kim told Shtykov of the personal toll that not being able to go to war was taking on him.

"Lately, I've been feeling very frustrated; I don't sleep at night. I am thinking all the time of how to solve the problem of unification of the whole country," he said, according to a cable Shtykov sent to Moscow. "If the cause of the liberation of the people of the southern portion of Korea and the unification of the country is postponed, then I can lose the confidence of the Korean people."

In his cable, Shtykov explained what Kim wanted: "He thinks that he needs again to visit Comrade Stalin and receive an order and permission for offensive action. Kim said that he himself cannot begin an attack because he is a communist, a disciplined person, and for him the order of Comrade Stalin is law."

When Kim said that for him Stalin's word was law, he was accurately acknowledging his status in the Communist pecking order. Still only thirty-seven years old, Kim was an exceedingly small potato in the Soviet Empire. Untraveled and unschooled, he led a poor, obscure, and strategically insignificant country that depended on Moscow for nearly everything.

Stalin, by contrast, was the *khozyain*, the owner, the Boss, the "custodian-in-chief of the Soviet order." He had dominated the largest nation on earth since the late 1920s. He had industrialized the Russian Empire, smashed Hitler's eastern armies, and seized control of the eastern half of Europe. Along the way, of course, Stalin had become a mass-murdering psychopath: starving millions with collectivized farming, exiling millions to the Siberian gulag, and, in the Great Terror of the 1930s, executing his political enemies on an epic scale. He also nurtured a cult of personality that marketed him to all the people in the Soviet Union as an all-knowing father with a soft spot for children.

When Kim wanted to talk war with him, Stalin was in his early seventies, playing what would be his last big game of geopolitical chess. His principal opponent was the United States, which he privately described as a "fascist" country. Although he had struck several international agreements with the United States, he viewed the promises he made in these treaties as short-term tactics in a long game of global Communist domination. Stalin still worked long days at his desk, still micromanaged the Communist brand around the world, and still took time to personally read cables from far-flung apparatchiks like Shtykov.

The best measure of how large Stalin loomed in Kim's imagination is slavish imitation. More than any leader of any Soviet satellite state, Kim swallowed Stalinism whole. Like Stalin, he collectivized agriculture, overbuilt heavy industry, created a gulag of political labor camps, murdered political enemies, geographically sorted civilians based on perceived loyalty, required people to obtain papers for internal travel, and incentivized citizens to spy on one another. Kim also copied Stalin's cult of personality, raising it to a religion of the absurd. He sold himself to the North Korean people as a caring father who also happened to be the smartest, most important individual ever to walk the earth. And like Stalin, Kim apparently had an outsized appetite for comely, compliant, and disposable young women.

In March 1949, ten months before his lunch with Shtykov, Kim had his first chance to meet his totalitarian role model when he led a North Korean delegation to Moscow. The visit did not go particularly well. For as much as Kim was eager to flatter Stalin, he was more eager to attack South Korea.

"Comrade Stalin, we believe that the situation makes it necessary and possible to liberate the whole country through military means," Kim said at one meeting. "The reactionary forces of the South will never agree on a peaceful unification and will perpetuate the division of the country until they feel themselves strong enough to attack the North."

He told Stalin that it was time to act because North Korea's army was stronger, it would receive the support of a powerful guerrilla army in the South, and the people in the South would rise up to help because they hated Americans.

Unconvinced, Stalin told Kim he did not have his facts straight.

"You should not advance to the South," Stalin said. "First of all, the Korean People's Army does not have an overwhelming superiority over the troops of the South. Numerically, as I understand, you are even behind them."

More worrying for Stalin were the Americans. Stalin reminded Kim that American troops were still in the South (although they would withdraw in June 1949) and would bite back if the North attacked.

"One should not forget that the agreement on the thirty-eighth parallel is in effect between the U.S.S.R. and the United States," Stalin said. "If the agreement is broken by our side, it is more of a reason to believe that Americans will interfere."

Kim pouted.

"Does this mean that there is no chance to reunify Korea in the near future?" he asked. "Our people are very anxious to be together again, to cast off the yoke of the reactionary regime and their American masters."

Stalin, in response, did not slam the door shut on war. He counseled watchful patience. If the South Koreans and the Americans "start the aggression," Stalin said, then "you will have a good opportunity to launch a counterattack [and] your move will be understood and supported by everyone."

When Kim returned to Pyongyang, he was watchful but hardly patient. Not even personal tragedy weakened his desire for war. In September, his wife died from complications of childbirth, a loss he grieved for many years. That same month, though, he told Shtykov that his intelligence sources had received "reliable information" that the South Koreans were preparing an all-out attack. Kim claimed the invasion would begin on the Ongjin Peninsula, on the west coast of Korea just north of the thirty-eighth parallel. To head it off, Kim proposed a limited preemptive strike. If that blow seemed to demoralize the South Korean army, then Kim's forces would move farther south. If not, the North would hold on to a new perimeter that would be easier to defend. Ever the advocate for Kim, Shtykov asked Stalin to consider the plan.

Again, Stalin said no, scolding Kim as more eager than wise.

"It is impossible to view this operation other than as the beginning of a war . . . for which North Korea is not prepared either militarily or politically," the Soviet Politburo wrote in a message for Kim.

An early draft of that message curtly dismissed Kim and his fever for war. It said that if the North attacked, "the Americans will certainly move their troops into South Korea, and you [Kim] cannot stop this, you cannot even defeat the South Korean army."

North-South border skirmishes in the fall of 1949 angered Stalin. In a telegram, he chided Shtykov for allowing Kim to incite these shoot-outs. "Such provocations are very dangerous for our interests and can induce the adversary to launch a big war," he wrote.

Between the Boss and his acolyte, the pattern seemed set: Kim begged for an invasion. His pleas produced forty-eight telegrams to the Kremlin. Each time, Stalin slapped Kim down, but not so hard that he did not dare beg again.

The pattern changed, though, after the lunch with Shtykov at the Soviet embassy in Pyongyang, the meal at which Kim bemoaned his sleeplessness, rehashed his hunger for war, and importuned the Soviet ambassador for a chance to return to Moscow. Shtykov sent a cable recounting that lunch to Stalin on January 19, 1950. Eleven days later, Stalin cabled back. He said the international situation had tilted in favor of war.

"I understand the unhappiness of Comrade Kim Il Sung," Stalin wrote. "But he must understand that such a big step regarding South Korea, which he intends to undertake, requires thorough preparation. It has to be organized in such a way that there won't be a large risk. If he wants to talk to me on this issue, then I'll always be ready to receive him and talk to him. Tell this to Kim Il Sung and stress that I am ready to help him in this matter."

Stalin, though, did not want the world to know of his helpfulness. Two days after notifying Kim that he was ready to talk war, he sent a follow-up cable to Shtykov: "Explain to Comrade Kim Il Sung that at this point the question he wants to discuss with me must be completely confidential. It should not be shared with anyone in the North Korean leadership, as well as with the Chinese comrades. This is dictated by the preoccupation with keeping the topic unknown to the adversary."

II

On an early spring morning in 1950, No Kum Sok and fifty other cadets from his class at the naval academy were sent down to the harbor at Chongjin. There, naval officers ordered them to unload wooden crates from a newly arrived Soviet cargo ship.

The unlabeled coffin-shaped boxes were extraordinarily heavy. It took four cadets to lug each one across the docks to waiting military trucks. The crates smelled of the shipping grease that firearms are packed in. Cadets guessed they contained rifles and machine guns.

They were right. In early February, Stalin had approved North Korea's request for enough arms to outfit three army divisions.

Naval officers told the cadets nothing about what was in the boxes. Their work was secret, the officers said, and they should not mention it to anyone, including other cadets back at the naval academy.

For No, classroom work at the academy had become much less mysterious. By reading the faces of his instructors, he had figured out how to be a successful naval officer for the Great Leader. Expertise in the hard sciences would not do it. Courses in calculus and physics, chemistry and navigation meant little to the apparatchiks who ran the academy. A gentleman's C would suffice.

The course that mattered was Soviet Communist Party history. If a cadet received a C or worse in this course, he would be given a formal reprimand. An A required long hours of memorization of a dull Korean translation of a dull Russian textbook, along with the ability to affect sincere enthusiasm while speaking in class about the invaluable life lessons to be found in Marxism, Leninism, and Stalinism.

Determined to impress his instructor and fearful that someone would eventually link him to his Communist-hating father, No stuffed his mind with party history. He became an expert on the doctrinal errors of Trotsky, explicated the schism between the Bolsheviks and the Mensheviks, and tracked the missteps of party hacks from Bukharin to Zinoviev. He memorized nearly every resolution of the Russian Communist Party dating back to 1898 and the First Party Congress in Minsk.

The instructor gave No an A and told him he was a bright young Communist with a future. In other subjects, No kept up with his peers, usually managing a B. He was never reprimanded.

III

Kim arrived secretly in Moscow on March 30, 1950. He stayed there for nearly a month, meeting three times with Stalin at Blizhnyaya, the Boss's heavily guarded dacha on the bank of the Moscow River. The dacha was only a few minutes by limousine from the Kremlin.

By reputation, Stalin expected facts from underlings at meetings, not emotion or theatrics. So Kim came ready to answer questions about the capacity of his military to punch a hole in the South's defenses and win a quick victory. Thanks to gifts from the departing Red Army and recent Soviet arms deliveries, Kim had already equipped a hundred-thousand-man army with small arms, tanks, and artillery. North Korean reconnaissance teams had captured soldiers from the South and learned through interrogation that the North had a huge advantage in men and machinery, while the South was ill-prepared for an attack. The North was clearly superior, with twice as many troops, seven times as many machine guns, and six and a half times as many tanks.

After listening avidly to the operational details, Stalin advised Kim to supercharge his army with elite, highly mobile attack divisions. To assist with this, Stalin pledged delivery of more weapons, trucks, and tanks.

But Stalin was up to something more devious and opportunistic than merely arming a client state for civil war. He wanted to isolate China from any possible deals it might make with the West and pressure Mao, whom he distrusted, into becoming an instrument of Soviet strategy in the Far East. He also wanted to embarrass and emasculate the Americans by crushing their new client state in Asia. All the while, Stalin wanted to operate in the shadows, minimizing his risk of being drawn into a full-blown war against the United States, which he regarded as militarily stronger than the Soviet Union.

"If you should get kicked in the teeth, I shall not lift a finger," Stalin told Kim. "You have to ask Mao for all the help."

If need be, Chinese troops would fight in Korea, Stalin told Kim, while emphasizing that the Soviet Union would help with weapons and advisers but never with soldiers on the ground.

In Stalin's chess game, Kim was a pawn: notably ambitious, commendably aggressive, but eminently expendable. Still, during their meetings in his dacha, Stalin took time to explain to his pawn the changed international circumstances that now made it possible for him to secretly help North Korea wage war.

The most important change, Stalin said, was that since Mao had won his civil war, his government was no longer preoccupied with an internal conflict and his troops could help in Korea without undermining Communism in China. Stalin also said the influence of the United States in Asia was fading. The American military had quietly pulled out of China, Stalin told Kim, and "did not dare to challenge the new Chinese authorities militarily."

The Americans, Stalin predicted, would be even more reluctant to challenge Communist states in Asia because China and the Soviets had signed a treaty of alliance and mutual assistance in February 1950. Stalin said the Soviet Union's possession of the atomic bomb—first exploded the previous August—contributed to American timidity in Asia.

"The prevailing mood is not to interfere," he told Kim.

Stalin's guess that the Americans would not go to war over Korea was apparently based on a January 1950 speech by Secretary of State Dean Acheson, which excluded the Korean Peninsula as a Pacific territory that the United States would fight to defend. A secret U.S. National Security Council policy paper on the Far East, which had been written thirteen months earlier and which Stalin obtained with the help of his spies in

Washington, said essentially the same thing. The defensive perimeter of the United States in the Pacific, it said, included Japan and the Philippines but not the Asian mainland and not the Korean Peninsula.

But Stalin was not absolutely certain that his intelligence people had it right. In his meeting with Kim, he wondered out loud if the Americans might interfere.

Kim was sure the Americans would not take the risk. At least, that is what he told Stalin. In a detailed and remarkably wrong analysis of how the war would unfold, he explained that North Korea's attack would be fast and victory would come in three days. Kim also said that a powerful pro-Communist, anti-American guerrilla movement would spontaneously rise in the South to assist the North Korean military. Finally, Kim predicted that the Americans would be caught off guard and by the time they figured out what to do, the Korean people would have rallied around a new Communist government.

As for Mao, Kim said he knew the Chinese leader would help North Korea—if necessary. But Kim was a nationalist. He was wary of China and mindful of the centuries it had dominated Korea. Back in Manchuria in the 1930s, he had personally witnessed what the Chinese were capable of, killing Korean partisans by the hundreds.

Kim told Stalin that he wanted to unify Korea without China's help. "We believe that we can do it," he said.

Stalin did not care what Kim wanted, telling him again that if he desired a war, he had to get approval from Mao.

Unlike Stalin, Mao was not yet an elderly dictator with the blood of millions of his own countrymen on his hands. His image had not yet been blackened by madness and mass murder.

That would soon come. Mao's Great Leap Forward (1958–61) forced farmers to abandon their land and produce steel in their backyards by melting down pots and pans. Farmers who complained were called counterrevolutionaries and severely punished. Farmers who obeyed starved to death by the tens of millions, along with their families. As a result, an estimated thirty-six million Chinese died. The Cultural Revolution (1966–76) was less lethal but perhaps even more disruptive. It exiled the urban elite to the countryside, blew up the economy, and squandered a generation of China's best minds.

But as of 1950, Mao still seemed sane, and his reputation was near its high-water mark. At fifty-six, he was fat, suffered from insomnia, and had a neurological disorder that caused sweating, hot flashes, and soreness in his fingers and toes. Yet he worked fifteen to sixteen hours a day and was the undisputed hero of a triumphant peasant revolution. As both a military and a political strategist, he had united the Chinese mainland after decades of civil war, routing the Nationalist army of Chiang Kai-shek and chasing it off to Taiwan. In the process, he had transformed a semicolony into an independent global power with the world's largest population.

Mao did not like or trust Stalin, who he believed had tried to have him killed in the 1930s. Privately, he made fun of the Soviet leader's "mechanical thinking." But publicly Mao linked arms with Stalin, stamping a gargantuan Red footprint on Asia and signing a treaty that would help China industrialize and build a modern military. As one of his longtime colleagues later said, "Had Mao died [in the 1950s], his achievements would have been immortal."

When Stalin ordered Kim Il Sung to seek China's approval before launching a war, Mao was well briefed on events in Korea. He knew that military action there was possible at any time. A year earlier, when Kim sent a secret emissary to China to inform leaders about the situation in Korea, Mao was sympathetic, and he owed the Korean Communists a favor. Tens of thousands of them had served in his army during the civil war against the Nationalists, fighting bravely and well.

"If the need arises, we can quietly send Chinese troops [into the Korean Peninsula]," Mao said. "We all have black hair, no one can tell the difference."

Yet when Kim Il Sung came calling in Beijing on May 13, 1950, aboard a Soviet aircraft, his secret meeting with the Chinese leader was strained and ended abruptly. Mao later said he had a strong dislike of Kim, viewing him as aggressive, doctrinaire, and rash. He came to regard North Korea under Kim's rule as "a number-one pain in the butt," according to Sidney Rittenberg, an American scholar and linguist who lived in China from 1944 to 1979 and often worked with Mao.

After his first meeting with Kim, Mao was furious with Stalin, who had not bothered telling him that the Soviet Union had given North Korea a conditional green light for war. For Mao, this was demeaning, disruptive, and extremely ill timed. He was then preparing to attack Taiwan. Most of his army was deployed on the southeast coast of China, within striking distance of the island. A war on the Korean Peninsula, Mao knew, would at best delay the fight for Taiwan; at worst, it could derail his most important military priority.

Mao broke off the meeting with Kim, whose word he did not trust, and sent his foreign minister, Zhou Enlai, to the Soviet embassy in Beijing to find out what the hell was going on.

"Comrade Mao Zedong would like to have personal explanations from Comrade Filippov [Stalin] on this issue," the Soviet ambassador N. V. Roshchin wrote in a cable that he immediately dispatched to Moscow. "The Chinese comrades expect a speedy answer."

Stalin replied the next day. But he did not apologize for cutting Mao out of the information loop. The cable said flatly that because of "the changed international situation," Stalin now supported Kim's plans for war. The final decision should be sorted out "by the Chinese and Korean comrades together." If China disagreed, Stalin said, an invasion would be "postponed pending further discussion. The Korean comrades can tell you the details."

Stalin had maneuvered Mao into a corner. China needed Soviet support to industrialize, build a more powerful military, and attack Taiwan. But Stalin now made it clear that he would not be happy unless China put off the war Mao wanted in favor of the war Kim wanted.

Mao had little choice but to swallow his fury and play the cards Stalin dealt him. He met two days later with Kim and agreed to support the unification of the Korean Peninsula by force of arms. But Mao warned Kim it could be a difficult and bloody slog, saying that the Americans—or perhaps the Japanese—were likely to join the war and prolong the fight.

Kim dismissed the warning. Victory would be quick and easy, he said. He predicted that the Japanese, should they dare return to Korea, would be crushed. Echoing what he had heard from Stalin, he told Mao that the Americans had slunk out of China without putting up a fight and would do the same in Korea.

Soviet advisers in Pyongyang soon wrote up a detailed war plan. The attack would commence early on Sunday, June 25. As prescribed by Stalin, it would be disguised to look like a defensive maneuver—a justifiable reaction to a South Korean invasion. The first stage would be a relatively small "counterattack" on the Ongjin Peninsula. Then a much larger force would hit the western coast of Korea.

Four days before the planned attack, there was an intelligence leak. Kim sent urgent word to Stalin: the South Koreans had learned of the North's plan. Kim now wanted a full-scale invasion. As Shtykov explained to Stalin in a cable, "Instead of a local operation at Ongjin Peninsula as a prelude to the general offensive, Kim Il Sung suggests an overall attack on 25 June along the whole front line."

Stalin cabled back the same day. Go for it, he told Kim, "advance along the whole front line," but be sure to make it look to the world as though South Korea were starting the war.

IV

When he heard the news, No Kum Sok had just returned to the naval academy after a punishing Sunday morning of infantry training. He had been crawling up a dusty mountain ridge on his belly carrying a rifle and heavy backpack.

A dour political officer dressed in navy blue spoke to No and other cadets as they lined up outside the mess hall for lunch. They were exhausted, sweaty, and caked in dirt.

"A full-scale war started early this morning," the officer told them. "The South Koreans suddenly invaded north of the thirty-eighth parallel and advanced two to three kilometers. Our People's Army counterattacked and has advanced twenty to thirty kilometers south of the border. The fighting is continuing."

The Great Leader was telling the same story that day on Radio Pyong-yang.

After rejecting North Korea's earnest proposals for peaceful unification, Kim told his listeners, the "puppet government of country-selling traitor Syngman Rhee" started the war. Kim said American stooges like Rhee would be hunted down and executed. An important reason for the war, he explained, was that American capitalists were forcing farmers off their land, closing factories, bankrupting businesses, creating mass unemployment, and starving the people.

"This war," Kim said on the radio, "is a war of righteousness for the cause of unification, independence, freedom, and democracy of the fatherland."

At the naval academy, a teacher of politics showed cadets "evidence" of the attack: an enlarged photograph of John Foster Dulles (then a foreign policy adviser and later secretary of state under Eisenhower) talking with the American ambassador and a South Korean general as they stood near the thirty-eighth parallel. The teacher did not take questions.

As No heard it, the story about how the war began did not make much sense. He wondered how a massive surprise invasion by the South Korean army, with the muscle of the U.S. military behind it, could have been stopped after advancing just two or three kilometers.

How could the North, as Kim said on the radio, already have "liberated" many towns and cities in the South? How could the South Koreans and the Americans have been thrown back so far and so fast?

But other cadets seemed to believe, and so did the people of North Korea. Just to make sure, North Korean state radio explained again and again that the invasion was instigated by the Americans and executed by their capitalist stooges in Seoul.

No heard this version of how the war started so many times that he came to believe it.

It would be years before he learned who attacked whom. But he never bought the idea that whipping the South Koreans—and the Americans—would be easy.

PART II

WAR

CHAPTER 4

The Great Liberation Struggle

I

For a few days, Kim Il Sung was a military genius.

His forces were all but unstoppable, particularly the ones howling south in Soviet tanks. South Korean soldiers abandoned their positions after discovering that shells from American rocket launchers bounced harmlessly off T-34 tanks. In less than forty-eight hours, the North Korean People's Army took Seoul, some thirty miles south of the thirty-eighth parallel. Three days into the war, nearly 80 percent of the South's army was unaccounted for, and nearly all its artillery, trucks, and supplies were lost.

Bristling with new Soviet weaponry, North Korean soldiers were not only better equipped than their counterparts in the South but better trained, more disciplined, and more ideologically committed. Nearly half of them were battle-hardened veterans who had fought, some for as long as a decade, on the Communist side in China's civil war. With Mao's approval, they had returned home to become the fist of the North Korean military. Most of them came from peasant families, and they despised Koreans in the South who had been Japanese collaborators. They viewed Americans as imperialist enablers of elites who ruled in Seoul.

The Americans badly underestimated their enemy, with a condescension bred of ignorance and racism. "I can handle it with one arm tied behind my back," General Douglas MacArthur, commander of U.S. forces in the Far East, said the day the war began. The next day, he said that if he sent just one cavalry division into Korea, "Why heavens you'd see those fellows scuddle up to the Manchurian border so quick, you would see no more of them." American soldiers believed officers who told them that North Korean troops would run and hide at the sight of a white man.

On the battlefield, as MacArthur himself soon acknowledged, the North Koreans were efficient, skillful, and tough. Combining Japanese infiltration skills with Russian tank tactics, they overwhelmed South Korean forces and alarmed the United States, along with much of the world. Two days after the invasion began, the United Nations Security Council authorized the use of force to stop North Korea. The Soviet Union's representative was absent from the vote and could not use his veto. On the fifth day after the invasion, President Harry Truman approved the use of ground forces. He told the American people it was a "police action."

Whatever its name, the United States was rushing into war. As Truman privately told his secretary of state, "We've got to stop the sons of bitches no matter what." Kim's preinvasion prediction of American passivity was wrong, as was his promise to Stalin and Mao that tens of thousands of South Korean Communists would rise up and help the North Korean army vanquish the imperialists.

Nothing of the sort happened. Stalin, too, had badly misread American foreign policy. He had no idea what the United States would fight for in Asia.

But for a couple of weeks, their misjudgments did not matter. North Korean troops crushed the first wave of American troops to arrive in Korea. Sixteen thousand soldiers and officers of the army's Twenty-fourth Infantry Division rushed into the war from cushy and undemanding duty in Japan, where they were physically unfit, poorly trained, and badly equipped. Few had combat experience. After two weeks in

Korea, about half of them were dead, wounded, or missing, including the division commander, General William F. Dean, who got lost in his jeep and became a prisoner of war. It was one of the most disastrous and humiliating showings in the history of the U.S. Army.

Korea, a place that had existed on the fuzzy, ill-informed edges of the American public's awareness of global trouble spots, became the center of the first major fight against Communism. And the United States was losing badly.

Stalin fretted when the Americans rushed into the war, sending an anxious cable to Shtykov, asking if the North Korean leadership was scared "or do they hold firm?" But by late August, the Boss had calmed down. Kim's army controlled the entire Korean Peninsula, save for an American toehold at Pusan, a city at its southeastern tip. As important to the Kremlin, Truman had refrained from publicly blaming the war on the secret machinations of the Soviet Union. To Stalin's enormous relief, the Americans, even though they were convinced that the Soviet Union had armed and enabled North Korea, did not use the Korean conflict as a pretext for a third world war. Stalin sent a cable in late August to Pyongyang, saluting "the great liberation struggle of the Korean people, which comrade Kim Il Sung is conducting with brilliant success. [I have] no doubt that in the nearest future the interventionists will be driven out of Korea with ignominy."

Stalin's pleasure was short-lived. Indeed, weeks before he sent his congratulatory cable, the North's army had begun to fall apart.

It was undone, in large measure, by Kim's impatience and incompetence as a war planner. In his rush to invade on June 25, he chose not to wait for most of the heavy armor that Stalin had given him. Eighty-nine T-34 tanks arrived by ship in July and August. Had he waited for them, the T-34s would have more than doubled the number of tanks in his invasion force and substantially increased his chances of winning a lightning victory. Kim could have raced into South Korea in the first days of the war with three armored divisions instead of one. Other Soviet military supplies, had Kim waited for them, would have outfitted another division's worth of infantry soldiers for the invasion. As important, Soviet equipment, food, and fuel would have substantially strengthened his combat supply lines.

As it turned out, many of North Korea's tanks and other mechanized units broke down within days on the rough terrain. Supply lines quickly collapsed. After the initial rout, several South Korean army units stood their ground, fighting with unexpected pluck and gumming up the North's effort to control the peninsula before massive numbers of American and international troops and their equipment could arrive. As they pushed south, many North Korean frontline commanders proved incompetent, turning certain victory into stalemate.

Desperate for better battlefield leadership, Kim begged Stalin to send Soviet military advisers to the front, saying that without them "the invasion would fail." Just two weeks into the war, Shtykov told Stalin "he had never seen Kim Il Sung so dejected and hopeless." In the weeks and months to come, Shtykov would have many opportunities to watch Kim come unglued. Delay and indecision in the North's offensive gave the Americans time to reinforce the Pusan line, which protected their precarious hold on the end of the peninsula—and allowed them time to plan a counterattack.

From the first day of fighting, North Korea had an insuperable vulnerability. The country could be devastated from the sky. Its infant air force was desperately short of trained pilots. A North Korean pilot shot down on the second day of the invasion told interrogators that the North had just eighty pilots, only two of whom were any good. When these pilots attacked the South, they flew World War II–era, propeller-driven aircraft that were easily shot down. Three weeks into the war, nearly all of the North's 132 combat planes had been destroyed. Most were strafed or bombed as they sat on runways.

"The air battle was short and sweet," said Lieutenant General George E. Stratemeyer, commander of U.S. Far East Air Forces during the first year of the war. "Air supremacy was quickly established . . . I need not dwell on the fact that had the enemy possessed a modern air force the whole picture in Korea—from the viewpoint of land, sea, and air forces— would have been vastly different."

To the delight of Americans drawing up bombing plans, North Korea revealed itself as a sitting duck of historic proportions: helpless and within easy striking distance of bombers based in Japan and Okinawa. The purpose of the air campaign, according to Major General Emmett O'Donnell, a veteran planner of the bombing of Japan during World War II, was to deliver "a very severe blow . . . and go to work burning five major cities in North Korea to the ground."

The official history of the air force campaign in Korea uses the word "leisurely" to characterize the first months of bombing. "Our bombing should have been good," said Colonel James V. Edmundson, a commander of the Twenty-second Bombardment Group. "We didn't have any opposition and the bombardiers had all the time in the world to make their bomb runs."

Bombs fell from the B-29 Superfortress, the hulking, long-range, four-engine plane that firebombed Tokyo and dropped atomic bombs on Hiroshima and Nagasaki. On board these aircraft, air force cameramen safely filmed the destruction. Their images soon appeared in newsreels shown in movie theaters across the United States. From ten thousand feet, the American response to Communist aggression looked efficient, overwhelming, and, with no visible corpses, rather tidy. Within a month, bombs from B-29s had methodically ruined North Korea's most important industrial cities. Within two months, there was—from the perspective of B-29 bombardiers—a critical shortage of targets.

Airmen aboard B-29s called it a "commuter war," with daily missions that took them out and back from comfortable quarters in Japan and Okinawa. They usually arrived home in time for dinner. They did not see the human cost of the bombs they dropped, and as the historian Kathryn Weathersby has noted, "Their memories of the war overwhelmingly focus on the performance of their aircraft, and secondarily on the painful loss of fellow airmen" who crashed or were shot down.

Outside the United States, the targeting of cities provoked outrage. In India, Jawaharlal Nehru complained of racist disregard for human life. In the United Nations, the Soviet Union accused the Americans of "barbarous and indiscriminate bombing of peaceful towns and civilians." There was sympathetic coverage of these charges in the international press, especially in British newspapers. But Americans did not read or hear much about it, and the wholesale killing of North Korean civilians never embarrassed politicians in the United States. It was a nonissue.

Thirty years after the truce that ended the conflict in Korea, the revised edition of the official history of the U.S. Air Force in the war said unambiguously that the "strategic air attacks destroyed none but legitimate military targets in North Korea, and the bombing was so accurate as to do little damage to civilian installations near the industrial plants [that were destroyed]." The official history noted, too, that the air force always dropped leaflets that "gave industrial workers ample warning that the bombers were coming."

In a congratulatory letter to the commander of the bombing operation, General Stratemeyer wrote, "The Far East Air Force Bomber Command, new as it is in the annals of the United States Air Force, has made history for which you and every member of your command can be justly proud."

II

No Kum Sok watched history being made in Chongjin.

American bomb planners had singled out the city in July, placing it on a list of major industrial targets to be destroyed. The naval academy and its three hundred cadets had moved there eleven months before the start of the Korean War. Chongjin then had a population of about 300,000 and was the political, industrial, and shipping center for the country's northernmost province.

When air-raid sirens first sounded in the city in July, thousands of leaflets fell from the sky. Few of them, however, found their way into the city; most were blown away by the wind. Like all residents of Chongjin, No and the other cadets had been given strict orders not to read leaflets dropped from enemy aircraft. They were supposed to turn them over to political officers. Soon after the leaflets were spotted, commanders at the naval academy ordered all cadets and school personnel to flee to the surrounding mountains.

Civilians stayed put.

As No ran for the hills, the first bombs exploded. Air force fighters did not escort the B-29s that dropped them, nor did a single North Korean aircraft rise up to try to defend the city. The American bombers struck their targets with precision, destroying No's school and most other military targets in Chongjin. That evening the naval academy set up a temporary barracks near the sea about ten miles northeast of the city. The cadets slept on cots in a long, low, unlit cave that had been cut through a mountain.

A few weeks later, on August 19, No was standing on that mountain at six o'clock in the morning, beginning his shift of sentry duty, when he saw a lone B-29 appear in the southern sky and swoop low over Chongjin. It was a reconnaissance plane, No guessed, taking photographs of the city. A half hour later, he saw four more B-29s lumber in from the south. Laying down his rifle, he crawled into a nearby foxhole and for the next five hours watched as the Americans carpet bombed Chongjin.

The B-29s started their work on the city's southwest edge. When bombs emerged from the belly of the planes, the pitch of their engines changed, as if sighing in relief, and the B-29s disappeared in the east. For a few moments, only a menacing whistle pierced the morning's quiet. Then explosions shook the earth, as smoke, flames, and screams filled the air. In his mountaintop foxhole, No began to tremble. Within two minutes, another wave of B-29s appeared, laying down their bombs a block north of the first row of explosions. So it went, as sixty-three B-29s carried out what the air force called "strategic bombing."

Like mowing a lawn, the destruction of Chongjin was a steady, systematic, and unhurried chore that moved block by block southwest to northeast. Again, the bombers did not bring a fighter escort. Again, they did not need one. North Korean aircraft did not interrupt their work, nor were any antiaircraft guns fired. In his foxhole, No could see how the residents of Chongjin responded to the bombing.

They did not evacuate before it started, nor did they flee as explosions devoured their neighborhoods. They stayed in their homes and apartments, dying by the thousands.

After the war, an American bomb damage assessment found that eighteen of the twenty-two largest cities in North Korea had been at least half demolished. It asserted that 65 percent of Chongjin had been obliterated. There is no official death toll from the bombing of Chongjin, but a postwar census found that the city lost about a third of its residents, about a hundred thousand people.

No had read newspaper stories about the Allied bombings of Berlin and Tokyo during World War II. Now he understood, as he cowered in his foxhole, the terror that people in those cities had experienced. The bombing horrified and revolted No. He was a witness to American savagery. But what he saw did not dim his desire to get out of North Korea. His goal did not change. He still wanted to live in the United States.

Waves of B-29s moved steadily north toward the mountain where No was trying to hide. He could see them coming and feared he would die in the dirt. But before they reached him, the B-29s veered away to drop their bombs on more populous targets. When the explosions ended and he climbed out of his hole, his hands were still trembling. On the beach that evening, he joined other cadets to listen to a political officer's speech. The naval academy was moving, the officer said, to a location less likely to be carpet bombed. It was sixty miles away, halfway between Chongjin and the Russian border. There was no rail line or road, not even a cleared path.

So they walked for two days and one night, bushwhacking through valleys and skirting around mountains. Commanders gave them a fifteen-minute break every two hours. All the cadets were in excellent shape, and no one collapsed from exhaustion.

When No was in elementary school, he had read stories about Japanese soldiers who somehow learned to sleep while on long marches in China. As he trudged toward the border carrying his heavy Russian rifle, No sometimes slipped into a walking sleep. He dreamed, briefly, of life before the Great Leader, when he was a schoolboy and his father was still alive.

His long march and short dreams ended when they arrived at the entrance to a dark railway tunnel near the coast. Newly excavated in anticipation of a railroad that had yet to be built, it cut through a mountain ridge high above the East Sea (Sea of Japan). There were no railroad tracks inside, just mud. The exhausted cadets, given no rest after their trek, barricaded each end of the tunnel with sandbags, strung electric lights and phone lines, and set up cots. Later they cut down trees to make bunk beds.

This would be the new naval academy. They slept in the cold, clammy tunnel and took infantry training out in the highlands. In between, they endured long political meetings that denounced the American aggression that they were told had started the war.

One evening on the hillside outside the tunnel, a cadet who was cleaning a Russian submachine gun accidentally pulled the trigger, firing three bullets into the stomach of a nearby classmate, killing him, and horrifying the other cadets. They had joined the naval academy to get a free college education and avoid dying on a battlefield. Now they were marching in the hills, apparently preparing to be infantry grunts, and one of their classmates was dead of gut wounds.

The day after the shooting accident, a political officer in the academy called the cadets together for a pep talk. His remarks, though, added to their collective dread. He told them that the academy trained officers for combat, not office jobs. It expected them to be leaders of men, fearless in battle, and willing to die for a glorious cause.

A few days after the cadets moved into the tunnel, American warships patrolling along the east coast of North Korea spotted them and began lobbing artillery shells in their direction. Explosions shook the ground around the clock, with shelling heaviest at night. From the tunnel entrance, No could see flashes of light far out in the East Sea. Then, within a minute or two, incoming shells would whistle briefly before smashing into the surrounding mountains.

III

Eleven weeks into the war, it was Douglas MacArthur's turn to be a genius, as forces under his command broke the back of the North Korean army. In doing so, they demonstrated to Stalin and Mao that Kim was an arrogant, inattentive amateur who had no business commanding a modern army. When he humiliated Kim and changed the course of the war, MacArthur was seventy and had been famous for much of his life. Perhaps more than that of any general in American history, his career had married battlefield creativity with theatrical self-promotion.

"He was a great thundering paradox of a man," his biographer William Manchester wrote. He had "great personal charm, a will of iron, and a soaring intellect." But at the same time "no more baffling, exasperating soldier ever wore a uniform. Flamboyant, imperious, and apocalyptic, he carried the plumage of a flamingo, could not acknowledge errors, and tried to cover up his mistakes with sly, childish tricks."

During World War I, MacArthur wore riding breeches and wrapped himself in a four-foot-long scarf; his men called him "the fighting dude." His baldness could never be photographed. Insisting on being larger than life, he ordered a photographer from *Stars and Stripes* to kneel while shooting his picture. He presented himself to the world, author William Styron wrote, as a great man who was "almost totally free of self-doubt" and was blessed with "a serene confidence untouched by that daily incertitude which afflicts most humans."

MacArthur's insatiable appetite for flattery was not unlike that of Kim Il Sung. Like Kim, he surrounded himself with mediocre, obsequious men who "catered to his peacockery." As Clare Boothe Luce put it, "MacArthur's temperament was flawed by an egotism that demanded obedience not only to his orders, but to his ideas and his person as well. He plainly relished idolatry."

A favorite of conservative Republicans, MacArthur harbored presidential aspirations and had a knack for annoying his commanders in chief. Yet he was so creative as a military strategist that Democratic presidents put up with him—that is, until Truman fired him in 1951, with the Korean War still raging.

For all his failings, MacArthur had an almost miraculous gift for winning huge battles without spilling American blood. He was "remarkably economical of human life." As commander of U.S. forces in the Pacific during World War II, MacArthur had saved countless American servicemen by perfecting an island-hopping strategy of hitting the Japanese where they were weak, cutting off their supply lines, and minimizing suicidal charges on dug-in machine guns. He believed in surprising his enemy with an attack that seemed impossible. The less likely it was to succeed, he believed, the less the enemy would be prepared to defend against it, and fewer American boys would have to die.

Guided by this audacious principle, MacArthur planned an amphibious marine landing at Inchon, a port about thirty miles west of Seoul. Everything about Inchon was risky—too risky, in the opinion of officials in Washington. Tides were among the highest in the world. There were no beaches for landing craft, just mudflats that could mire marines in gluey muck if the landing did not time the tides exactly right. In addition, mining the harbor would be an easy and obvious task for North Korea. It would be the first priority of a competent commander.

MacArthur bet that Kim was incompetent. He also wagered that superb planning and perfect execution would overcome all other obstacles. If he was right, the landing would allow Americans quick access to Seoul while severing the North's supply lines and stranding Kim's best troops at the southern end of the Korean Peninsula, where they could be picked apart by fighter-bombers.

"I can almost hear the ticking of the second hand of destiny. We must act now or we will die," MacArthur said in a briefing on the proposed landing on August 23. "Inchon will succeed. And it will save a hundred thousand lives."

The invasion was supposed to be a military secret. It could succeed only if the North Koreans failed to anticipate and prepare for it. Yet weeks before it happened, Chinese intelligence saw it coming. They watched a huge American buildup of troops and warships, then guessed that an amphibious invasion was taking shape. They guessed, too, that MacArthur, based on the surprise tactics he had often used in the Pacific against Japan, would probably land at Inchon. In two meetings with a North Korean official who had come to Beijing to brief the Chinese leadership on the progress of the war, Mao specifically warned of an American attack at Inchon and advised the North to retreat and deploy troops to prevent a catastrophe. Soviet advisers made similar warnings. Eleven days before the attack, China's ambassador in Pyongyang met with Kim to discuss what exactly he was doing to protect his overextended army from an Inchon-like attack.

Kim was reluctant to share military information with Beijing. His government had not bothered telling China about the timing of its invasion of the South. Chinese officials learned about it by reading news accounts. Similarly, after fighting began, Kim did not seek China's advice, and when it was offered, he almost always ignored it.

"We estimate that presently, a U.S. counterattack is not possible," Kim told the Chinese ambassador. "They do not possess sufficient troop support, and therefore a landing in our rear ports would be difficult."

Five days before the Inchon invasion, with Beijing in a near panic over what they feared MacArthur was soon to spring on the North Koreans, the Chinese ambassador again met with Kim. Again, he implored the Great Leader to consider a strategic withdrawal and protect the North from an Inchon-style attack.

"I have never considered retreat," Kim replied.

Back in Manchuria in the 1930s, Kim had been a resourceful and cunning guerrilla leader, as skilled in retreating from the Japanese as he was in attacking them. But his command skills were dated and limited. He had led two hundred partisans armed with rifles and knives, not tens of thousands of troops with tanks, artillery, and supply lines that extended for hundreds of miles. Compounding his incompetence was fear on the part of his advisers. Like the officers who surrounded MacArthur, they were afraid of the great man's displeasure. No one close to Kim dared warn that the North's army could soon be lost. When the Chinese and the Soviets did warn him, he would not listen.

On the morning of September 15, 1950, the weather proved perfect for the landing at Inchon, and so did MacArthur's plan. Thirteen thousand marines stormed the piers and seawalls, overwhelming a scant two thousand North Korean soldiers based in the area. On the first day, only twenty marines were killed. After three days, seventy thousand American troops had come ashore. Within ten days, marines were in Seoul. Down in the far south of the peninsula, where Americans had broken out of the Pusan perimeter, the North Korean army collapsed and was fleeing north. Kim's army was decimated, losing as many as fifty thousand soldiers (out of the estimated ninety-eight thousand it had sent into South Korea). Nearly all of his Soviet-supplied tanks and mobile armor were destroyed or abandoned. All the while, American bombers pounded North Korean cities. In late September, Shtykov reported to Stalin that Kim was confused, lost, hopeless, and desperate.

Stalin had explicitly warned Kim in April before the war that if the North Korean army got "kicked in the teeth," Moscow would "not lift a finger" and he would have to ask Mao for help. But Kim begged for Soviet help anyway. On September 29, 1950, three months and four days after the war began, MacArthur officially restored the South Korean government to power in Seoul, and Kim sent an urgent cable to Stalin.

"We consider it necessary to report to you about extremely unfavorable conditions for us," he wrote. "The enemy's air force, possessing about one thousand planes of various kinds, is not encountering any resistance from our side, and has full control in the air. It conducts bombing at the front and in the rear daily, around the clock."

Kim begged Stalin for Soviet MiGs and Soviet help in teaching North Koreans how to fly them. He predicted (accurately) that the Americans and the South Koreans would soon march into North Korea. "At the moment that the enemy troops cross the thirty-eighth parallel," Kim wrote, "we'll be in dire need of direct military assistance from the Soviet Union."

Stalin refused to send soldiers. He had no taste for a distant ground war against the Americans. Instead, two days after reading Kim's help-me telegram, he wrote to Mao, explaining that the "situation of the Korean comrades is becoming desperate." China, he said, must clean up the mess.

Stalin blamed the North Koreans for military ineptitude and for failing to heed his advice to move troops north in time to repulse the landing at Inchon. "Korean comrades don't have any troops capable of resistance," Stalin told Mao. "The road in the direction of the thirty-eighth parallel can be considered open."

To save Kim's government, Stalin told Mao that he should "without delay" dispatch five or six divisions of Chinese "volunteers" (about a hundred thousand soldiers) to stop the Americans. He closed his message by saying, "I don't intend to inform Korean comrades about this, but I have no doubt they'll be glad when they learn about it."

IV

In the muddy tunnel turned naval academy, a political officer called all the cadets together. The Americans, he said, had landed at Inchon. He did not elaborate or explain. From that day forward, cadets would be given no more official news about the war. They only heard rumors, nearly all of them frightening.

The American landing thrilled No Kum Sok. He suspected that Inchon—and the information blackout that followed it—meant the beginning of the end of the Great Leader and of Communism in North Korea. Less happily, he suspected that the crippled army would soon be clamoring for infantrymen to send to the front. More than ever, he needed an excuse not to go.

It came a week after Inchon. A dozen doctors arrived at the tunnel to give an elaborate physical test to a hundred randomly chosen cadets. No was not among the chosen, but he was curious about what the doctors were doing and hung around to watch. The doctors asked a few teachers at the academy to assist with scoring the tests. One of them was the history professor who had given No an A in Communist Party history. This professor kept score on two "spin tests." In the first, a cadet sat in a swivel chair and was spun around twenty times. Then he stood and tried to walk straight. In the second test, a cadet held a finger to the ground, ran twenty circles around it, and, again, tried to walk straight. A few of his classmates, having spun, fell down when they tried to walk.

As he watched his dizzy classmates, No realized that the doctors were looking for pilots. Those selected, he guessed, would have to be trained for at least a year. By then, he hoped, the war would be over. Pilot trainees might never have to fight. They certainly would not be sent to the front as cannon fodder.

"May I take the test, Professor?" he asked.

The teacher hesitated and tilted his head to stare for a moment at his star pupil, who seemed to be such a fervent Communist.

"Yes," he said, "go ahead and take it."

The test did not make No dizzy. He passed it easily and scored well on the rest of the physical exam. Much later, No would learn of the life-or-death importance of the spin test. Most of those who did not take it—or flunked it—were killed in ground combat against the South Koreans and the Americans.

That evening, on the mountain ridge outside the tunnel, No was asked to line up with the eighty cadets who had passed the test. It was late September, a cloudless, moon-bright night with a cold wind. The North Korean winter would come soon. Echoing up from the sea, the sound of whitecaps breaking against the rocky shore could be heard by No. That night, led by the professor of Soviet Communist Party history, they marched twenty miles by moonlight to another railroad tunnel. At one rest stop on the way, the professor told them that discipline in the naval academy had been stupidly harsh. He said that when they became commanders, they should be more tolerant and humane.

No was jubilant during the night's long walk, convinced that he was heading off to flight school, where Kim Il Sung's government would teach him the skills he needed to fulfill his teenage dreams: he would learn to be a pilot, steal a plane, and fly away.

The rail tunnel at the end of the march offered a surprising improvement in accommodations. Freshly made beds awaited the cadets. When they awoke in the morning, they had an even bigger surprise—a promotion. An orderly gave No a new uniform with one star on each shoulder. He was now an ensign. Walking out of the tunnel to the officers' mess for breakfast, he encountered two sergeants who were much older than he was. They unnerved No by saluting him. At breakfast, the waiters were eager and the tablecloths white. In the officers' mess, the food was plentiful, hot, and tasty.

On his first day, No saw several Russian officers. They were living in the rail tunnel, eating at the officers' mess, and advising the North Korean navy. One of them strutted around outside the tunnel with a dog. The Americans also put in an appearance that day. They flew over the tunnel in B-29s, dropping bombs, chasing the Russians and the North Koreans into the tunnel for shelter.

That night, No's jubilation about the future was confirmed by the vice-commander of the naval academy. He told the new ensigns they would become pilots. He did not say when or where, but ordered them to pack up immediately. They marched again that night and stopped at a small depot, where a two-car train took them north. It stopped at dawn inside a railroad tunnel to avoid American air attack. No took a delicious swim that day in a nearby river and ate a leisurely lunch in a small village. At dusk, they resumed their journey, rolling farther north. At midnight, they stopped to change trains in a station on the south side of the Tumen River, which marks the border between North Korea and China.

"The crossing will be made in complete silence," an officer announced after they boarded a Chinese train pulled by a black steam locomotive. "Take off your uniforms and all signs of rank. Put on these clothes."

No was given padded black cotton pants and a jacket. At first he thought they were work clothes. But as the train chugged across the river, he realized he was wearing the uniform of the Chinese People's Liberation Army.

CHAPTER 5

Kicked in the Teeth

I

Thanks to Kim Il Sung's stubborn refusal to listen to his tactical betters, he had lost, in less than four months, most of his army and much of its weaponry. He was helpless to stop American aircraft from devastating his cities and slaughtering his retreating troops. As one of his commanders later wrote, the bombing "tormented" the Korean army: Soldiers "could neither fight nor move during daylight . . . As soon as the aircraft sound was heard, one could see the serious neurotic state in which the soldiers were terrified out of their wits."

Kim's war spun completely out of control in the first two weeks of October. South Korean and American troops advanced north across the thirty-eighth parallel and began taking control of his country. He fled the capital and hid near the Chinese border. Fearing attack from the air, he and nearly everyone in his government lived in bunkers, caves, and tunnels during the day, traveling only at night. The future of Kim Il Sung and the continued existence of North Korea were now in the hands of Stalin and Mao.

Stalin had applauded the idea of Communist expansion on the

Korean Peninsula and was enthusiastic about forcing the Americans to spend treasure and spill blood to try to stop it. But he did not want a ground confrontation with the United States. After Inchon, when it seemed likely that North Korea would be lost, Stalin bluntly told Khrushchev that Moscow would never use troops to stop the Americans unless they invaded the Soviet Union itself. The Great Leader and his country were expendable. If he had to, Stalin said, he could tolerate Americans on the border with China and the Soviet Union.

"So what? Let the United States of America be our neighbors in the Far East," he said. "They will come there, but we shall not fight them now. We are not ready to fight."

Like Stalin, Mao lost little sleep worrying about the survival of Kim Il Sung, viewing him as an irritating incompetent. Kim himself was to blame for this. Before the war started in June, at his first meeting with Mao, when he broke the news that Stalin had given him a thumbs-up to invade South Korea, Kim acted uppity. That impression deepened in the early months of the war as Kim failed to keep Beijing informed about the fighting, turned down Chinese aid offers, and ignored advice from Mao that might have prevented the disaster at Inchon.

But unlike Stalin, Mao could not stomach the idea of Americans prancing around on his country's eastern border. He worried that they might cross into Manchuria or perhaps arm the Nationalists in Taiwan for an invasion. "If the American imperialists are victorious," he told his Politburo in early August, "they will become dizzy with success, and then be in a position to threaten us. We have to help Korea; we have to assist them."

Soon after Kim's catastrophic defeat at Inchon, China began making substantial preparations to do exactly that. On October 8, Mao issued an order that created a Chinese volunteer force, named a famous general as its commander, and began assembling troops near the North Korean border. In a telegram to Kim, Mao said, "We have decided to send volunteers to Korea to help you fight against the aggressors." The plan was for Chinese soldiers to begin moving into Korean territory around October 15.

The Great Leader, by then in dire need of rescue, was giddy with happiness.

"Well done!" he said. "Excellent!"

Mao, however, did not tell Kim that China had a key precondition before it would fight the Americans: air cover.

The Chinese military did not have a modern air force. Aware of this weakness, Stalin had told Mao back in July that "we will do our best to provide air cover" for Chinese soldiers if the Americans crossed the thirty-eighth parallel.

Mao wanted more than words. Fearing that his soldiers would be slaughtered, as the North Koreans had been, by American air supremacy, Mao wanted an ironclad commitment from Stalin. He expected the Soviet air force to work with the Chinese infantry and push the Americans south.

On October 9, 1950, just a day after delighting Kim Il Sung with news that the Chinese infantry was coming to the rescue, Mao secretly sent two senior officials, Zhou Enlai and Lin Biao, to talk to Stalin. Their orders were to tell him that China would *not* rescue North Korea without a commitment of air support. The Chinese argued with the Boss for two days at his villa on the Black Sea.

"We asked, 'Can you help with your air force?'" Zhou said later. "[Stalin] vacillated, saying that if China had difficulty, then it was better not to send troops, that if North Korea was lost, we would still be socialist, and China would still exist . . . We just wanted the Soviet Union to send some of their air force, and then we could go in, but without the air force, we would be in trouble. Stalin said he could not send [his] air force."

Exasperated by Stalin's games, Mao pulled the plug. In an October 12 telegram, he told the Soviet leader that China had changed its mind. It would not bail out North Korea. At the same time, though, Mao kept Chinese troops near the Korean border and continued their training.

Mao's telegram weighed heavily on Stalin because a week earlier the Soviet Politburo had decided to abandon North Korea rather than risk a ground confrontation with the Americans. In Moscow the morning after he heard from Mao, Stalin received still more discouraging news about North Korea. The chief of the Soviet navy told him that MacArthur was uncoiling yet another amphibious assault, this time off the east coast of North Korea. A massive naval flotilla, including three aircraft carriers, a battleship, three heavy cruisers, twelve destroyers, two squadrons of minesweepers, and hundreds of assault landing crafts, had been spotted in the East Sea. It was headed for the harbor of Wonsan, which Stalin feared would complicate an already disastrous situation and give the Americans control over all of North Korea.

That afternoon, Stalin decided to cut his losses. He composed an extraordinary telegram. Without ceremony and without delay, Stalin wrote, Kim and his army must flee the Korean Peninsula, head for the Manchurian boondocks, and await further instructions.

"The Chinese have again refused to send troops," Stalin wrote. "Because of this, you must evacuate Korea and retreat in the northern direction in the shortest possible period."

Kim was stunned. He said it was "very hard" to give up, according to a telegram sent to Stalin by Shtykov, who had delivered the crushing news to Kim late at night in his makeshift headquarters in the town of Kosangjin near the Chinese border.

Yet the Great Leader began preparations to skulk away as instructed. On the same night that Stalin ordered him to retreat, Kim asked Shtykov for advice on leaving the country and requested that the Soviets give him an evacuation plan. He called a trusted member of his Front Military Council, Major General Choe Kyong Dok, to his headquarters and told him to leave at once for Manchuria and scout out bases. Over the next few hours, Kim reportedly told his closest associates, partisans who had fought with him in Manchuria, that they would again have to become guerrilla fighters.

Then, shockingly, Mao changed his mind again.

Just hours after Stalin sent the cable that terminated the existence of North Korea, he received a cable from Mao that said China had decided to fight, with or without Soviet air cover. Within a week, 260,000 Chinese troops began crossing the Yalu River into North Korea.

Mao simply could not accept American domination of the entire Korean Peninsula. MacArthur's demands for the North's unconditional surrender, together with his threats against China, had exacerbated Mao's insecurity. He and the entire Chinese leadership, fearing that the Americans might soon march into China, decided it was best to go to war on Korean soil.

Stalin welcomed China's final flip-flop. He wrote a letter to Kim, saying that he "was glad that the final and favorable decision for Korea has been made at last."

Kim, meanwhile, had become a passive observer of his mouse-like insignificance.

Upon the whims of Stalin and Mao, he and his country had ceased to exist. A day later, upon the whims of Stalin and Mao, he and his country were permitted to exist again. The Great Leader's status as a player in the power struggles of the Soviet Union and China was painfully clear: North Korea and its people were expendable. So was he.

Kim's humiliation—and the bitterness it engendered—would permanently stain North Korea's relations with the Soviet Union and China. In the long run, Kim would get revenge. He would play the Communist powers off each other while milking them for development aid, industrial expertise, and military hardware. But in the short run, as China took command of the war he had so eagerly started, Kim's degradation was just beginning.

II

Inside China, No Kum Sok traveled north by train and then by truck to Yanji airfield, which had a wide dirt runway and a handful of low brick barracks. Thirty Soviet-built, propeller-driven training aircraft were parked out in the weather, which soon turned bitingly cold. The flight instructors at Yanji were North Koreans whose planes and home air bases had been destroyed by American air attacks in the first weeks of the war.

The airfield was in Jilin Province, a region that in the 1950s was still commonly referred to as Manchuria. It had been part of the guerrilla-war turf of the young Kim Il Sung in his fight against Japanese colonial police, and most of the population was still ethnic Korean. In the city of Yanji, No felt as though he had never left Korea. Newspapers were printed in Korean script. Courses at the city university were taught in Korean. No heard Korean music on local radio, ate Korean food in local restaurants, and attended a Korean drama in a local theater. It was only when performers in the play referred to "our country" and meant China that No was jolted into remembering he was in a foreign country.

Being inside China was the necessary condition that allowed him to learn how to fly. If the planes, pilots, and students at Yanji airfield had been back in North Korea, they would have been obliterated by American bombs.

Location defined safety in the Korean War, which was fought under a curious set of unwritten superpower rules. They were intended to confine all shooting, bombing, and killing to the Korean Peninsula and prevent violence from spreading into a broader war. Leaders in Washington, Moscow, and Beijing who could have expanded the war chose not to do so. Truman ordered American pilots not to go after ground targets in Manchuria or the Soviet Far East. His restraint was sorely tested when the Chinese troops poured into Korea. His generals drew up plans to drop nuclear bombs on Manchuria, and U.S. combat pilots slipped over the border to hunt airborne enemy aircraft. Still, ground targets in Manchuria remained safely out-of-bounds throughout the war.

As a result, No found that his new quarters were tranquil—and surprisingly comfortable. Instead of shivering in a cave or a tunnel, he slept on a new straw mattress in a well-heated barrack. There was plenty of meat in his soup. Because the mission at Yanji was to teach young men how to fly as quickly as possible—and not to torment them with discipline and physical hardship—the students were allowed a reasonable amount of sleep. They awoke at six in the morning and were encouraged to be in bed by nine or ten at night.

No had never flown in an airplane, never been near one. He had never even driven a car. To his relief, other naval cadets were just as green. They began their careers as combat pilots with four weeks of classroom basics, learning the principles of flight, how an internal combustion engine worked, and the names of an airplane's parts—rudders, flaps, ailerons. By early winter, as snow blanketed Manchuria, they had left the classroom and climbed aboard the World War II–era propeller planes that Moscow had shipped east by train. Instructors taught them how to fly Yak-18s, a light, fabric-covered two-seater with a three-hundred-horsepower engine and a passing resemblance to the Japanese Zero, the fighter No would have flown had his father not nipped his adolescent urge to be a kamikaze pilot in the bud.

On his first flight, No sat in the front seat of a Yak-18 with an instructor seated behind. The takeoff was so smooth that No did not realize he was airborne. Gradually, the instructor allowed him to take control while explaining what speed to maintain to avoid stalling. No understood and memorized everything. On his next flight, he repeated the routine precisely. He had a good mind for navigation, an intuitive feel for flying, and preternatural self-confidence. His stomach never got upset, even when he flew upside down. Most important, learning how to fly gave him hope. He had a means to get out of North Korea.

He soloed in the Yak-18 after thirty hours of training, then moved up to the Yak-11, a heavier, faster, all-metal, prop-driven fighter that was more difficult to master. A day after his first solo in the bigger plane, on a morning when the airfield was covered in fresh snow, he volunteered to be the first to go up. Thirty minutes later, as he returned for landing, the flat winter light, a gusty wind, and the snowy runway confused his vision. Losing track of his altitude, he stalled the plane, bounced it on the runway, became airborne, bounced it again, and finally came to a stop. The base commander, who happened to be watching, gave No a dirty look.

"That was the lousiest landing I have ever seen," he said.

The lousy landing, though, did not damage No's standing in the Korean People's Air Force, which paid much more attention to a pilot's political loyalty than to his flying skill. Political officers closely monitored pilot trainees, trying to identify and weed out those who might take advantage of a solo flight and defect to South Korea.

Because defection was exactly what he had in mind, No needed a cloak of patriotism to hide his intentions. He created a pro-Communist newspaper for the airfield and made himself its hyper-Communist editor in chief. In the pages of the *Battle Gazette,* No affirmed his devotion to the Great Leader and flattered senior officers at the airfield.

No had few close friends among the cadet pilots, even though they had worked, slept, and eaten in close quarters for more than a year. Keeping them at a distance made his Red act easier and less exhausting. All North Korean pilots were required to snitch on each other, reporting regularly on conversation and behavior that could be interpreted as disloyal or suspicious.

No trusted only one person at Yanji, Kun Soo Sung, who had been a naval cadet and was now a student pilot. Six years older than No, Kun was better educated and more worldly than most of the other North Koreans, having attended a merchant marine school in Korea run by the Japanese during World War II. Like No, Kun was a fake Red. The two young pilots could sense the pretense in each other and intuit a mutual loathing of Kim Il Sung's government. They told each other their secrets. Kun said he wanted to move to England when the war ended. He believed that the best way to survive was to put on a show of his love for the Great Leader and the Workers' Party of Korea, of which he was a member.

Kun became No's partner in the production of the *Battle Gazette.* They worked every night to write and illustrate three or four news items for the paper. Each was handwritten by No, while Kun drew sketches and caricatures. There were no typewriters or mimeograph machines at the airfield. No and Kun pressed down as hard as they could with pens on sheets of paper separated by carbon paper. Then they pasted the original and a few faint copies on cardboard, which they passed around in the flight line rest area, where student pilots, instructors, and some senior officers gathered every day.

The *Battle Gazette* used humor to exhort students to perfect their flying skills while minimizing flight hours and maximizing fuel savings. It warned them to avoid mistakes that could damage aircraft and runways. No and Kun also took pains to praise the bravery and self-sacrificing spirit of the North Korean military, particularly those in the infantry, who were fighting the Americans at the front. Everything in the newspaper emphasized the need for young pilots to obey their wise and hardworking superiors.

Political officers took notice. They praised No by name during ideology meetings. Whenever he could, No stood up at these meetings, denounced American imperialism, and thanked the Great Leader for his courage and wisdom. No's standing as a patriot also benefited from the long hours of parade-ground marching that he and the other naval cadets had been required to do back in North Korea. The commander in Yanji beamed when they marched smartly around the airfield, singing—in Russian—revolutionary songs. He called them the Special Group.

A voice No did *not* hear that Manchurian winter was that of Kim Il Sung. The volume on the Great Leader's propaganda machine was uncharacteristically low, which disturbed No. To become an air force pilot, No needed to be perceived as a reliable Red. Publicly praising the most recent pronouncements of the Great Leader had always been the easiest way for No to impress his superiors with his sincerity.

Now there was nothing to praise. The Great Leader had gone silent.

III

As Chinese soldiers prepared to surge into North Korea, their commander, Peng Dehuai, sized up Kim Il Sung's performance as a battlefield commander and concluded that he was a risk-taking fool.

"There are no long-term plans, and adventurism is all one can see!" Peng wrote in an evaluation of the leadership Kim demonstrated during the first months of the war. "Military control has been extremely childish."

This was not just a Chinese view. "He was the type of adventurer who left his fate to contingency and luck," wrote one former colleague of Kim's. "He always ordered reckless attacks and did not compose effective nor timely retreats."

Peng's judgment carried enormous weight in Beijing. He was China's top general, a hero of the Chinese civil war, and a close friend of Mao's (although they later disagreed and Peng died in a Chinese prison). In a poem, Mao described Peng as "our only general." Born a peasant and raised in grinding poverty, he was an idealistic Communist and a career soldier who believed an army must understand and adapt to enemy strengths. In winning the civil war against Chiang Kai-shek and the Nationalists, he never risked a head-on assault. Instead, he attacked from the shadows, using stealth and speed. In Korea, he assessed the Americans as lethal in the air and increasingly strong on the ground. If the Chinese were to have a fighting chance against them, Peng believed, Kim's foolishness had to be neutralized. Peng wanted absolute command of Chinese *and* North Korean forces. In asserting his military dominion over North Korea, he shouted at Kim and denigrated him in front of other officials.

"You are just hoping for a quick victory and are not making concrete preparations, and this is only going to prolong the war," Peng told Kim. "You are hoping to end this war based on luck . . . I resolutely oppose this mistake you are making in misunderstanding the enemy."

Kim resisted Peng for months, even as his shattered army was being protected by Chinese troops. The North Korean leader would not agree to a unified command structure; he wanted the Chinese People's Volunteer Army to be controlled from his headquarters. He demanded that Chinese soldiers use North Korean currency and pay for their firewood at prevailing market prices. Chinese and North Korean forces soon began obstructing each other's ability to travel, fight, and deliver supplies. In the first Chinese campaign of the war, when Peng's Thirty-ninth Volunteer Army moved in October to surround a U.S. Army division near the town of Pochon, North Korean tanks mistakenly attacked the Chinese, allowing the Americans to slip away. As Peng's frustration with Kim grew, the Chinese general complained to Mao, who complained to

Stalin, and Kim was ordered to accept his emasculation. China soon took control of roads, railways, ports, airports, food storage, and recruitment of men to fight and deliver supplies.

As he asserted his command, Peng surprised and overwhelmed the Americans, who in late November had begun a massive push north to flush the Chinese out of North Korea and end the war. MacArthur, underestimating the Chinese infantry just as he had underestimated the North Korean ground troops at the outbreak of the war, said the offensive would "get the boys home by Christmas." Instead, about 180,000 Chinese troops shattered the U.S. Eighth Army as it tried to move up the west side of the Korean Peninsula.

By December 2, 1950, the home-by-Christmas offensive "had turned into a bloody nightmare." The Eighth Army abandoned Pyongyang and fell back 120 miles to the thirty-eighth parallel—the longest retreat in American military history.

At the same time, the Chinese sprang another trap on the east side of North Korea near the Chosin Reservoir, a man-made, high-country lake created by the Japanese. No Kum Sok and his parents had often summered at the reservoir to escape the suffocating lowland heat. But in winter the area was murderously cold, particularly in late November 1950, when American troops, many of them ill-dressed for winter, were enveloped by a Siberian front. The temperature dropped to minus thirty-five degrees Fahrenheit. Weapons would not fire. Blood plasma froze into chunks of ice in medical tents. With twice as many troops on the ground, Chinese generals tried to destroy the U.S. Army X Corps and the First Marine Division. Only brilliant leadership and ferocious fighting by the marines saved the Americans, enabling them to break out of the trap and escape Chosin Reservoir without devastating loss of life. Still, it was a retreat. Under Peng's leadership, the Chinese had routed the Americans, humiliated MacArthur, and taken back all of North Korea's territory in less than three months.

The Great Leader played virtually no role in these victories.

While stewing in his irrelevance, Kim devised a pie-in-the-sky plan to revive his army in eastern China. His plan depended on help from

Stalin, whom he appealed to via Shtykov, the supportive Soviet ambassador.

"Our North Korean friends will withdraw to Manchuria with the personnel for organizing nine divisions," Shtykov wrote to Stalin. "Once again, our comrades are requesting that ninety Soviet advisors . . . help them organize the nine divisions and establish education and training institutions. The North Koreans state that if they do not have this help, it will take them a year before they can prepare for combat on their own."

Stalin refused.

When Kim heard the news, he was silent for a moment and then asked, "How can matters come to this?"

For Kim, matters soon deteriorated further. At the end of 1950, Stalin fired Shtykov, who for five years had been Kim's most sympathetic Soviet supporter and his only direct line to the Boss. The longtime ambassador, it seems, sabotaged his own career by being too close to Kim and his battlefield blunders.

The man who replaced Shtykov was not a confidant of Stalin's, and Kim's complaints no longer reached the Soviet leader directly. North Korea soon became just another distant Soviet satellite. Its importuning to Moscow was filtered through Beijing. To appeal to the Soviets for money, matériel, and advisers, Kim had to win sympathy from Peng, who thought the North Korean leader was an ass, and from Mao, who agreed with Peng. In his memoirs, Khrushchev wrote that the Soviet ambassador in Pyongyang sent "very tragic reports concerning Kim Il Sung's state of mind."

In the fall of 1950, Kim was a thirty-eight-year-old widower, still mourning the deaths of his wife, who died the previous year, and of his second son, who drowned in a pond in 1947. He was head of a nearly nonexistent state, living on the run and hunkering down in bunkers with his son and daughter to escape American bombing.

Being kicked when he was down, however, was not an unfamiliar experience for Kim. As a guerrilla commander in Manchuria, he had endured crushing military defeats at the hands of the Japanese and survived murderous backstabbing from the Chinese. He had been weaned, as the historian Adrian Buzo put it, "in a predatory, political subculture of force which encouraged in him an outlook that accepted callousness and criminality as a daily reality."

Kim began to emerge from his wartime funk and assert his predatory instincts at the end of 1950, shortly after Chinese forces retook Pyongyang in December and secured control of all of North Korea. Change in the war's momentum gave him a chance to convene a party plenum on December 21 in the bomb-shattered city of Kanggye. There he "attacked almost everybody." He blamed his failings as a commander on the incompetence, cowardice, and lack of discipline of underlings. At considerable length, he damned his own military, his own propaganda machine, his own internal security apparatus, and all the wannabe Communist guerrillas in the South who he had predicted would help him during the war but who had done nothing. Then he censored his own speech, leaving many North Koreans (including No Kum Sok at Yanji airfield) with only a vague idea of what the Great Leader was up to.

China had grabbed control of the war, but unlike the Soviet Union it did not meddle in the internal affairs of the North Korean government.

Paradoxically, Kim benefited from his own incompetence. The Chinese did the dirty work of ground fighting, freeing him from day-to-day management of the war and giving him an opportunity to begin eliminating his political rivals. His incompetence also weakened his ties to Soviet advisers who had guided his behavior. Cut loose from them, his Manchurian-bred callousness could assert itself.

At the party plenum in December, Kim showed glimpses of the dictator he would become. When it came time to praise Stalin, he was less the lickspittle and more the enforcer. Gone were his references to the great Soviet Union and the Glorious Leader of Worldwide Revolution. Instead, he demanded that the party act "as one man upon the orders of the Chief."

As General Peng saw it, Kim was too childish and too impatient to run a military campaign against a formidable enemy like the United States. But politics were different. Kim could win at home because he alone made up the rules. His official biographer explained the new world according to Kim: "Only when the entire Party membership and working people had established the unitary ideological system, firmly arming themselves with the ideas of the Leader, being boundlessly faithful to his teachings, defending with their lives Comrade Kim Il Sung, the respected and beloved Leader, without vacillation in any storm and stress, at any time and at any place, and unconditionally accepting and carrying out the teachings of the Leader and the decision of the Party, would they be able to win the war."

In the last weeks of 1950, Kim moved back to Pyongyang, which Americans continued to bomb and burn. The U.S. Air Force estimated it destroyed 75 percent of the capital, while the North Korean government said every modern building in the city was destroyed, save two. The Great Leader, stripped of command over his own war, often had to live underground.

IV

In the early spring of 1951, No Kum Sok's war took a turn toward luxury.

He ate imported caviar and wiped his lips with freshly laundered cloth napkins. He slept, for the first time in his life, on a bed with a spring mattress. Every third night, he watched a new movie from Moscow. In a dining hall packed with chatty pilots, many of whom were tall, blond, and pale Russians, he feasted on borscht and vodka, piroshki and fish pie, black bread and gobs of butter. Much of the food was flown in from the Soviet Union and prepared by chefs who had been recruited from international hotels in China. The waiters, also imports from first-class hotels, wore clean white linen and glided around the dining hall, busing as many as five plates in one hand. When No asked for seconds, they smiled and fetched. The best thing, by far, about learning to fly was the food.

No began eating it after qualifying for jet training, as did nearly all of the North Korean naval cadets who had been sent to Manchuria. The excellent food was served at a Soviet-run airfield near Anshan, China, a steelmaking city about 150 miles northwest of the North Korean border, where the mountains of eastern Manchuria give way to a dusty plain.

Almost as soon as No arrived there by train on March 7, 1951, he felt more comfortable than he had in years. The Russian flight instructors he dined with were in their late twenties. They were welcoming, intelligent, and urbane—far more amiable companions than his stressed-out North Korean peers. Part of it was language. To enhance his performance as a No. 1 Communist, No had been working for years to learn conversational Russian. After high school, he took three years of college-level Russian at the chemical college in Hungnam and at the naval academy.

At Anshan, where most Korean pilots could not communicate without help from translators, No talked directly with Russian instructors and aircraft mechanics, few of whom could speak Korean or Chinese. As a result, he learned more about flying a jet and he learned it faster than other cadet pilots.

Although they had been in Manchuria for nearly half a year, many of the cadet pilots remained traumatized by the punitive ordeal of their training in the North, particularly in the naval academy's caves and tunnels. They feared demotion, even death, if they crashed a plane, failed to pass ideological muster, or said the wrong word.

The few cadet pilots who did not qualify for jet training—and were then relegated to older, propeller-driven aircraft—were not necessarily inferior pilots. More often, they were poor actors. Unlike No, they failed to flaunt their dedication to the Great Leader. At ideology-improvement meetings, which were an endless, mind-numbing component of flight training, they neglected to flatter political officers. One of these unfortunate cadet pilots, Lee Yong Chol, who had been No's classmate in high school in Hungnam and at the naval academy, was upset when he learned he would not be allowed to fly a jet. Someone overheard him saying that if he had to fight the Americans in a Russian propeller plane, he would just as soon defect to South Korea. For his pique, he was executed, supposedly in secret, although word of his death spread among the cadet pilots, with sobering effect.

By comparison, the Russian pilots, as No watched them in the dining hall and on the flight line, behaved like free men, like the Americans he imagined meeting one day. They were self-confident, opinionated, and funny. Drinking vodka, they could become loud and playful but rarely violent or cruel. They were nothing like the Russians he had encountered five years earlier in Kanggye: beefy, unwashed dregs who raped North Korean housewives and puked in the streets.

No's instructor at Anshan, Captain Alexei Nikichenko, was a patient man and a sophisticated Muscovite: slender, gentle, and articulate. He showed No photographs of his wife and two young sons and often said that he missed his family.

The instructors at Anshan were by far the best jet fighter pilots in the Soviet Union. Many had flown hundreds of combat missions against Germany during World War II. Before Manchuria, they were stationed in Moscow, where they protected the capital from possible American air attack and marched in air parades in Red Square.

Their commander was Colonel Ivan N. Kozhedub, one of the most famous military men in the Soviet Union. A skilled and fearless pilot with hawk-like blue eyes, he was credited with shooting down a record sixty-two German aircraft during World War II. Three times he had been named a Hero of the Soviet Union, the country's highest honor.

The fame and status of Kozhedub, along with the superb flying skills of his men, helped explain the luxury treatment at Anshan airfield. The orders that sent them there, which came directly from Stalin, explained the rest. In a coded message on November 20, 1950, Stalin promised Kim Il Sung that he would send Soviet instructors to teach two regiments of North Korean pilots how to fly jet fighters. A month later Kozhedub and his men left Moscow on trains heading to the Far East. When No showed up in March as part of the first class of North Koreans to be taught to fly jets, the Russians had been waiting for them for more than two months.

The elite Russians were supposedly there to teach, not fight, as Stalin wanted to minimize his risk of an all-out confrontation with the United States. But the unchecked ferocity of American airpower—after China entered the war—forced the Boss to rethink. American pilots were blowing up bridge after bridge over the Yalu, disrupting supply lines, and slaughtering Chinese units that were fighting in North Korea without air cover.

MacArthur had revved up the bombing to compensate for his ego-centric mistake: he had bathed too long in the adulation generated by his triumph at Inchon while neglecting intelligence reports that Chinese troops were moving into North Korea. When the Chinese started killing GIs and clawing back territory, MacArthur demanded a scorched-earth response. He approved the use of incendiary bombs and ordered the air force "to destroy every means of communication and every installa-tion, factory, city, and village" in North Korea. He instructed bombers to create "a desert" incapable of supporting Communist troops between United Nations lines and the Chinese border.

Prior to the Chinese incursion, the air force had pounded North Korea with conventional explosives. These bombs, as No had witnessed in Chongjin, tore buildings apart, knocked bridges down, and killed tens of thousands of people. But rarely did they start fires that engulfed entire cities. Politicians and generals in Washington had been unwilling during the war's first few months to allow the air force to drop bombs contain-ing incendiary chemical compounds like napalm, a gel that sticks to human flesh and burns for an extended period. During World War II, incendiaries, dropped from B-29s, created firestorms in cities across Japan. On a windy night over Tokyo in March 1945, American bombers dropped nearly 800,000 pounds of napalm in less than an hour, creating an epochal fire that reduced fifteen square miles of the city to ashes and killed about a hundred thousand people. The fire was so intense it burned paint off the bellies of air force bombers and pilots smelled updrafts of "roasting human flesh."

After Chinese soldiers overran American infantry positions, Wash-ington put aside its qualms about using napalm on North Korean cities. It quietly agreed with air force strategists who claimed that the stuff was "economical, efficient, and expeditious." The first firebombing in the North occurred on November 4, 1950, when twenty-six B-29s took off in search of Kanggye, the city where No had attended middle school. Bad weather diverted them to a secondary target, Chongjin, where they burned the rubble that was left after the devastating conventional bomb-ing that No had witnessed back in August. Two days later, the Pentagon ordered the air force to use all available means against Yalu bridges on the border with Manchuria. The border city of Sinuiju was attacked by seventy B-29s carrying incendiary bombs. Firestorms burned the city to the ground, killing more than two thousand civilians.

In the three devastating months that followed, as the air force dropped 40 percent of the bombs and two-thirds of the napalm used in the entire Korean War, most major cities and many minor towns in the North were set afire. American fighter-bomber pilots often preferred napalm. As one explained, "When you've hit a village and have seen it go up in flames, you know you've accomplished something."

The Americans dropped more than thirty-two thousand tons of napalm on Korea, about double the amount that fell on Japan in 1945. During an "average good day" it amounted to about seventy thousand gallons. The human toll even horrified MacArthur. After Truman fired him, he told Congress, "I have seen, I guess, as much blood and disaster as any living man, and it just curdled my stomach, the last time I was [in Korea]. After I looked at that wreckage and those thousands of women and children and everything, I vomited."

Stalin never used airpower to protect major North Korean cities from American napalm. Mass death of civilians in the Korean War, Soviet archives show, meant nothing to him and was never a factor in his strategic calculations. But as the war heated up, as MacArthur's airborne ferocity gathered momentum, as Chinese forces absorbed devastating losses from American air strikes, Stalin reversed his own policy of not helping China from the air. He committed more and more fighter jets to the Yalu River corridor to protect Chinese troops and their supply routes into North Korea.

For a while, Stalin tried to keep his best jet pilots out of this fight, sending his second team instead. But they did not have the flying skills, combat experience, or self-confidence to mix it up with the hotshot American fighter pilots who now escorted B-29s to and from their targets. By March 1951, after several months of crashing into each other and getting shot down, these neophyte Soviet pilots "began evading and breaking off combat," and the Communist side of the conflict over the Yalu River became "one of flight and panic," according to Lieutenant Colonel Yevgeny Pepel-yaev, who commanded an elite flight squadron.

So Stalin reluctantly played his aces.

Just as No was preparing to move from classroom to runway, from jet propulsion principles to the cockpit of a MiG-15, Stalin ordered all the excellent Russian instructor-pilots at Anshan air base into combat. The airspace over the Yalu River soon became world famous as MiG Alley. The first jet-powered aerial war was on. No's instructor, Captain Nikichenko, the homesick family man, joined the fight.

No, too, would be thrown into the air war, but not for several more months.

He had yet to get his hands on a MiG.

And now, thanks to Stalin, he could not find one. When his instructors rushed away to war, they took all sixty-five of their MiGs with them.

CHAPTER 6

MiGs

I

The Great Leader left his Pyongyang bunker in early morning darkness, bringing along Kim Jong Il, his nine-year-old son and future heir. In a Russian-built limousine painted olive drab, they traveled northwest toward the Chinese border. Their convoy included seven sedans and five trucks carrying a security detail with about a hundred plainclothes police and uniformed soldiers.

It was early October 1951, and the convoy was bound for Uiju, a border town in the heart of MiG Alley. Chinese engineers there had just completed construction of a concrete runway. Located about a half mile south of the Yalu River, it was the only airfield in North Korea built for fighter jets.

When the limousine stopped at the runway's edge and the Great Leader emerged, eight newly trained North Korean fighter pilots saluted. They had landed minutes earlier in MiG-15s after a short hop from Anshan airfield on the Manchurian side of the border. The pilots had been told that the Great Leader wanted a firsthand look at the fighter jets that would soon be based in Uiju. If he offered to shake hands, they were told not to squeeze too tight.

The youngest pilot on the runway that unseasonably warm autumn morning was No Kum Sok, then nineteen. He was still playing the faux-Communist role he had chosen for himself more than three years earlier, after seeing the Great Leader on the fertilizer mountain. But jet training had stirred his imagination and complicated his performance. He fantasized about exiting the war in his MiG-15. So far, though, he did not have the flying skills, the nerve, or a plan. He was torn between escape fantasies and cold feet.

At Uiju, No's second sighting of Kim triggered a new and suicidal fantasy: he would shoot the Great Leader. With an inchoate rage that had been smoldering since his father's death, No blamed Kim for splintering his family and ruining his childhood. He also hated him for poisoning Korea with Communism, paranoia, and fear.

As he eyed the men protecting Kim and his son, it seemed that the plainclothes bodyguards were worried more about the uniformed soldiers, each of whom carried a submachine gun, than about the MiG pilots. No had a loaded service pistol at his side, a Russian-made Tokarev TT-33 semiautomatic. He was a decent shot. He reckoned he could draw his gun and pump several bullets into Kim Il Sung before security guards could open fire.

But he did not touch the pistol. He had come too far to give in to a postadolescent urge for instant justice.

Shaking off his daydream, he watched and listened to the two Kims, who had dressed for the morning's MiG inspection in matching Mao suits with puffy Mao caps. War seemed to have aged the Great Leader. For a man who was thirty-nine years old, his face was wrinkled and careworn. His hair, jet-black three years earlier, was flecked with gray. He was fatter than before.

As Kim Il Sung walked around one of the MiGs, the three guns in the plane's snout caught his eye. He was especially taken with the biggest one, a 37 mm cannon, which fired high-explosive shells that weighed one and a half pounds each and had a range of up to a mile. A MiG-15 could shoot eighty of these rounds in five seconds. Two direct hits could bring down an American fighter jet, Soviet engineers believed, while eight could knock a fifty-two-ton B-29 out of the sky.

"This is quite a weapon," Kim said, seeming to think out loud. "With a weapon like this we could kill even the granddaddies of Americans."

He turned to his son and asked if he would like to fly a MiG when he grew up.

"Yes," said Kim Jong Il, who climbed a ladder to look down into the jet's cockpit.

"If you want to fly this plane," his father said, "you will have to study hard."

The father-son inspection ended as abruptly as it began.

Without giving a speech or shaking a hand, Kim walked back to his limousine and climbed in. He and his son were whisked away, having come and gone in less than fifteen minutes. No and the other pilots followed suit, climbing into the cockpits of their jets and roaring back to Manchuria. In a month's time, Uiju would become the first and only MiG base in North Korea.

Brief though it was, No's encounter with Kim and his son was on-the-ground proof that something fundamental had changed in the air war over Korea in 1951. The Great Leader felt safe enough to risk exposing himself—and his precious son—to a possible American air attack while strolling around on an exposed runway under clear blue skies.

Kim took the risk because American bombers had been stymied. In the Yalu River corridor, they could no longer embark on leisurely, risk-free missions to blow up bridges, supply depots, and airfields.

MacArthur attributed the change to the murderous rise of the MiG. "Modern high performance type jet aircraft" operating out of Manchuria, he said, were seriously challenging American air superiority.

In the month that Kim visited Uiju airfield, fifty-five American airmen were killed, as MiGs shot down eight B-29s. It was the worst month of the war for the U.S. Air Force. The worst day was October 23, which became known as Black Tuesday, when eighty-four MiGs shredded an American bombing formation, damaging all five of its B-29s and shooting down three. In the process, MiGs outmaneuvered and out-fought fifty-five American Thunderjets, which were escorting the bomb-ers and trying to protect them. American claims to the contrary, not a single MiG was lost, and only three were damaged. It was "one of the most savage and bloody" air battles of the Korean War, according to the official U.S. Air Force history of the war.

MiGs were itching for a fight. UN pilots counted more than twenty-five hundred of them in the Yalu River corridor in October, and 85 per-cent behaved in a manner suggesting they were eager to engage in aerial combat. So many B-29s were shot down that month that the Americans canceled daylight bombing operations in MiG Alley.

On the ground in the fall of 1951, the conflict between Chinese and UN forces had settled into a grim World War I–style, trench-warfare stale-mate. The first cease-fire negotiations began in July amid nasty but incon-clusive ground fighting that would go on for two more years. The real action in the Korean War—the stuff that made front-page headlines—was no longer on the ground. It had risen into the sky over MiG Alley.

II

The MiG pilots responsible for Black Tuesday—and for the Com-munist surge that made Kim Il Sung feel secure enough to visit Uiju airfield with his son—were the Russians who had eaten caviar with No Kum Sok.

Beginning in April 1951, while based in Manchuria's Dandong air-field, a few miles from the North Korean border, they confronted, out-flew, and outgunned some of the best combat pilots in the U.S. Air Force. With respect and fear, American pilots called them "honchos," from a Japanese word for "boss."

The honchos flew under orders from Stalin that were as secret as they were bizarre. Before they could engage the Americans, they had to pre-tend to be Chinese. They took fake Chinese names and wore Chinese flight uniforms, with blue pants, orange-red boots, and khaki jackets.

They never flew with identification papers. Colonel Kozhedub's unit painted its MiGs with the colors of North Korea, while another elite Soviet fighter unit disguised its fighters with Chinese markings.

The Russians signed nondisclosure forms, promising not to tell anyone they were fighting in the Korean War. In case of capture by the enemy, they were supposed to explain their white skin by saying that they were European Chinese of Soviet extraction. In case of capture by the friendly forces of China or North Korea, their lack of identification papers could be a life-threatening problem, because Chinese and North Korean ground troops were inclined to view Caucasian pilots as imperialist bastards.

On the radio in their MiGs, the Russians were ordered to speak Chinese, a ridiculous, much-resented, and utterly impossible order, given that they did not speak the language. They secretly buried their recovered dead (with the exception of senior officers, who were transported back to Moscow) in the Far East Soviet enclave of Port Arthur.

The orders from Stalin were part of a "carefully orchestrated ballet" intended to protect the Soviet Union's Chinese allies without provoking the United States into a wider war. It never fooled the Americans, who often heard MiG pilots speaking Russian on the radio. The United States, though, decided not to react. It was, as Shen Zhihua, a Chinese scholar of the Korean War, has called it, "a curious case of double deniability."

Like Stalin, Truman did not want to pour gasoline on a regional fire. He and other officials in Washington believed it would be imprudent to tell the American public that Russians were blasting American boys out of the sky. They feared the rise of popular sentiment for a larger retaliatory war against the nuclear-armed Soviet Union.

So everyone lied for the sake of a larger peace. The Soviet air force contributed about seventy thousand pilots, artillery gunners, and technicians to the war. And the United States publicly blamed the catastrophic turn in the air war on China. It was then a much less formidable military power, and the American public already knew that Chinese soldiers were fighting in Korea. After returning from a visit to the Far East in the fall of 1951, General Hoyt Vandenberg, the air force chief of staff, gloomily and mendaciously explained the air-war crisis to the Washington press corps: "Almost overnight, Communist China has become one of the major air powers of the world."

The cover-up continued on the American side through the end of the Korean War and on through the Eisenhower administration. The Soviet Union never officially acknowledged its role in the Korean War, an omission that probably helped keep the cold war cool.

Russian pilots, though, were irritated by the pretense. So they made racist jokes about it.

First Russian: We have the best pilots in the world.

Second Russian: How is that?

First Russian: Because they can fly with no hands.

Second Russian: Why do they do that?

First Russian: They use their hands to slant their eyes so the Americans will think they're Koreans.

On Stalin's orders, the Russians could not go on the offensive. They never coordinated with Chinese ground forces or flew close air support to help the Chinese or North Korean infantry. They were under strict orders not to fly over the sea, over any American-held territory, or even near a battle line, lest they get shot down and be discovered as Russian. These orders seem to have been carefully followed. During the war, not one of them was taken prisoner by UN forces.

The Russians had to be patient predators, waiting for American bombers and jet fighter escorts to attack bridges and supply lines along the Yalu River. Only then, with American aircraft already in the air, could the Russians swoop in and try to shoot them down.

This, too, annoyed the Russians.

"We had to sit stewing in our cockpits for hours on end," said Lieutenant General G. A. Lobov, commander of the 303rd Soviet Air Defense Division. "We had to be on duty waiting, but the Americans could choose the time. This was extremely demoralizing. When a report came in of an American sortie, I had only seconds to prepare my men. I could never plan an operation in advance."

For all their frustration, for all their disguises, for all the Stalinist red tape they had to wrap themselves in, the elite Russian pilots and their MiGs were extraordinarily effective. For nearly a year, they protected the Chinese, contributed significantly to the survival of North Korea, and tormented the entire U.S. military operation. MiGs chased off bombers and reconnaissance aircraft. They gave the North Koreans and the Chinese a chance to build new bases and repair old ones. Without eyes in the sky, American generals struggled in 1951 to keep tabs on the whereabouts of Chinese reinforcements pouring into the ground war.

III

With the MiG-15, Stalin had hit on a winner. It was much faster—by a hundred miles an hour—than any aircraft the Americans had in the Far East during the first six months of the war. More important, it could climb quicker and fly higher than any American fighter.

On his first solo flight in a MiG-15, No was astonished—and unnerved—by the jet's thrust. Off the runway, the cigar-shaped jet could climb at nearly two miles a minute. It was like riding a rocket with wings.

The Soviet Union manufactured about twelve thousand of these fighters, and in the early 1950s most of them were sent by train to Manchuria.

For all its speed, however, the MiG-15 was flimsy, uncomfortable, and difficult to control. Chuck Yeager, the legendary American test pilot, called the MiG-15 "a flying booby trap" and "a quirky airplane that's killed a lot of its pilots." Another American test pilot, Tom Collins, described it as "a little, light, peashooter machine." The plane pitched up its nose unexpectedly, stalled without warning, and rarely recovered from a fatal spin. Its instruction manual warned that flying for more than ten minutes at full throttle could set the engine on fire. Poor quality control in Soviet factories meant that a MiG-15's two swept-back wings were almost never the same exact size. As the plane approached the speed of sound, the mismatch caused sudden and uncontrollable rolling movements.

The cockpit was an ergonomic horror. It forced a pilot to sit low in a cramped seat that offered poor visibility. Bad heating and air-conditioning made the MiG-15 intolerably warm on a hot tarmac and freezing cold at high altitude. Cabin pressure and the oxygen supply were reliable, if a MiG was expertly serviced. If not, a pilot sometimes had to fiddle with a little knob beside his seat to maintain cabin pressure, and to breathe safely above forty thousand feet he had to pay careful attention to a valve on the oxygen system. Open it too much and all the plane's oxygen could be lost. Open it too little and a pilot's fingernails would turn a bluish purple, the early sign of oxygen deprivation, which could quickly lead to loss of consciousness and death.

In several dangerous and infuriating ways, the cockpit inhibited a pilot from seeing an enemy fighter creeping up on his tail. There was no rearview mirror. At high altitude, the Plexiglas cockpit canopy could ice over if it was not serviced properly. Ice began forming at the rear of the canopy at about forty thousand feet and then crept forward until it covered the pilot's entire field of vision.

"At forty-five thousand feet, you felt as though someone had pulled a white bag over your head," said Collins. "If you had sharp fingernails or a knife, you could scrape a little hole to look out. [At lower altitudes], this ice melted, but it became a wet vapor on top of the canopy that obscured your vision."

Even when the canopy was not shrouded in ice or occluded by fog (and good maintenance usually kept it clear), the MiG's T-shaped tail had a high horizontal stabilizer that kept pilots from seeing planes approaching from above and behind.

Russian flight instructors told young North Korean pilots to lift weights so they would be strong enough to manipulate the stick on an early model of the MiG-15 that arrived in Manchuria in late 1950. The stick did not have hydraulic assist and was almost impossible to control at high speed and low altitude. No did a hundred push-ups a day (part of the regimen he began in the naval academy) but still struggled to control the stick. That early MiG model also had quirky German-made buttons on a cramped control panel. During flights, a pilot trying to press a single control button often pressed several others by mistake.

At the relatively low speed (for a MiG) of 130 miles an hour, the lateral stability of the plane "goes to pot," according to Collins. "The MiG starts wallowing around and you're sitting up there really whopping the stick around to try to hold it steady . . . You can see that a guy could be approaching a stall, lose control and the airplane would immediately go into a spin."

When all else failed on the MiG-15, the ejection seat occasionally failed as well.

Then the MiG-15's high T-shaped tail functioned as a kind of guillotine. It sometimes dismembered escaping pilots who crawled free from the cockpit. When the ejection seat worked, there was still a significant risk of death, although North Korean pilots were not told about it. They were taught that they could safely bail out at any altitude above sixteen hundred feet. During the war, they never learned about several MiG pilots who bailed out above thirty-three thousand feet and froze to death before reaching the ground.

To master these "quirks," to transform the MiG-15 from a flying booby trap into an effective fighting machine, most pilots needed several years of flying experience in other kinds of aircraft, then a year of expert fighter-jet instruction, and about three hundred hours (seven forty-hour weeks) of solo flight time in the cockpit.

With this kind of training, they could take maximum advantage of the aircraft's speed, high-altitude maneuverability, and astonishing climbing ability. They could also get in many hours of gunnery practice, which they needed in order to hit an enemy flying at several hundred miles an hour. The MiG-15's gun sights were rated as somewhere between poorly designed and useless.

The Russian honchos—the pilots No had dined with, the ones who rattled American nerves in the fall of 1951—had this kind of experience and training. The majority of them, before coming to the Far East, had spent about three hundred hours in jet fighters.

So had American fighter pilots in Korea. In fact, they usually had more. Most of the fighter pilots from the U.S. Air Force Fourth Fighter-Interceptor Wing, which flew the hottest fighter jets, were combat veterans of World War II. All of them had spent a year and a half with their fighters before they began arriving in Korea at the end of 1950.

IV

No Kum Sok did not get enough training to become a honcho. Neither did the other North Korean pilots, and neither did the Chinese.

Stalin had no patience for it. He sent angry telegrams to his air force generals in Manchuria, scolding them for "very slowly" training Koreans to fly jets and for trying to "make professors rather than battle pilots out of the Chinese."

To push them to the front faster, he ordered that the typical Soviet pilot training course be cut in half, from a year to six months. This was a hurry-up-and-die order, given the educational background of most of the student pilots taking flight training in Manchuria.

Few spoke Russian, and many of them, particularly the "peasant soldiers" of China, had left school between the ages of eight and fifteen. In any language, they struggled to understand aviation and navigation concepts. It took at least twice as long to teach aviation basics to these students as it did in the Soviet Union—so even the best of the Chinese and Korean students were exposed to about a quarter of the information that was drilled into the greenest Russian pilots.

Then, for those Chinese and Korean pilots who had stumbled through a basic aviation course, jet training was squeezed into two months.

By the time a Chinese pilot flew off to fight the Americans, he had somewhere between fifty and eighty hours of total flight time—and about sixteen hours in a MiG-15. This was not nearly enough training to prevent Chinese MiG pilots from killing themselves by mistake. In the first half of 1951, more than a hundred died in accidents. China's own air force regulations called for at least three hundred hours of flight time before entering combat.

When Chinese-piloted MiGs confronted the best American fighter jets, they became prey. This quickly led to a widespread reluctance to engage. When the Chinese saw the enemy coming, they fled. Chinese veterans who piloted MiGs in the Korean War have attributed this well-documented pattern of flight, not fight, to a rational understanding of their own inexperience and incompetence.

No's training was marginally better—thanks to his conversational Russian, his educational background, his aptitude for flying, and his good fortune in finding time for a few extra pre-combat hours in the jet.

His training, however, did not start well.

In mid-April 1951, after his Soviet instructors suddenly departed to fight the Americans, taking their MiGs with them, No and the other North Korean pilots traveled to another Manchurian airfield. Dongfeng air base had a runway, but it did not have any MiG-15s or any aircraft of any kind. Nor was there a single instructor who had ever flown an airplane.

The instructors were North Koreans who had been selected because they spoke Russian. They translated Russian-language MiG flight manuals into Korean, and from these translations No and the others tried to grasp the theoretical principles behind the operation of the jet engine that powered the MiG-15. The teachers were usually confused by technical language in the manuals. No stayed at Dongfeng for a month and learned next to nothing.

His next stop was Tianjin, a sprawling Chinese city near Beijing and far from the war. Serious instruction finally began there, with classes and jet training flights from dawn to dark seven days a week for two months. The pace was grueling, but No felt exhilarated. Within a few days, he soloed in a Yak-17, a straight-wing turbojet with a top speed of about four hundred miles an hour.

His Soviet instructor-pilots were part of a newly arrived MiG division. They wore brightly colored sport shirts and enjoyed vodka, often to excess, and sometimes did not show up in the morning because of headaches. But the Russians were friendly, talkative, and skilled as teachers.

No liked nearly all of them, the pilots and the mechanics. As a Russian speaker, he was eager to hang out with them on the flight line.

Stuck on a Chinese air base with nothing to do but work, the Russian jet mechanics loved to talk about their sexual triumphs. No listened keenly and learned lots of dirty words. North Korean pilots were not supposed to talk about women; wartime love affairs were strictly forbidden. But with the Russians, No ignored the rules and began telling spicy tales of his own romantic triumphs.

As a storyteller, No could not rely on firsthand experience with women, sex, or romance. He was a nineteen-year-old virgin. He had never had a girlfriend. He did not even have a sister. But he had been to the movies, and his imagination had been working overtime for the past three years as he pretended to be a loyal North Korean Communist. It was not that much of a stretch to pretend to be a Casanova who specialized in Russian maidens.

So he invented a lover and called her Natasha (a name he remembered from a Soviet film called *The Melody of the Great Siberian Land*). His exploits with Natasha tickled the Russians, perhaps because of his boyish face, his iffy understanding of sex, and his determination to sound worldly while speaking Russian in a Korean accent. They teased him about his lover, asking, "How is Natasha?"

No soloed in a MiG-15 near the end of his two-month stay in Tianjin. Because the jet was damnably difficult to control and because North Korean student pilots often damaged them on their first solo flights, only one student was allowed to solo at a time.

On that first go, a Russian airman stood on a ladder that leaned against the MiG's cockpit and strapped No into his parachute and then into his seat. A green flare gun fired a signal for him to take off, and within minutes he was several miles high. When he stopped accelerating and tried to level off for the first time, the altimeter began spinning backward, giving him the alarming news that he was descending at an uncontrolled rate. He was barely in control.

He had, as always, memorized the landing procedures he had learned in class. But he was not at all confident he could do them. He approached the runway too fast and, at touchdown, scraped his right wingtip on the tarmac. But he did not wreck his MiG, as many other students did.

At the end of June, No and the other pilots moved closer to the North Korean border—and to the war—for final flight training at Anshan air base, where seventy shiny MiG-15s were waiting for them. Each pilot was assigned his own fighter. No's had the number 008 painted in red on both sides of its nose. Because of manufacturing mistakes, some of the MiGs had asymmetrical airframes; others had buggy engines or stiff control sticks. No's MiG was one of the good ones, or so he was told by one of the Russian instructors who sometimes borrowed it. Every morning, No participated in simulated dogfights. His jet instructor was a Ukrainian, Captain Pisanenko, who taught him how to fly in formation while maintaining a constant speed of 620 miles an hour. The Ukrainian told him that if he flew slower than that, he would not have a chance against the Americans.

When No's training concluded at the end of the summer of 1951, he had fifty hours of flying time in a MiG, more than twice as many jet hours as the average Chinese MiG pilot who flew in the Korean War. No considered himself to be the best pilot in the North Korean air force, based on what he had seen of his peers' flying ability. He had soloed in four different Soviet planes earlier than most student pilots. His aerobatic skills, as demonstrated in training drills, were unsurpassed. He won a simulated dogfight against his flight leader.

But compared with Russian honchos—and the American pilots who would soon be trying to kill him—he was easy pickings. His flight instructors had neglected to teach him how to fire the guns on his MiG, and he had not asked how to shoot them, assuming that it would come up later.

CHAPTER 7

Return to North Korea

I

In November 1951, Kim Il Sung ordered twenty-six newly trained MiG pilots to leave their sanctuary in Manchuria, fly across the border, and establish a combat presence on North Korean soil. The pilots and their MiG-15s were sent to Uiju, with the newly constructed airfield that Kim and his son had inspected a month earlier. The timing made some sense. The total number of MiGs in the war—flown by pilots from the Soviet Union, China, and North Korea—had mushroomed to more than five hundred. They created a formidable shield along the border between China and North Korea.

The real intent of the move, though, was political. Marginalized and living underground in Pyongyang, Kim desperately needed to blow his horn and assert his greatness. China controlled the ground war he had bungled, and he feared that after the war Mao would force him into a subservient role or get rid of him altogether. Moving MiGs to North Korea showed gumption. It suggested that Kim's war-battered government was getting up off its knees, standing up to American airpower, and defending the homeland with Korean pilots flying the Communist world's most ferocious fighter jet.

But the move also showed, yet again, that Kim was a reckless adventurer, more concerned with image making than with military strategy or the well-being of his men. Had he allowed his elite fighter pilots to remain at air bases in Manchuria, where they had excellent support, reliable communications, and quick access to the fighting in MiG Alley, they could dogfight all day and rest easy at night. American bombers and fighter jets could not attack them on the ground. But if Americans spotted MiGs on the ground at Uiju, they and their pilots were fair game for annihilation.

So it was that No Kum Sok, on orders of the Great Leader he had chosen not to shoot, began his career as a combat pilot at an air base ripe for destruction from above.

After a quick flight from Manchuria, No landed at Uiju on November 7. It was more landing strip than air base, with a runway that stretched for seventy-two hundred feet, plenty long enough to accommodate a MiG. Administrative offices, such as they were, consisted of a few wooden huts made from railroad containers the Soviets had used to transport MiGs to the Far East. Flight orders were relayed to the huts by radio from Dandong air base in Manchuria, where Soviet and North Korean radar monitored American aircraft as they flew north from airfields in South Korea, Japan, and Okinawa. An apron ramp at Uiju connected the runway to twenty bunker-like revetments (parking places for aircraft) lined with sandbags, each of which could shelter two MiGs. At each end of the airfield, sandbag bunkers protected antiaircraft batteries. Scattered in the nearby hills, other antiaircraft guns were draped in camouflage.

In the expectation that American bombs and fighter jets would soon come, No and all the MiG pilots bunked five miles from the airfield in farmhouses with boards nailed over the windows. On his first evening in the farmhouse, with combat coming in the morning, No was too worried to eat. Lights went out soon after dinner, and most of the pilots went to bed. No lay awake for hours in the long darkness, as fear seized his body like a contagion, causing cramps in his stomach. It would be many years before he could shake the night terrors that infected him in Uiju.

Like all the young North Korean pilots, No was untested. He doubted that his flying skills were good enough to survive air-to-air combat. Yet that was only part of what kept him awake. Returning to North Korea had awakened his long-suppressed terror of being exposed as a fake. He would be shot for sure in this combat zone, he thought, when commanders found out he was a pretend Communist.

With his first mission in the morning, there was something new to dread: killing an American.

No had volunteered for the air force in the hope that this day would never come. He had convinced himself that Kim's malignant reign and his disastrous war would come to an end long before he learned how to fly a fighter jet. Since childhood he had wanted to make a life in the United States; the last thing he wanted to do was kill one of its citizens. All through flight training, political officers had assured him that American pilots were bullying weasels who only cared about money. When confronted by a swarm of MiGs, the political officers predicted, "the cowardly Americans will flee and desert their comrades to certain death." As he lay awake on that first night in Uiju, No found himself hoping that for once the political officers had told him the truth.

He learned they were liars as he flew in formation with seven other MiGs at forty thousand feet in scattered clouds near Pyongyang. He had been flying sorties for a week, without seeing a single enemy aircraft. But on the morning of November 15, four American fighter jets screamed out of the sun and attacked his formation from the rear. Machine guns blazing, they sliced down through the North Koreans, who panicked and skittered off in all directions. One MiG managed to veer away, lock in behind an American jet, and put its tail in his gun sights. But before the MiG pilot could fire, three other American jets counterattacked, forcing him to flee.

The attack taught No a simple and sobering lesson: what he had been told about the Americans was nonsense. With his own eyes, he saw that they were better fliers than the North Koreans—and at least the equals of the Russian honchos. The Americans hunted like wolves in a pack, protecting one another at great personal risk. No was frightened by their will to fight and win.

Russian advisers had told No how fortunate he was to be flying a MiG-15, which they proudly described as the world's best jet fighter. But the Americans attacked in a fighter jet—the F-86 Sabre—that performed as well, if not better.

Days after his first dogfight, No discovered that a Sabre could dive faster than a MiG. He watched from a distance as a Sabre pursued a MiG descending at its maximum safe speed of Mach 0.95, just below the speed of sound. The MiG pilot dared not go faster because as his jet approached Mach 1 it began to shake uncontrollably and the control stick became unmanageably heavy. Not so for the Sabre. In a dive, it smoothly pushed past the speed of sound and closed rapidly on the fleeing MiG.

When No returned to Uiju to break this alarming news to his North Korean commanders and his regiment's Russian adviser, they already knew. They did not want to talk about it.

II

The cold war race to build the best fighter jet dates to the final days of World War II, when the Americans and the Soviets marched into Germany. Both armies discovered records of the Third Reich's advanced aerodynamic research—the Americans in Bavaria, the Soviets in Berlin—showing that fighter jets could fly at or beyond the speed of sound if they were designed with swept wings, a high tail, and a stubby, open-nosed fuselage.

The Soviet Union's version of this design was the MiG-15; the name comes from the initials of Artem Mikoyan and Mikhail Gurevich, founders of an aircraft design bureau. The fighter was rushed into military service in June 1949. Five months earlier, the U.S. Air Force sent its first version of the Sabre, the F-86A, into the field.

The two fighter jets looked alike and had similar capabilities. Engineers in both countries tweaked newer models of the planes throughout the Korean War, keeping them roughly equal when flown by pilots of equal skill. Broadly speaking, the MiG could climb faster and operate at higher altitudes, but the Sabre was easier to fly, especially at low altitude. It was also more comfortable and less prone to shakes, sputters, and death spins because of mismatched wings and other manufacturing flubs. Unlike the early MiG-15 model that No trained on, the Sabre had hydraulic controls; pilots need not lift weights to handle its stick.

The cockpit of the Sabre was roomy and ergonomically sound, with gauges and toggle switches logically positioned. The fighter had good cockpit pressurization and temperature controls. Visibility was excellent, with a bullet-resistant, blown-plastic canopy that did not fog up. Pilots could see who was attacking from the rear. Guns on the Sabre, six .50-caliber machine guns, three on each side of its nose, were smaller and less lethal than those on the MiG. A Sabre pilot usually had to fly close to an enemy aircraft and hit it repeatedly to bring it down. But unlike a MiG pilot, he had radar to calculate distance to his target, and gun sights used gyroscopes to show him how far to fire in front of an enemy aircraft in order to hit it. "We were driving Cadillacs while they had Fords," one Sabre pilot said.

The Truman administration had hoped to keep these Cadillacs out of Korea, holding them in reserve in case the cold war turned hot in Europe. But Stalin forced the Americans to play their first team. Soon after MiGs began prowling the border region in November 1950, one of them shot down a B-29, unmasking the hulking bombers as vulnerable prey and alarming the air force. To protect them, the air force chief of staff, Vandenberg, decided within one day to send Sabres to Korea. Within a week, the first squadron of F-86As was loaded as deck cargo on navy tankers bound for Japan. The first seven flew into Kimpo Air Force Base near Seoul in mid-December.

Eleven months later, around the time No's nerves were rattled by his first encounter with a Sabre, the number of America's premier fighter jets in Korea had increased to 127. They were still outnumbered, more than four to one, by MiGs piloted by Russians, Chinese, and North Koreans.

But with each passing month, the Americans brought in more Sabres and more highly trained pilots. And with each passing month, the air war over Korea took on a superpower-versus-superpower life of its own. The aviation historians Douglas C. Dildy and Warren E. Thompson describe a high-speed, high-altitude, high-tech contest waged above the gore and muck of the ground war: "The best [pilots] from both sides sparred and dueled, fought and killed—or died—in an arena almost completely detached from the World War I–like trench warfare far below . . . It was a battle much more for the prestige of the nations engaged—and the reputation of their respective aerospace industries—and for the glory of the fighter pilots involved than for its effect on the conduct or the outcome of the conflict."

No was not ready for this kill-or-be-killed game. His lack of readiness began with his lightweight blue cotton pants.

In a fighter jet, a pilot is subjected to extraordinary g-forces that can cause exhaustion and blackouts. Coming out of a dive, a pilot can experience up to nine g's—nine times his body weight—slamming against limbs and torso, slowing the flow of blood to his brain.

Specialized pants—the kind found in a G suit, the kind that automatically squeeze a pilot's legs, ensuring that plenty of blood reaches his brain—were standard equipment for American fighter pilots in the Korean War. MiG pilots did not have them.

No had never seen a G suit, although he knew the Americans wore them. His commanders assured him that as long as his plane could endure the strain of dogfights, so could he. But the more he flew, the less he believed. Veteran Soviet MiG pilots, he noticed, looked old at twenty-five.

The guns in the nose of No's MiG were even more problematic than his pants.

Prior to going into combat, he had never fired them. And they remained silent on his first few combat sorties because he did not see anything to shoot. When that first flight of Sabres attacked, he did not have the time or presence of mind to shoot back.

When he finally managed to fire a few rounds on a later mission, he was frightened by the vibration from the cannon and the noise. Hitting anything with the plane's two 23 mm cannon or the slower-firing 37 mm cannon was almost impossible. At speeds above five hundred miles an hour, the World War II–era gun sights on his MiG did not provide a reliable read as to where the shells might go. Kill-minded MiG pilots had to fly behind their target, squeeze off a couple quick bursts of tracer bullets, and then guess at a trajectory that might hit the enemy. On nearly all of his combat sorties, No flew out and back in large formations of twenty or more MiGs, which gave him little opportunity to maneuver into a position with a legitimate shot at an American aircraft.

He knew, though, that the North Korean air force expected him to shoot down Americans. To keep his superiors happy and burnish his reputation as a kill-hungry Red, No began blazing his cannon across the sky, spraying shells at impossibly distant targets, and flying home with his ammunition patriotically wasted. He fretted less, over time, about harming an American. Even if he had wanted to, he could not shoot well enough to do it. As far as he could determine, he never hit anything. Neither did most of the other North Korean MiG pilots.

III

As dogfights escalated and Americans continued punishing his country with bombs and napalm, Kim Il Sung needed to find a way to escape responsibility for the devastation he had unleashed. He knew that when the war ended, he would be vulnerable and that many North Koreans would demand his head. His cold-blooded genius was to give them the heads of rival Korean politicians, particularly those who had come to Pyongyang from the Soviet Union, China, and South Korea and held powerful positions inside his government.

By making a scapegoat of these rivals, he increased his own power, distracted the masses with showy, Stalinist-style human sacrifice, and danced away from accountability for his failures as a military commander.

It was quite a show, and each performance consisted of three acts, according to Yu Song Chol, Kim's onetime translator and a top commander in the war. First, an elaborate plot was concocted to trap a rival. Second, the trapped individual was publicly criticized at party meetings. Finally, he was stripped of power, imprisoned, and in most cases killed.

Kim had to strike quickly. Many of the men he wanted to ruin had loyal followers and foreign backing and were smart enough to use the failed war to ruin him. Before they could act and long before the war was over, Kim began scheming. His first target, in the fall of 1951, was Ho Kai, the highest-ranking Soviet Korean in the North.

Ho was conscripted in the mid-1940s by Soviet authorities to go to the Korean Peninsula as a translator. He joined thousands of other ethnic Koreans who had been born and raised in the Soviet Union and spoke Korean and Russian. Yet Ho was always a cut above the bilingual schoolteachers and low-level bureaucrats who, on Stalin's orders, seeded Communism on the Korean Peninsula.

Ho had joined the Soviet Communist Party in 1930, at the precocious age of twenty-two. He had become well known in the Soviet Far East by the mid-1930s as "a young Korean of remarkable willpower, intelligence, and organizational skills," writes the historian Andrei Lankov. He was accomplished enough to become the second-ranking official in a district that was home to the Soviet Union's largest group of ethnic Koreans, and he was nimble enough to dodge a purge by Stalin that eliminated many of his peers.

Arriving in North Korea in November 1945, Ho moved immediately to the upper ranks of the bureaucracy that the Soviets erected around Kim Il Sung. He was the only high-ranking Korean speaker who knew from personal experience how to assemble a Stalinist party machine. Prior to the war, his organization worked more efficiently than government ministries in American-financed South Korea. Ho became known as the "Party doctor."

His skills as a politician and public speaker, however, were negligible. He had no grassroots political support. In the spring of 1950, he gave a speech to naval academy cadets, including No Kum Sok, who had lined up in the academy parade ground. Ho was memorably fat and did not speak Korean very well. He read his speech in a monotone, and none of the cadets understood what he was talking about.

As the war began, he was first secretary of the Korean Workers' Party, a post that made him second, after Kim Il Sung, in the Communist hierarchy. Working with Kim, Ho was involved in early planning for the invasion of South Korea and in trying to mobilize underground Communists in South Korea. Ho also helped groom Kim as Great Leader, according to Lim Un, a onetime colleague of both men.

"Ho Kai was not only the closest cooperator of Kim Il Sung, he was virtually his patron and guardian," Lim wrote. "He played the role of maternity nurse when the leader Kim Il Sung was born. These facts were for Kim Il Sung sufficient reason to purge Ho Kai."

Kim had another compelling motivation: his souring ties with Stalin.

In the days before China's army rescued North Korea, Stalin had made it humiliatingly clear that he viewed Kim as a man of no consequence. As long as the Soviet Koreans, led by the coolly competent Ho, exercised power in Pyongyang, Kim feared that it might please Stalin if he were killed and replaced.

Fortunately for Kim, the presence of Chinese troops in North Korea had weakened the Soviet Union's influence. The time was ripe for Kim to embark on a purge of Ho.

It began when Kim asked Ho to examine the behavior of party members who lived briefly under UN occupation during the early months of the war. When American and South Korean soldiers controlled the North, many cadres had burned their party cards, renounced Kim's government, and welcomed the occupiers. Ho zealously checked out these turncoats, denying party reinstatement to nearly everyone who could not produce an old membership card. He also tightened qualifications for new party members, embracing factory workers but excluding poor farmers.

At a plenum of the party's Central Committee in November 1951, Kim announced that Ho had gone too far. He criticized Ho for denying membership to toiling peasants who gave the party a populist base and for refusing to readmit party members who had done nothing wrong. His crimes were called "closed-doorism" and "liquidationism."

Ho was soon caught in another trap. He was asked to edit a draft document that contained flowery language praising the all-knowing magnificence of Kim.

"Is this really necessary?" Ho reportedly asked the man who gave him the document. Ho then used red ink to edit out florid passages. A politician who wanted Ho's job took the document directly to Kim. When Ho later visited Kim in his office, the Great Leader slyly pulled out the edited draft.

Criticized in the party plenum and humiliated in Kim's presence, Ho was stripped of his leadership position and expelled from the party. Kim then opened the door for party membership to peasant farmers, which swelled the ranks to more than a million and helped Kim claim a popular mandate. Later, Kim assigned Ho an impossible task: fixing American bomb damage at a major water reservoir. When Ho failed to complete the repair work on schedule, Kim accused him of "bureaucratism" and mismanagement.

With his life unraveling, Ho visited the Soviet embassy in Pyongyang, where he told a Soviet diplomat that he was being punished, in part, because he had been skeptical about "excessive praise" for Kim. Two days later, Ho was dead in his own house.

Officially, it was suicide. But Lankov found strong circumstantial evidence of murder and suggests three motives: Kim feared Ho was plotting against him, he saw Ho as an instrument of Soviet control, and he worried that Ho would return to the Soviet Union and cause trouble.

"His body lay in the small bed of his son, with a hunting rifle in his hands and a belt from his wife's dress tied to the trigger," Lankov writes. "Some of those who were there during the first minutes and hours thought that he had definitely been murdered and that the appearance of a suicide was merely a set-up. All the people I met during my studies who had known Ho well, including those whose orientation was pro–Kim Il Sung, were almost unanimous in believing that he was murdered."

Ho's father-in-law, Choe Pyo Dok, was a senior general in the North Korean army who commanded armored troops that seized Seoul in 1950. Choe had gone to see Ho on the night before he was supposed to have committed suicide. They spent the evening together, and the general detected nothing that made him believe Ho would want to end his life. Instead, he talked about his desire to get out of Korea and perhaps return to the Soviet Union. He also talked lovingly about his young son.

After learning that Ho was dead, Choe became convinced that he had been murdered. He was so certain that he telephoned Kim and accused him of murder, according to Lankov. Choe then resigned from the army and left the country.

Ho's wife, who was outside Pyongyang when she heard that her husband was dead, rushed home to bury him. By the time she arrived, he was already in the ground. She tried to talk to aides, servants, and a driver, but they had all been transferred to new jobs.

IV

Three days after the Great Leader moved his MiGs inside North Korea, the Americans spotted them.

An air force reconnaissance aircraft reported on November 10, 1951, that more than twenty MiGs were parked on the runway at Uiju airfield. That sighting prompted mission planners in the Fifth Air Force headquarters in Nagoya, Japan, to draw up a full-scale attack. They planned to pulverize the runway and destroy all the MiGs they could catch on the ground. The attack would include B-29 and B-26 bombers and an escort of fighter jets.

Before the mission could be approved, four American Sabres happened to fly over Uiju on the morning of November 18, and one of the pilots noticed MiGs parked in a zigzag pattern at the south end of the airfield. Two Sabres circled above to provide cover while Captain Kenneth Chandler and Lieutenant Dayton Ragland swooped down. Flying ten feet above the runway at near supersonic speed, they strafed the airfield with .50-caliber fire. In his report on the raid, Chandler said he destroyed four MiGs and damaged several others.

No Kum Sok got up at five that morning in his farmhouse bunk. He washed his face, brushed his teeth, put on his flight suit, and ate breakfast before riding a truck to the airfield. There he and the twenty-three other pilots in his fighter squadron were ordered to go on Alert One, the highest level of combat readiness. A third of the pilots had to climb into the cockpits of eight MiGs parked on the runway's apron, where they were expected to be ready to start their engines. The pilots hated Alert One. They believed that sitting in a fighter jet on an exposed runway made them sitting ducks. If there were a good reason for the highest-possible alert, they reasoned, why not take off and go to it? But they dared not complain to their commanders.

Starting at 8:00 a.m., in rotating shifts lasting one hour, they began an Alert One rotation. The squadron's first battalion went first, while pilots from the second and third battalions stood around and shot the breeze. No, who belonged to the second battalion, chatted with Senior Lieutenant Chung Young Tae, a friend from the third battalion.

"You've grown taller," Chung told No.

They had first met at the naval academy two and a half years earlier, when No was seventeen, short, and skinny. Chung was about three years older. They had a friendly argument over which Chinese city—Tianjin or Shenyang—had the larger population. No said, correctly, that it was Tianjin. Chung changed the subject, talking about the phenomenal number of aircraft the Americans manufactured to win World War II.

After an hour, it was No's turn to sit in a cramped cockpit and try to stay alert.

At ten, when pilots of the third battalion took their turn, No climbed down from his MiG and began walking along the edge of the runway to stretch his legs. That's when he noticed his regimental commander, Colonel Tae Kuk Sung, waving his arms wildly and screaming at the pilots to take cover. No also saw two VIPs, senior officers, walking together on the tarmac. One was a Soviet air force general, the top adviser to the North Korean air force. The second was the North Korean air force commander, General Wang Yong.

When General Wang heard the colonel shouting, he looked up at the sky.

"Look out!" he hollered in Russian.

No turned his head toward the northern end of the runway. Two planes were coming in fast, dragging contrails of dark smoke. No thought at first that they were Soviet MiGs hit in dogfights and approaching for emergency landing. But they did not slow down. Then he saw red tracers and heard machine-gun fire. He dove to the ground, pressing his face in the dirt as bullets kicked up dust on the runway and punched two holes in the MiG he had just gotten out of.

Not far away, General Wang and the Russian general had thrown themselves into the dirt, while the panicked airfield ground crew ran around in circles.

The raid's toll, as measured by destroyed aircraft, was not nearly as impressive as Captain Chandler later reported, an exaggerated tally that would find its way into the official air force history of the Korean War. One MiG, not four, was destroyed. Its fuel tank was hit, setting it ablaze. The airfield did not have a fire truck, and the burning MiG melted down to a few bits of blackened metal. It had been unoccupied, and no one near it was hurt.

Three other MiGs were slightly damaged. In one of them, a .50-caliber shell grazed a pilot sitting in the cockpit; it scratched the chin strap of his flight helmet. The pilot sitting in the cockpit of the MiG that No had occupied was also unhurt.

But the pilot in the third MiG—Chung Young Tae, No's friend—was not so lucky. A bullet cut through his neck. Before he could be removed from the cockpit, he was dead.

That strafing was just the beginning. More robust American efforts to wreck Uiju airfield and blow up its MiGs would soon begin. Twelve B-29s dropped eighty tons of explosive on the runway within two weeks, leaving 454 craters on the runway and making it unusable. Some of the craters were twenty feet wide. Trying to destroy hidden MiGs, night-flying bombers blanketed the Uiju area with five-hundred-pound bombs that exploded before they hit the ground, spraying shrapnel in all directions.

No and the other North Korean pilots could not take off at night to fight the Americans. (Only one North Korean air squadron was trained for night flight during the war, but it never entered combat.) Instead, the pilots stayed on the ground and hoped that shrapnel would not find the farmhouses where they struggled to sleep. No went to bed in his clothes, listening for the drone of B-29s, ready to run if he sensed that a bomb was heading his way.

American bombing tested the sanity of North Korean jet mechanics. Unlike the pilots, they slept in tents next to the airfield. A chief mechanic who befriended No was in his bunk beside the runway when he felt a dull, ground-shaking thud in the middle of the night. The next morning he looked out and saw a one-thousand-pound bomb—a dud—sticking out of the earth.

The Great Leader's decision to park MiGs at Uiju airfield lasted five weeks. When it was reversed on December 15, Chinese army engineers were called in to repair the cratered runway so the MiGs could take off. After two days, it was ragged but serviceable. No and the other pilots happily flew away and resumed operations in Manchuria.

CHAPTER 8

An International Sporting Event

I

Back in Manchuria, No could sleep at night without fear. He was back with the honchos, dining opulently at tables covered with white linen and indulging his fondness for steaming-hot borscht, which eased the winter chill. The convivial Russian pilots persuaded him to apply thick layers of butter to his black bread. Supposedly, it eased the pain of g-forces during dogfights. For the hell of it, No would top off the butter with a thick smear of caviar and wash it down with vodka, courtesy of his comrades, whose drinking had increased over eight harrowing months in MiG Alley. No also began smoking Great Production cigarettes, a supposedly premium Chinese brand that was bitter and often rotten. Still, they calmed his nerves.

His new airfield was near Dandong, just north of the Yalu. It had become the primary forward base for the Communist air war, with 170 MiGs flown by pilots from the Soviet Union, China, and North Korea. It had one narrow, congested, and intermittently deadly runway. The Chinese were based at the runway's east end and always took off to the west. The Russians and North Koreans were on the west end and took off to the east. All the MiGs, especially the newer models with bigger engines, were extraordinary fuel guzzlers. Most of them ran low on fuel in about an hour; a few could fly at full power for only thirty-five minutes. Then they returned to Dandong in panicky flocks, often landing from the east and the west at the same time, squeezing past each other at high speed on the narrow runway. Pilots struggled to keep to the right, and a few collided head-on. No had many near misses, but in the process became accustomed to landing amid runway chaos that would horrify most pilots.

From nearly a year of studying MiG pilots over MiG Alley, American fliers were wise to who was good (most of the Russians) and who was not (most of the Chinese and North Koreans). The Communists unwittingly assisted the Americans' ranking system by color coding some of their jets. The MiGs in No's regiment, with poorly trained pilots who could not shoot straight, had a red nose and a red ring painted around the fuselage behind the wing. The distinctive pattern seemed to say to Sabre pilots, "Come kill me."

In early 1952, to No's enormous relief, the red on every MiG was covered with silver paint.

On New Year's Day 1952, the twenty-four MiGs in No's regiment took off, climbed to forty-two thousand feet, and headed south. Following the regimental commander, Colonel Tae Kuk Sung, they flew over bomb-shattered Pyongyang and continued south. The day was clear. Visibility was excellent. Best of all, the Americans were celebrating the New Year's holiday by keeping their fighter jets on the ground. No's usual stomach-churning fear had ebbed. He relaxed and enjoyed the view.

"That smoky scene in the southern horizon is Seoul," Colonel Tae told his pilots over the radio.

No had never flown so close to South Korea. It struck him that this might be his best chance to make a run for it. He could peel away from his formation, dive to a lower altitude, and perhaps find a landing strip in South Korea before Sabres could be scrambled to shoot him down. If he made it, he could quit pretending.

Exhilarated and terrified at the same moment, he had only seconds to take inventory of his chances. Other MiGs, he guessed, would give chase and fire at him. If he eluded them, where, exactly, would he land? He knew little about runways in South Korea. He worried, too, that the Americans would spot him on radar and target him with antiaircraft fire.

Over the radio, the regimental commander ordered his pilots to turn north and head back to Manchuria. In tight formation, No made the turn.

A cold calculation had canceled his daydream of defection: he figured he would not survive. The same calculation had stopped him from shooting the Great Leader on the runway at Uiju. No had no interest in making a grand statement. He did not want to die as a symbol of opposition to Kim Il Sung. He wanted to live in the United States.

To improve his odds, he reasoned, he needed more experience as a pilot. As important, he needed precise map coordinates for airfields in South Korea. He needed to know which ones could accommodate a MiG. He flew back to Manchuria, at peace with his decision to wait for a better opportunity to escape and relieved to see that the Americans were still taking the day off.

But for the rest of the year, indeed for the rest of the war, the risk of his being killed in air-to-air combat continued to build.

II

The honchos were going home. Their mastery of the MiG and appetite for confrontation had remade the air war: providing essential cover for Chinese supply routes, seizing superiority over MiG Alley, and forcing the Americans to rush their best fighter jets to Korea. Thirty-nine honchos had shot down five or more American aircraft; eighteen were proclaimed Heroes of the Soviet Union.

A final accounting of the air war between Sabres and MiGs shows that the Americans won an overwhelming victory, with an overall "kill ratio" of nine to one. But that ratio included all of the MiGs in the war, as flown by Chinese, North Korean, and lesser-trained Russian pilots. When the Soviet pilots of the elite 324th and 303rd fighter divisions were in the cockpit, the kill ratio was nearly even. The honchos fought the Americans to a draw in the air, just as the Chinese fought them to a draw on the ground.

By March 1952, though, the elite Russian fliers were exhausted and breaking down. One pilot had a heart attack after landing, another vomited into his oxygen mask and nearly collided with his group leader, a third blacked out and fell into a spin. Doctors gave them injections to increase their strength, but between a third and a half of them were no longer fit to fly. All were eager to leave. Thirty-two had been killed, including No's former instructor and friend, Captain Nikichenko.

The night before the honchos left Dandong, No heard them carousing all night in their barracks, drunkenly singing Russian folk songs. The next morning, one pilot told No it had not been a victory celebration. They were relieved to be alive.

Soviet replacement pilots were not nearly as good, and many were soon killed. Stalin seemed to be losing interest in the war, sending rookies to fight it. These pilots arrived from the Soviet Union with fewer than fifty hours in the latest-model MiG. Less than 20 percent of them were veterans of World War II. In Moscow, their training had focused on instrument flying, not dogfighting. They were not much better than the Chinese or the North Koreans. With each passing month, Sabres shot them down in steadily increasing numbers—and with fewer American losses.

As the best Russian fliers left, the Americans brought in more deadly aircraft. The new F model of the Sabre had a more powerful engine and slightly larger wings. It could climb to high altitudes that had been the exclusive preserve of MiGs. Once there, the new Sabres could maneuver more precisely. By the middle of 1952, No believed it was suicide for any MiG to engage a Sabre, especially at low altitudes. He was not alone. Russian MiG pilots began shying away from air-to-air combat.

Many others refused to fly, claiming chronic battle fatigue. A Soviet commander in charge of the laggards was sent home in disgrace. By the final year of the war, Sabre pilots could plainly see that many MiG pilots were "pitifully incompetent" and did not have the stomach for any kind of fight. At least seven times, American fliers watched as MiG pilots failed to execute tight turns above thirty-five thousand feet, fumbling their aircraft into deadly spins from which pilots usually ejected before the MiG crashed. Some MiG pilots surrendered immediately in response to attack. When a Sabre fired at them, they bailed out and floated down in a parachute. An air force intelligence report noted, "A new inexpensive, highly efficient 'MiG Killer' technique has been found! If the pilot sees you, he bails out; if he doesn't see you, you shoot him down. What could be more effective?"

For No and many North Korean fliers, the fear of being blasted out of the air was compounded by anxiety about being punished on the ground. A pilot in No's regiment, Sin Yoon Chul, who had flown more than fifty combat missions, was suddenly dismissed from the air force after a security officer learned the pilot's brother had fled to South Korea early in the war. The commander of a division of propeller aircraft flying out of Manchuria, Colonel Kim Tal Hion, was suspected of planning to defect—and was executed by firing squad.

As mortifying for No was the incompetence of senior flight officers in his regiment. Instead of flying in tight clusters of four fighters that could hide behind clouds, these senior officers almost always led large formations of twenty to twenty-four MiGs, which created massive vapor trails that could be seen for at least eighty miles. These formations, No observed, invited attack and usually resulted in the deaths of North Korean pilots. As stupid, No believed, his commanders did not take advantage of the MiG's greatest strength: its capacity to operate above forty-five thousand feet. His division often entered MiG Alley at much lower altitudes and at less than maximum speed, making it easy for Sabres to pick them off.

One of No's worst scares occurred when he was flying east of Pyongyang in a formation of twenty-four MiGs at about forty-one thousand feet. A smaller formation of Russian MiGs—presumably under more experienced command—was flying well above them.

From behind, four Sabres attacked, scattering the North Koreans and shredding their capacity to fight back. No lost his wingman, who was supposed to stay behind No but had turned away to elude machine-gun fire. No veered sharply to the right and was accelerating north for Manchuria when he saw red tracer bullets over his cockpit. A Sabre flew directly behind him at a distance of about three thousand feet. It kept on shooting. No panicked, swerved his MiG sharply to the left and then to the right, and accelerated into a climb. The Sabre could not keep up. No was out of range. If the American pilot had been more patient, if he had held his fire until he closed to within a thousand feet, No probably would have been shot down.

On the ground, No could not relax or unwind. There were no weekend passes. He had not had a single day off since the war started. Although he had written his mother many letters, there was never a reply from her or from anyone in his family. He believed his mother must be dead, killed by American bombs. Then, in the spring of 1952, his risk of dying increased exponentially.

The Manchurian sanctuary—the single most important advantage that Communist air forces enjoyed during the Korean War—suddenly evaporated. American Sabre pilots decided to start killing MiGs inside China, ignoring the rules of combat that governed the Korean War. They did so with a wink and a nod from their commanders in South Korea.

No watched it happen in early April, on a sunny morning when he was not flying. Shortly after the morning fog lifted at Dandong airfield, about fifty Russian-piloted MiGs took off for MiG Alley. They returned about an hour later, desperately low on fuel. As No, who was standing on the southwest apron of the runway, listened to the throaty roar of MiGs decelerating to land, he heard an unexpected whine: the high-pitched signature of Sabre engines. He looked up and saw more than a dozen of them.

Flying at low altitude and high speed, they converged on the airfield from three directions, seeking out MiGs that had slowed down and were on approach to land. No watched Sabres hit three MiGs with machine-gun fire. None of the Russian pilots managed to eject before their jets crashed and exploded. Two other wounded MiGs crashed northeast of the airfield, sending towering plumes of black smoke into the sky.

From then until the end of the war, Sabres showed up almost daily over Communist airfields inside Manchuria. The Americans were highly selective. They never strafed aircraft parked on the ground, as they always did inside North Korea. Instead, they swooped and soared around Manchurian airfields like eagles, picking off MiGs when they were easiest to kill. In the first six months of 1952, one Russian fighter division lost twenty-six planes over its own airfields. Chinese losses also soared.

"We shot them down in the landing pattern, we shot them down on local test hops, we shot them down on training flights, and we shot them down anywhere we could find them," explained Colonel Walker "Bud" Mahurin, who organized and participated in many attacks inside China. "We considered it slightly dirty pool to shoot them down just as they were trying to land, but each victory added up."

No observed that American pilots had no compunctions about killing MiGs as they tried to land. Indeed, it was their preferred moment, with MiGs low on fuel and in no position to fight back.

Mahurin and American pilots had to screen and destroy cockpit film that showed them operating in Manchuria. "We just couldn't let anything incriminating get away from our base," Mahurin said in his autobiography. "Our pilots were coming back from missions [in Manchuria] with some of the damnedest pictures."

The United States never officially approved this predation, and for decades the air force minimized it or tried to cover it up. *Air Force Magazine*, in an article published a half century after the start of the Korean War, misleadingly said, "The air war was a fluid encounter conducted almost solely over North Korean territory. The exceptions were rare . . . a few inadvertent excursions across the Yalu River by wandering U.S. airmen."

Throughout the war, air force generals frequently sought but never received top-level approval for a policy of "hot pursuit," which would have allowed Sabres to chase MiGs into Manchuria. On this subject, MacArthur had been categorical. "The border," he said, "cannot and must not be violated." The air force commander in East Asia, General Stratemeyer, said he was "ready" to take the air war to China, but only if politicians gave the order. The decision to use "our fighters beyond the confines of Korea is not one that should be made by the field commander," he said. "It might be wise to point out that the military man implements foreign policy in our democratic form of government—the military do not formulate foreign policy."

Yet the Sabre pilots who formulated and implemented the policy of shooting down MiGs inside China got away with it.

Their commanders rarely disciplined them, unless incontrovertible evidence of Manchurian mischief reached Washington. Such evidence included cockpit film and, most damningly, radar records. Air force radar monitoring stations could monitor and record unauthorized border incursions, but only if a Sabre pilot turned on a small device in his plane called an IFF (identification, friend or foe) set, which sends a unique geo-location signal to friendly radar.

When incriminating radar records did not exist, air force generals ignored the games Sabre pilots played. Mahurin described how it worked:

> One day the six of us [pilots] were summoned to Fifth Air Force Headquarters. Our commander, General Frank Everest, came storming in and he was as mad as could be. He pounded the table and said, "You guys are violating the demarcation line; you're crossing the Yalu River. It's got to stop! All the trouble this will cause with the State Department! I am going to court-martial every one of you. I was in my control center just the other day, watching on radar. I saw your pilots take off, fly over the Yalu River . . . My God, this has really got to stop!"
>
> We all stood up at attention. He stalked out of the conference room and slammed the door. We were all looking at each other, when he poked his head back in and said, "If you're gonna do it, for

God's sake, turn off your IFF system, because we can track you on radar."

Soon, all Sabre pilots felt competitive pressure to kill MiGs in Manchuria. As Major Thomas Sellers told his wife in a letter, "I'm determined to get a MiG as are most of the boys around here and it seems there is only one positive way of doing it and that is to go north of the Yalu." A month later, on a mission inside Manchuria, Sellers saw fourteen MiGs taking off from an airfield and led an attack. He shot down two of them before his Sabre was hit by enemy fire and crashed. His posthumous Silver Star citation said he died inside North Korea while protecting American aircraft from MiG attack.

After interviewing fifty-four Sabre pilots who fought in the war, the historian and former air force pilot Kenneth P. Werrell asked in his account of the air war why pilots "took it upon themselves to cross the border." His answer: "To paraphrase the famous 1950s bank robber Willie Sutton, that's where the MiGs were. And therein lay the fame, glory, and the essence of being a hot fighter pilot: killing MiGs."

III

As seen from the United States, the conflict in Korea was mostly a downer. Its main event, the bloody ground war, was an unsatisfying, inconclusive bore. As the historian Bruce Cumings has written, the war "began to disappear from consciousness as soon as the fighting stabilized."

Air battles in MiG Alley were much sexier. For starters, the U.S. Air Force won most of them, especially after the honchos went home. As important, the air war plugged into a powerful postwar ethos of self-congratulation: our boys were whipping those nasty Commies with new-fangled American technologies and old-fashioned American guts.

Hollywood loved jet-age dogfights and churned out movies like *Sabre Jet* and *Jet Attack*. The fight over MiG Alley sold newspapers. When a Sabre downed a MiG, it was often front-page news—much more so than when the air force napalmed North Korean cities and killed large numbers of civilians.

Sabre pilots themselves were smitten by their own sexiness. The best and most aggressive of them became obsessed with shooting down MiGs. The coveted goal was five kills, and those who reached it became aces. During the war, the significance of being an ace was difficult to overstate—for career advancement, for bedding women, for respecting oneself as a man.

"If you shoot down five planes you join a group, a core of heroes. Nothing less can do it," the novelist James Salter—himself a Sabre pilot—explains in *The Hunters,* his first novel. "There were no other values. It was like money: it did not matter how it had been acquired, but only that it had. That was the final judgment. MiGs were everything. If you had MiGs you were a standard of excellence. The sun shone upon you. The crew chiefs were happy to have you fly their ships. The touring actresses wanted to meet you. You were the center of everything—the praise, the excitement, the enviers . . . If you did not have MiGs, you were nothing."

Before they arrived in Korea, the air force drummed MiG killing and risk taking into Sabre pilots. At Nellis Air Force Base near Las Vegas, where many of the Sabre pilots who fought in Korea learned to fly, the average death rate from flight-training accidents was one a week. The "overriding philosophy was that if you weren't having accidents you weren't training realistically," writes John Lowery, a Sabre pilot who trained at Nellis before heading to Korea. "The lack of concern for safety was exacerbated by the demand for seemingly mindless aggressiveness."

The tone was set at the top. Colonel Clay Tice, base commander, gave a welcoming speech that one incoming pilot remembered as "Welcome to Nellis AFB, men. The finest fighter weapons school in the world. We're going to do one of three things to you here—wash you out, kill you, or make you one of the best fighter pilots in the world. The choice is yours. Now I want you all to go out, drink a pint of 'panther piss,' eat a pound of raw meat, find yourselves a strange woman, and we'll see you bright and early Monday morning."

During and after the Korean War, the air force reveled in the glory of its fighter pilots and their machines. The Sabre was "the vehicle in which the new aces of the jet age were achieving stardom, and MiG Alley was their stage," explained General T. R. Milton in an official air force history. Changing metaphors, Milton said the dogfights "had taken on the aura of an international sporting event."

The sport—which grew in popularity as it tilted in America's favor—produced thirty-nine aces. By their own admission, these pilots found addictive pleasure in risking death to kill MiGs. "The one thing that never left me was the intense, gripping anxiety and excitement that occurred when I saw some kind of movement which indicated the enemy pilot had seen me and one of us wasn't going home. That remained and has to this day been the greatest thrill of my life," wrote Major Frederick "Boots" Blesse, who shot down ten MiGs.

For the pilots who shot down the most MiGs, the push to risk everything had tragic, if predictable, consequences. Four out of five of the aces with thirteen or more "victories" died violently and before their time, one lost in action, two in aircraft accidents, and the fourth in a car accident. Major George A. Davis, a remarkable marksman with a .50-caliber machine gun and a daredevil pilot with fourteen kills, won a posthumous Medal of Honor for attacking a dozen MiGs on February 10, 1952. He shot down two before a third MiG got him. His peers later said Davis had more self-confidence than good sense: he believed all MiG pilots were his inferiors.

Aces played an outsized role in winning the air war. Only 4 percent of the thousand pilots who flew Sabres in Korea shot down five or more MiGs, yet they accounted for 40 percent of confirmed kills. Flying skill and courage were not the whole story behind these numbers. Aces tended to be flagrant violators of combat rules, crossing into Manchuria and picking off MiGs that were taking off or landing. As many as twenty-five of the thirty-nine aces flew into Manchuria.

Fame and touring actresses notwithstanding, risking everything for glory did not make sense to most American fighter pilots in Korea. The great majority flew a hundred mostly dull missions and went home, unfamous but alive. Bud Mahurin, the rule-breaking air force colonel with the Fifty-first Fighter-Interceptor Wing based near Seoul, said only a fraction of his pilots would seek out a fight. Out of the one hundred pilots whom Mahurin regularly addressed in preflight briefings, he said, "I could pick, say, eighteen who could actually be depended upon to mix it up with the enemy and perhaps do some shooting. Another seventy would never see the enemy or fire a gun. The rest would inevitably develop some sort of mechanical, mental or physical difficulty sufficient to cause them to turn back home."

These careful, cautious, unexciting Americans were No Kum Sok's soul mates. To his great relief, they were the kind of pilots he encountered most often.

From Dandong airfield, No flew nearly every day, sometimes two sorties a day. On two-thirds of these missions, he did not see a single Sabre, which suited him just fine. Even when he saw the enemy, nothing would usually come of it. No and a Sabre pilot would eye each other at a range of several miles. Both would squirt off a few rounds in the general direction of the enemy. No would skedaddle to a higher altitude and head north. In almost every case, the American pilot did not try to follow him home.

IV

By midsummer of 1952, Kim Il Sung had had enough of his dreadful war. It had wrecked Korea without unifying it. Searching for a way out, the Great Leader sent an urgent message to Stalin. He complained that armistice talks, already a year old, seemed likely to go on indefinitely, as the misery of North Koreans increased daily.

"Over the past year of negotiations we have virtually curtailed military operations and moved to a passive defense," Kim said. "Such a position has led to the fact that the enemy almost without suffering any kind of losses constantly inflicts on us huge losses in manpower and material values."

He complained, too, that American bombing had destroyed "all the electrical stations" in North Korea and that U.S. Air Force patrols do "not allow us the possibility to restore them." Most upsetting, Kim said, was the constant bombing of Pyongyang.

"In only one twenty-four hour period of barbaric bombing . . . more than six thousand peaceful inhabitants were killed and wounded," Kim said, referring to a massive American bombing operation on July 11, 1952, five days before Kim sent his plaintive telegram to Stalin.

That bombing involved nearly every operational UN air unit in the Far East. Characterized in an official U.S. Air Force history as "savage," it was the Korean War's biggest air assault up to that point. The 1,254 aircraft sorties that day managed a direct hit on an air-raid shelter for the elite, reportedly killing more than four hundred North Korean government officials. This was apparently the hit that riled the Great Leader.

Air force generals had been unhappy for months with their bombing campaign, which had failed to force Communist concessions in truce talks. So they launched Operation Pressure Pump, which was intended to use "destructive power as a political tool" and have a "deleterious effect" on North Korean morale. The air force began bombing hydroelectric dams and then strafed them to prevent repairs. It also used fighter-bombers to drop napalm and delayed-action bombs on seventy-eight towns and villages suspected of sheltering the enemy. "Lucrative targets" became increasingly hard to find. So six weeks after pounding Pyongyang with the ferocious all-day bombing that caused Kim to complain to Stalin, the air force did it again—this time over two days with more than fourteen hundred sorties. Again, it was a leisurely exercise in destruction, with no North Korean, Chinese, or Russian MiGs to fight back. (The MiGs almost always stayed well north of Pyongyang, patrolling only the Yalu River area.)

The stepped-up American bombing campaign was intended to demoralize Kim Il Sung, and it apparently worked. In his telegram to Stalin, Kim asked for antiaircraft weaponry and help in preparing for active military operations. He also implored Stalin for permission to talk more seriously with the Americans about ending the war.

"We need simultaneously to move decisively toward the soonest conclusion of an armistice, a ceasefire and transfer of all prisoners of war on the basis of the Geneva Convention," Kim wrote. "These demands are supported by all peace-loving peoples and will lead us out of a passive position."

Because the Chinese were fighting his ground war, Kim sent the same urgent end-the-combat message to Mao in Beijing. But his requests fell on deaf ears. Mao wanted the war to continue—and so did Stalin. Human suffering aside, they felt that the war was turning out to be a good and galvanizing thing for global Communism. They also viewed it as a useful device for humiliating the United States, weakening the Truman administration, gathering intelligence about America's weapons, killing its soldiers, and bleeding its treasury while teaching Communist soldiers how to fight against a superpower. Stalin also found value in the war because it required China to depend on military and economic assistance from the Soviet Union. This lessened the chances that Mao would follow Yugoslavia's lead and wander off the Communist reservation.

Mao wrote back to Kim to say that negotiating an end to the war "is highly disadvantageous to us." He conceded that continuing the war would kill many more Koreans and Chinese soldiers but argued the sacrifice was justified because it provided useful "experience in the struggle against American imperialism" and inspired "peace-loving peoples of the whole world." As important, Mao said, the war "limits the mobility of the main forces of American imperialism and makes it suffer constant losses in the east" while allowing the Soviet Union to rebuild from World War II and spread revolution around the world.

A month later, Stalin weighed in with an even more enthusiastic endorsement of prolonging the war. His blanket refusal to consider Kim's desire to stop it included a cold-blooded assessment of the insignificance of the dead and dying in North Korea.

"This war is getting on America's nerves," Stalin said in a meeting in Moscow with the Chinese prime minister, Zhou Enlai. "The North Koreans have lost nothing, except for people."

Stalin said that of course he knew death and destruction were making North Korean leaders panicky. But they should take a deep breath, he said, and understand their "many casualties" in the proper context—a context that would encourage "patience and lots of endurance."

By dying without surrendering, Stalin said, North Koreans were performing a useful service for international Communism.

"The war in Korea has shown America's weakness," Stalin said.

Every American soldier is a speculator, occupied with buying and selling. Germans conquered France in 20 days. It's been already two years, and U.S.A. still has not subdued little Korea. What kind of strength is that? America's primary weapons . . . are stockings, cigarettes, and other merchandise. They want to subjugate the world, yet they cannot subdue little Korea. No, Americans don't know how to fight. After the Korean war, in particular, they have lost the capability to wage a large-scale war. They are pinning their hopes on the atom bomb and air power. But one cannot win a war with that. One needs infantry, and they don't have much infantry; the infantry they do have is weak. They are fighting with little Korea, and already people are weeping in the U.S.A. What will happen if they start a large-scale war? Then, perhaps, everyone will weep.

This chilling pep talk was not intended for the ears of the leadership in "little Korea." But the core message found its way, via the Chinese, to Pyongyang: The war, the bombing, the destruction, and the dying would continue because they suited Stalin.

Living in a bunker, utterly dependent on Mao and Stalin for his survival, Kim Il Sung had no leverage. He had to play the toady, saying in one telegram, "We consider that your analysis of the present situation is correct."

In the late summer of 1952, with the ruins of Pyongyang still smoldering from American bombs, Kim was invited to Moscow for his third and final visit with Stalin. The Soviet leader had heard from Zhou Enlai that the North Koreans were getting "panicky." So he sent a special plane to fetch Kim.

At their meeting on September 4, Kim was shrewd enough to tell the Boss what he wanted to hear.

"What is the mood of the Korean people?" Stalin asked.

"The mood is good," Kim lied.

"What about in the armies?" Stalin asked.

"In the armies the mood is also good," Kim lied.

Then, almost as an afterthought, Kim dared to prick Stalin with a sliver of truth.

"The overall situation is favorable," he said, "if you do not include the bombing raids."

Stalin knew, of course, about the catastrophic effects of American airpower. But he had no intention of investing enough Soviet resources to stop it. Instead, he promised to give Kim some additional fighter aircraft and antiaircraft artillery—and quickly changed the subject.

For all his kowtowing to Stalin and Mao, Kim was never completely acquiescent. Before his September meeting with Moscow, he had asked for his patrons' approval in taking the offensive to the Americans. The North Korean air force had no large long-range bombers trained for night action inside enemy territory, but he told Mao that he did: "It is necessary to send already trained air force bomber units on night actions deep in enemy [territory], to boldly carry out air battles [and] subject to bombardment a number of airports."

One of the North Korean pilots who had been trained to attack airports in enemy territory was No Kum Sok.

CHAPTER 9

Attack Maps and Defection Bribes

I

No received the order for secret training in June 1952, when he was twenty. Along with seven other North Korean pilots, he left Dandong airfield and flew deeper inside Manchuria. After they landed at Anshan air base, where two years earlier Russians had taught them to fly, their regimental commander said they would soon attack American jets inside South Korea. Because North Korean MiG pilots could not seem to hit Sabres in the air, Kim Il Sung's government had decided they would hit them on the ground.

"We are here to train you to destroy Sabres before they get into the air," Colonel Tae Kuk Sung said.

The target was Kimpo Air Force Base, on the western outskirts of Seoul. Western reporters called it "the Home of the MiG Killers." The U.S. Air Force Fourth Fighter-Interceptor Wing was stationed there, and its Sabre pilots were responsible for more than half of the MiGs shot down in the Korean War. Out of the thirty-nine American aces in the war, twenty-five of them flew for the Fourth Fighter-Interceptor Wing. Between missions, they slept, ate, showered, and drank near the airfield in steel Quonset huts and in poorly insulated wooden huts called hootches.

Using live ammunition, No and the other pilots practiced destroying American Sabres by strafing wooden fences laid down on the tarmac at Anshan. When exploding fragments from cannon shells bounced up and punched holes in their MiGs, they stopped firing live ammunition and did flyovers while shooting pictures. At night, No studied maps and models of Kimpo. He learned the orientation of the runway, north to south, and saw what longitudinal degree to follow across North Korea to reach it.

The planned attack on Kimpo was by far the most audacious plan he had ever been a part of. Whoever came up with it, No thought, would surely be aware that it could provoke an all-out American counterattack on air bases in Manchuria, one that could annihilate all the aircraft that the Soviet Union had shipped east for the war. The plan suggested to No that the Communists were becoming desperate. The Chinese could not train pilots quickly enough to replace those who had been killed. Newly arriving Russian pilots were inexperienced and increasingly unwilling to engage the Americans. The air war was all but lost.

What motivated No to study the maps and models so diligently was his own audacious plan. When he flew to Kimpo, he did not intend to strafe the runway. He would land on it. He would surrender himself and his MiG to the famous aces of the Fourth Fighter-Interceptor Wing. He would ask to be taken to America.

His fear of defecting had faded.

For that, he could thank the North Korean air force and his Great Leader. They gave him access to superb maps of South Korea's airports and ordered him to memorize them. Back in January, when he was flying a mission near the South Korean border and thinking about defecting, he had hesitated because he was not sure where to land. Now he knew. There were three airports in the South with runways long enough for a MiG. Thanks to the maps, he had calculated the distances to the airports, the times, the approaches, and the required fuel—and filed it all away in the top secret and hyperactive part of his mind where for five years he had been pretending to love Communism. Although his training with all-weather navigation instruments on his MiG was rudimentary, he convinced himself that his mastery of the maps would allow him to find Kimpo or another airport, even in cloudy weather.

No could also thank a North Korean aircraft mechanic who told him the thrilling story of Lieutenant Lee Kun Soon.

Lee was a flight instructor in the North Korean air force and the best pilot in his training division. At twenty-four, he was in charge of the first generation of cadet fliers. He was also a devout Catholic, which he tried to keep secret. His faith became known when he was promoted from sergeant to lieutenant, but his commander tolerated him because of his flying and teaching skills. As a flight instructor, Lee had a reputation for being tough and uncompromising. He was harsh in enforcing military discipline, and students dreaded flying with him.

Two months before the start of the Korean War, Lee defected. Leaving his wife behind, he took off from Pyongyang in an Ilyushin Il-10, a Soviet-made single-engine propeller aircraft of World War II vintage. He landed in the South Korean city of Pusan, where he was greeted warmly and welcomed into the South Korean air force. Had he stayed in the North flying an Il-10, he probably would have been killed. Americans shot down nearly all of these outdated attack planes.

At the time of Lee's defection, there was no law in North Korea that authorized the government to punish, imprison, or execute family members of defectors, so nothing happened to his wife or parents. Lee's good fortune held throughout the war. When South Korean forces moved north in the first year of fighting and briefly occupied Pyongyang, Lee went along and found his wife and parents. They all fled together when the Chinese pushed UN forces south. Lee and his wife raised four children in South Korea, where he rose to the rank of colonel in the air force and became vice-commander of the South Korean Air Force Academy. After retiring, he worked as a civilian adviser until he was killed at age seventy near Seoul in an automobile accident. The North Korean mechanic did not, of course, know the entire story of Lee's defection. But he told No enough to dispel his fear.

If one North Korean pilot can do it, No asked himself, why can't I?

The North Korean government never publicly acknowledged Lee's defection, and few North Koreans were aware of it. But Kim's regime was taking no chances. In the fall of 1951, it authorized the execution of family members of any defector and publicized the decree.

When No read about the decree in a newspaper, it did not change his plans. His father was dead, and he believed his mother was too. As for his Uncle Yoo, No had been careful never to contact him or his family. He did not trust or like his uncle, but he certainly did not want to harm him, his wife (the sister of his mother), or their children. He hoped that by keeping his distance, he would keep them safe.

After six weeks of training, No and the other pilots returned to Dandong and waited for orders to attack Kimpo. The orders never came. The mission was canceled without explanation, and No could only guess what happened. He thought that the Soviet high command must have judged North Korea's plan to attack American air bases too provocative and scrubbed it.

II

He guessed right.

The airport attack proposed by Kim Il Sung was discussed by Stalin and the Chinese prime minister, Zhou Enlai, in Moscow during their meeting in August 1952.

"The Korean comrades have asked about launching a new offensive," Zhou told Stalin, quickly adding that the Chinese government thought it was a bad idea and had said as much to North Korea.

Stalin agreed. He did not want to give the Americans an excuse to bomb Manchuria, nor did he want to introduce a complicating factor into the armistice talks with the Americans. Stalin did not want those talks to end the war, but neither did he want them to collapse, which might provoke the Americans into using their superior airpower to widen the war's footprint—and perhaps drop nuclear weapons.

The North Koreans "should not be launching either strategic or tactical offensives," Stalin told Zhou. "They shouldn't be launching any offensives."

Stalin, in effect, was ordering the Great Leader to twist slowly in the wind: do nothing, keep quiet, and endure North Korea's continuing annihilation.

And Kim's response?

He turned up the volume on North Korea's official adulation of all things Stalin.

"The Korean people look up to Marshal Stalin as to the sun—the savior of mankind, the benefactor of the Korean people's liberation, our father," said a page-one editorial published on May 22, 1952, in the *Rodong Sinmun*, the official newspaper of the North Korean Workers' Party. "We praise him with joy and song, and call on his name as the symbol of happiness and peace." Similarly effusive editorial tributes to Stalin's genius, wisdom, and countless tender mercies toward the North Korean people were published several times in the party newspaper throughout 1952.

Kim's decision to worship Stalin in public—even as Stalin privately betrayed him and the people of North Korea—was driven by political desperation. Throughout 1952, as the American bombing grew more savage, as Stalin and Mao shortened his leash, Kim struggled to reclaim the popularity he had lost in the war. He needed to rebuild his ruling party and the government's shattered bureaucracy. He needed intelligence officers to identify rivals and police muscle to neutralize them. For these needs, Stalin—the backstabbing old bastard—was not at all helpful.

But Stalinism was.

So Kim began wrapping himself up in a full-blown Stalinist cult of personality. He had done this at times before the war, but now he pulled out all the stops. Buildings and monuments were commissioned in Kim's honor. More and bigger photographs of him were printed. Idealized life histories were published. The party newspaper that sang Stalin's praises also sang about Kim: "In his revolutionary activities and entire career, [Kim] has totally devoted his creative energies and genius to the cause of the freedom, independence, happiness, democracy, and peace of the fatherland."

"The focus on Kim became ever more conspicuous" in 1952, according to the historians Robert A. Scalapino and Chong-Sik Lee. "Kim was now being featured by official Party and state organs in a manner roughly parallel to the homage being paid Stalin in the Soviet Union."

For Kim to sell himself as Stalin-like, even as Stalin undercut him, was remarkable political theater. It also demonstrated Kim's lifelong ability to take a punch, stay on his feet, and find a creative way to survive. It helped, of course, that his humiliations by telegram from Moscow and Beijing were secret. The world did not learn about them until the mid-1990s, after Stalin, Mao, Kim, and the Soviet Union were all dead. The people of North Korea have yet to hear about Stalin's casual willingness to treat them and their Great Leader with contempt and indifference.

In 1952, Kim needed to be creative—and wary.

His bungled war had weakened his political grip and emboldened his rivals, the most worrisome of whom was Pak Hon Yong. A former newspaper reporter who spoke English, Pak had been by far the best-known Communist in Korea during the Japanese occupation. After the peninsula was divided and the Soviets installed Kim as leader in the North, Pak became a partner with Kim in running the new North Korea and steering it toward war. When Kim traveled to meet Stalin and plan the invasion, Pak went along as foreign minister.

Yet Pak always retained his own political power base. He commanded the loyalty of Communists who had grown up on the Korean Peninsula— the so-called domestic faction. As the war went from bad to worse, members of this faction began to organize an effort to overthrow Kim and install Pak as leader. "Kim's failure to unify Korea militarily gave rise to a conviction that Kim was indeed a puppet who had falsely claimed the leadership of the Korean Communist movement," writes Kim's biographer Dae-Sook Suh.

No Kum Sok, age three, wearing a pith helmet, with his father, No Zae Hiub (left), an all-star pitcher for his company's baseball team, in Sinhung, Korea, in 1935.

No Kum Sok, age four, with his mother, Veronica, in Sinhung. The family was well off, and his mother was one of a handful of Korean women who owned a Singer sewing machine.

Kim Il Sung, age fourteen, in 1926, while in school in Manchuria. In his memoirs, Kim says he read *The Communist Manifesto* at this time; historians doubt it.

Kim, seated, in Chinese dress, in Manchuria circa 1926. This photo was taken before he was expelled from middle school for anti-Japanese activities.

No Kum Sok, age five, riding his tricycle. No's father, who worked for a large Japanese company, had shopping privileges at a company store.

No, age seven, with his father on the first day of elementary school in April 1939. No's father died of cancer in 1949, when his son was seventeen.

No's mother wearing furs in a studio photograph taken in the early 1940s. After the Soviets entered Korea in 1945, his parents struggled financially, selling many of their possessions.

Kim Il Sung in Manchuria in the late 1930s, around the time he became an effective anti-Japanese guerrilla leader and a legend to many Koreans.

Kim in a propaganda painting depicting his guerrilla forces in snowy Manchuria. By 1941, his fighters had been crushed by the Japanese, and he fled to the Soviet Far East.

Kim with his first wife, Kim Jong Suk, in an undated photo. She was a guerrilla who fought the Japanese in Manchuria in the early 1940s and followed him to the Soviet Union, where they married.

Kim Il Sung with his wife and infant son, Kim Jong Il, who was born on a Soviet Army base in 1942. Kim Jong Il succeeded his father in 1994 as the leader of North Korea.

South Korea's first president, Syngman Rhee, greets General Douglas MacArthur near Seoul in August 1948, shortly after Rhee was elected to lead the U.S.-sponsored government.

MacArthur devised the amphibious invasion at Inchon, which devastated Kim Il Sung's army in September 1950. But MacArthur's misjudgments and insubordination led President Harry Truman to fire him the next year. This photo was taken in 1944 after U.S. forces liberated the Philippines.

Senior Lieutenant No Kum Sok, age twenty-one, after landing a North Korean MiG-15 at Kimpo Air Force Base in South Korea on September 21, 1953.

No in his flight suit on the day he landed in South Korea. Hours after he climbed out of his MiG, U.S. Air Force photographers asked him to pose in the suit and oxygen mask.

The Weather

Today—Cloudy with occasional rain, with high at 78. Tuesday—Partly cloudy and cooler. Yesterday—High, 80 at 2 p. m.; low, 84 at 4:40 a. m. Ragweed count—28. (Details on Page 16.)

The Washington Post

SEP 25 1953 *Bankers Convene*

For complete coverage of the American Bankers Association meeting this week. The Post is turning lanes several reporters and making big plans. It's The Post for economic news.

Seventy-Five Years in the Nation's Capital

NO. . . 28,221   Phone NA. 8-4200   MONDAY, SEPTEMBER 21, 1953   WTOP-AM (1500) FM (96.3) TV (CH. 9)   FIVE CENTS

Red MIG-15 Brought to Seoul

Intelligence Officers of AF Question Pilot of Jet

Offer of $100,000 Made Before Truce By Gen. Clark for Soviet-Built Craft

SEOUL (Monday). Sept. 21 (AP).—The Fifth Air Force announced that a "Communist MIG-15 jet" landed at Kimpo Airfield near Seoul at 9:24 a. m. today.

An Air Force spokesman said "the pilot is now under interrogation by Air Force intelligence officers."

The spokesman said Lieut. Gen. F. E. Anderson, Fifth Air Force commanding general, "is on his way," to see the pilot.

Before the armistice, Gen.

Mark Clark, supreme Allied commander, had offered $100,000 to any Communist pilot who would fly a Russian-built MIG-15 jet to an Allied airfield in South Korea.

Elaborate arrangements were set up to assure a safe flight when the Allies controlled the skies over Korea, but the MIG pilots stayed north.

[The pilot of the MIG was identified as a Communist by the Fifth Air Force, the United Press reported. Of the $100,000 offer by Clark, the United Press quoted a Far East Command spokesman as saying it had never been withdrawn.]

© 2014, *The Washington Post.* Reprinted with permission.

San Francisco Chronicle

THE VOICE OF THE WEST

FINAL

VOL. CLXXVIII, NO. 68 CCCCAAA—   SAN FRANCISCO, MONDAY, SEPTEMBER 21, 1953   GA 1-1112 DAILY 10c, SUNDAY 20c

MYSTERY RED MIG LANDS NEAR SEOUL

Security Lid Clamped On

Pilot Roars Into U. S. Jet Base---Air Force Says He's Not a North Korean

$100,000 Once Offered For Plane

By the Associated Press

SEOUL, Sept. 21—A Russian-built MIG-15 roared out of the Communist North today (Monday and landed at a U. S. jet base 15 miles northwest of Seoul.

American airmen clustered around the pilot as he stepped down from the MIG but he was rushed into headquarters for questioning.

A Fifth Air Force officer said the pilot's nationality could not be disclosed "at this time" but "he is not a North Korean."

The spokesman said the pilot "will not be interviewed or identified for fear of retaliation."

A tight security guard was clamped around the base. Special officers watched all entrances. Everyone entering or leaving was checked. No visitors were permitted.

U. S. AIR CHIEF

Lieutenant General Samuel Anderson. Fifth Air Force commander, rushed to the airfield at Kimpo, home base for American Sabrejets which tangled with the MIGs throughout the air war in North Korea.

"The pilot is now under interrogation by Air Force intelligence oficers." the spokesman said.

His plane was placed in a hangar by itself. A cordon of

U. S. air police armed with .45 caliber pistols guarded it.

During the last days of the Korean war. General Mark Clark offered $100,000 to the first Communist pilot to land a MIG in Allied territory in Korea. The offer was beamed to North Korea and Manchuria by radio for days but there were no takers.

POLISH DEFECTIONS

However, two Polish flyers landed MIGs last spring on the Danish island of Bornholn in the Baltic sea. The two, Lieutenant Franciszek Jarecki and Lieutenant Zdislaw Jazwenski, were granted political asylum in the United States.

A convoy of Allied reporters and cameramen was stopped at the gate of Kimpo Airfield and held there until the base commander, Colonel J. R. McDoug-

Continued on Page 5, Col. 2

No's theft of a Soviet-built fighter jet, long coveted by the U.S. government, and his arrival at a U.S. air base in South Korea triggered banner headlines around the world.

Fearing a Communist air attack that might destroy the stolen MiG-15 before it could be examined, the U.S. Air Force quickly hid it in a hangar and disassembled it for shipment out of South Korea.

F-86 Sabre fighter jets, photographed in November 1952 at Kimpo Air Force Base, were the only American warplanes that could challenge MiGs in dogfights during the Korean War.

Chuck Yeager, shown here in 1947, was the first pilot to fly faster than the speed of sound. He was sent to Okinawa to fly the stolen MiG.

No's MiG was transported to Okinawa, where it was repainted and secretly tested in the fall of 1953 by Yeager and other top American test pilots.

On Okinawa, where No was interrogated for six months in 1953–54, he became friends with Shigeo Morisato, a U.S. Air Force intelligence officer and English teacher.

To convince the press that it had paid a promised reward for the stolen MiG, the U.S. Air Force staged this photo of No depositing $100,000 in a bank. The check was a fake; the money was later put into a trust fund for him.

No chatted with Vice President Richard Nixon in his office on Capitol Hill in May 1954. Nixon wished No good fortune in running for political office.

No in June 1954 at the University of Delaware, where he studied engineering. Known on campus as Kenny No, he was admitted to the university with the assistance of the Central Intelligence Agency.

In 1954, No worked for several months for the Voice of America, speaking out against Communism and describing his new life in the United States.

No worked hard to find a way to bring his mother to the United States. She arrived in Washington, D.C., in November 1957 and lived near her son until her death in 2004.

After No became an aeronautical engineer named Kenneth H. Rowe, he married Clara in 1960 in New York City. His mother played matchmaker, selecting Clara, an immigrant from South Korea who worked in the Empire State Building.

Rowe and his family in December 1986 in Daytona Beach, Florida. From left, Edmund, Bonnie, Kenneth, Clara, and Raymond.

Kim Il Sung ruled as dictator until his peaceful death in 1994 at age eighty-two. In this undated propaganda photo, he poses on Mount Paektu, the highest peak in Korea and the sacred mountain of his revolution.

Kim Jong Un, grandson of the Great Leader, tours an air force unit in March 2014. Kim Jong Un became the third dictator in the Kim dynasty in December 2011, after the death of his father, Kim Jong Il.

Rowe on the beach near his home in South Daytona, Florida, in April 2014. In his early eighties, he often attends conferences with American fighter pilots and does sixty pushups a day.

In the fall of 1952, twelve of Pak's supporters plotted in the living room of his house, although Pak was not home at the time. Pak's most loyal friend, Yi Sung Yop, a former mayor of Seoul and minister of justice in Kim Il Sung's cabinet, was in charge. Yi had trained guerrillas in South Korea and helped establish a military training school in the North. The Kumgang Political Institute taught party cadres how to organize and lead underground fighters. Nearly all its instructors, the staff, and even the kitchen help had grown up in the South and were loyal to Pak. The plot to overthrow Kim leaned heavily on the skills of officers from the institute, and by November 1952 Yi had begun putting together a unit of four thousand men, or at least that is what he was later accused of.

The meeting in Pak's living room was a final stage in coup planning. Its leaders even named ministers in the government that they envisioned would take power after Kim was ousted and, presumably, killed.

III

At air bases in Manchuria, No Kum Sok discerned a consistent pattern of behavior among North Korean air force officers who rose to senior positions of power and trust.

They were fanatics, shouting Kim Il Sung's praises and denouncing one another for insufficient loathing of the enemy. They joined the ruling Workers' Party of North Korea and at party meetings turned fanaticism into performance art, the noisier the better.

Having witnessed all this, No imitated it.

He joined the party in 1952, at age twenty, with help and recommendations from two former cadets from the naval academy. One of them was Kun Soo Sung, No's best friend and collaborator on the *Battle Gazette*, their flight school newspaper. In an autobiographical essay that accompanied his party application, No again lied about his father, saying he had been a loyal party member who admired the Great Leader. No assumed, apparently correctly, that records about his father had been destroyed by American bombs.

The more No thought about defecting, the more fanatical he tried to appear. It was a way of self-medicating for his growing anxiety. When three thousand airmen and officers were assembled for a division meeting at Dandong airfield, No stood up and ranted against American imperialism. It seemed to impress political officers. They picked him to be a designated reader of statements released in the name of Kim and Stalin. While reading the words of the great Communists at public gatherings, No spoke loudly, gestured broadly, and tried to look as if he were deeply moved. This also impressed political officers. In July 1952, he was named vice-chairman of his battalion's cell of the Workers' Party. A month later, he was promoted to senior lieutenant and became a flight leader for four MiGs flying out of Dandong. He won two medals—the Red Flag Medal, which many combat pilots received, and the Gold Medal, an award similar to the Distinguished Flying Medal, for having flown fifty combat missions.

After joining the party, No perfected the art of public denunciation—and used it to protect himself from superiors he suspected might one day question his sincerity. Public denunciations were an aggressive North Korean variant of Stalinist criticism and self-criticism. Stalin preached that criticism was a core Communist principle that allowed the party to correct its excesses and fine-tune its service to the masses. Stalin also said that criticism could go uphill: the masses could criticize party bosses (not including him). But in practice, criticism and self-criticism were invaluable tools for extracting and compiling incriminating information about party members, which was later used as leverage for control, extortion, purges, and executions.

For North Korean pilots in Manchuria, the nagging fear of being shot down by American Sabres was compounded by on-the-ground paranoia about each other. Like his fellow pilots, No worried about every word he said, even as he spied on his colleagues, looking for embarrassing missteps to denounce. The finger-pointing turned his stomach, but as vice-chairman of the party cell in his battalion he was obligated to do it energetically and with venom.

The selfishness and blunders of senior officers became his focus. He criticized his battalion's chief of staff, Colonel Chae Kil Yon, a non-pilot, for having a stove in his room while many pilots shivered without heat. He humiliated a prominent party member, Major Lee Choon Tuk, who got lost while flying in bad weather and crashed his MiG.

"Comrade Lee outwardly appears to be a good Communist," No said in a party meeting. "But this farce shows that he is a lazy man who does not care about his expensive equipment. Perhaps he does not hate the enemy enough or doesn't love our glorious leader, Kim Il Sung?"

By the end of 1952, No was disgusted with himself. He was not sleeping well and had become exhausted. He had been in the air force for more than two years without a day off. He worked from 5:00 a.m. to bedtime seven days a week. Unlike Russian pilots, who napped or partied in their barracks between flights, No was always burdened with party work. As vice-chairman, he had to represent his battalion at divisional party meetings. He organized pilots who spied and reported on each other. Every few months, he was allowed a quick trip into Dandong city, but rules prevented him from having a drink in a bar or chatting with a woman. Pilots had been warned that all women who spoke Korean were South Korean agents.

IV

Stalin died on March 5, 1953, and the Soviet Union's interest in prolonging the Korean War died with him.

China, too, wanted out. In Moscow for Stalin's funeral, Zhou Enlai "urgently proposed that the Soviet side assist the speeding up" of armistice talks. The Soviets sent a special emissary to Pyongyang, where Kim "showed a clear aspiration for the most rapid cessation of military activity," according to a Soviet Foreign Ministry memo.

Two weeks after Stalin's death, the Soviet Union announced to the world that it had agreed with China and North Korea to seek "the soonest possible conclusion of the war in Korea." A week later, the United States realized they were serious. The Communists accepted a previously ignored American request to exchange ailing prisoners of war—and then proposed a resumption of armistice talks that had been frozen for half a year. In Washington, the new American president, Dwight Eisenhower, was also willing to deal.

It was not just Stalin who died in the Soviet Union. It was Stalinism. And the Kremlin's next generation of leaders was happy to be rid of both. In Moscow, Stalin's "Hate America Campaign" abruptly ended. Anti-American placards were removed from the streets. Radio Moscow conceded for the first time that the United States helped defeat Hitler. A meeting was proposed between the new Soviet premier, Georgi Malenkov, and Eisenhower to discuss the control of atomic weapons. The change in Moscow's foreign policy was sudden, sharp, and sustained.

In three years' time, Khrushchev would astonish the world by denouncing Stalin as a vain and brutal despot. At a party congress, he said Stalin had murdered his political rivals and perpetuated his power by using fear, terror, and a phony cult of personality.

For Kim Il Sung, Stalin's death was a mixed blessing. The ghastly destruction of North Korea could finally end. An armistice would allow Kim to climb out of his bunker. Rebuilding could begin. No longer would Kim have to play the poodle to a distant and devious bully.

Kim, though, could not stay in power without Stalinism. It suited the gangster instincts he had honed as a young man fighting the Japanese in Manchuria. It gave him the tools he would need to survive postwar power struggles. When the fighting stopped, Kim knew, his rivals would be bolder, and the North Korean people would want to know why he had failed to unite Korea. Like Stalin, Kim needed a cult of personality to whitewash reality. Like Stalin, he needed to dispose of wrong thinkers.

With Stalin dead and Stalinism fading fast in the Soviet Union, Kim faced an existential threat. He hinted at the seriousness of the threat in the eulogy he published on the front page of the party newspaper five days after Stalin died. "The ardent heart of the great leader of progressive mankind has ceased to beat," he lamented. "The very being of Korea has seemed to bow down."

Stalin's death did not immediately end the war. An armistice would not be signed until July 27, 1953. In the intervening months, ground fighting continued, much of it pointless and bloody. A famous example was Pork Chop Hill, an exposed American outpost on the outer edge of UN territory. The hill had no strategic value. But Americans possessed it, and the Chinese wanted it. They attacked in late March and were driven back while taking control of a nearby hill called Old Baldy. They attacked again in April with about twenty-three hundred men, gaining control of the hill and then losing it as the Americans showered them with one of the most intense artillery barrages in history. To clear trenches, the Americans killed Chinese with hand grenades, flame-throwers, and hand-to-hand fighting. In early July, the Chinese tried again, with heavy casualties on both sides. After five days of fighting, Lieutenant General Maxwell Taylor decided Pork Chop Hill was not worth it. American soldiers quietly walked away.

The U.S. Air Force, meanwhile, kept looking for new targets to blow up. In the month Stalin died, bomb planners located twenty dams around Pyongyang that controlled irrigation water for about half a million acres of rice. Because enemy soldiers ate rice, the fields that grew it could be classified as "war materiel." Bombing the dams after the May planting season could wipe out an entire year's crop and destroy a quarter-million tons of rice.

"Attacks on the irrigation dams, it was believed, would produce useful psychological reactions, since farmers would tend to blame the war, and thus the Communists, for exposing their crops to attack and destruction," said an air force staff study written in 1953.

The Toksan Dam, about twenty miles north of Pyongyang, was hit first. Fifty-nine fighter-bombers attacked on May 13, dropping one-thousand-pound bombs that caused the earth-and-stone dam to collapse. A flash flood ripped across twenty-seven miles of river valley and spilled into the bombed-out streets of Pyongyang. Floodwaters knocked down five railroad bridges, destroyed seven hundred buildings, and inundated an airport. They also scoured out five square miles of prime rice crop. "The damage done by the deluge far exceeded the hopes of everyone," reported the Fifth Air Force.

Two days later, another dam north of Pyongyang was blown up, creating another flood that wrecked "field after field of young rice."

Air force generals worried that destroying food would trigger adverse press coverage.

But the American press did not care. It ignored the attacks and then ignored North Korean government protests against "barbarous raids" on the civilian food supply. Instead, American reporters focused on the American fighter aces who in the final months of the war were shooting down MiGs in record numbers with almost no losses. Each MiG that the Americans shot down received more coverage than the flood-generating bombing raids.

Fifteen days after Stalin died, the American government dreamed up another plan to pressure and annoy the Communists.

They called it Operation Moolah. It was a bribe that offered $100,000 (worth about $900,000 today) to the first Russian, Chinese, or North Korean pilot to defect in a "modern, operational, combat-type jet in flyable condition," which meant a late-model MiG.

To advertise the bribe, the Far East Command sent two B-29s on an April night flight over the Yalu River. They dropped more than a million leaflets, explaining the offer in Russian, Mandarin, Cantonese, and Korean. Fourteen radio stations in Japan and South Korea broadcast the offer into North Korea and China for a week. For good measure, in May the air force dropped another half million leaflets. The leaflets invited "all brave pilots who wish to free themselves from the vicious whip" of Communism to "proceed to Kimpo Air Base at 6,100 meters altitude and circle with his [landing] gear down." After landing, the leaflet said, every pilot would be offered "a new and better life with proper honor in the free world."

The origin of Operation Moolah is murky. General Mark W. Clark, commander of U.S. forces in the Far East in the last year of the Korean War, writes in his memoir that a war correspondent came up with the idea while "communing with a bottle of brandy" and then wrote it into a fictionalized interview with an air force general. That piece of fiction found its way to air force headquarters in Tokyo, Clark said, where it was judged to have "merit" and then sent on to Washington for approval.

The war correspondent Edward Hymoff, bureau chief in Korea for the International News Service, told a less romantic but more probable story. He said that on a flight to Tokyo in the fall of 1952 he had a long conversation with General Clark and mentioned his concept of offering a defecting MiG pilot a large cash reward and political asylum in the United States. "He wouldn't have any worries the rest of his life, plus, he would be a rich man, tax free," Hymoff said he told the general.

Credit for the idea has also been claimed by an air force psychological warfare unit in Washington. Its chief, Captain Alan K. Abner, said his staff had seen intelligence reports suggesting that younger Russian pilots in Manchuria "felt they were not respected" and were good candidates for defection "if properly motivated." The plan was to circulate news of a $10,000 reward for a MiG through enemy lines by word of mouth, which would give the American government "a certain advantage of deniability." Abner says he sent the plan to the Pentagon on a Monday in the fall of 1952 and was "shocked" to see that it had been changed, hyped up, and leaked to the *Washington Post* the following Saturday, under the headline "General Mark Clark Offers $100,000 for Russian Jet." Abner and his psychological operations staff felt "disillusionment with the way [their] proposal had been distorted."

The reward was made public the day after armistice talks resumed in April 1953. Clark said the timing was intended to vex the enemy and sow suspicion among enemy commanders, which it might have done.

A month after the first leaflet drop, Kim Il Sung delivered an unusual radio message. He told North Korean pilots to "strengthen their discipline and protect their equipment." Clark claimed in his memoir that Russian-language broadcasts of the offer were electronically jammed. He also claimed that after Operation Moolah was made public, only "the worst" Communist pilots were allowed to fly.

"These pilots flew far fewer missions in the last ninety days of the war than in the preceding three months, but American Sabre pilots shot down twice as many," Clark wrote. "Sabres destroyed 165 MiGs against three friendly combat losses—a record ratio of 55 to one."

The last three months of the war were indeed a one-sided American slaughter. Sabre pilots who were veterans of World War II compared the easy pickings to the "Marianas Turkey Shoot," when Japanese pilots were shot down in extraordinary numbers. But it is unlikely that Operation Moolah had much—if anything—to do with it. An air force analysis found "no positive information" that the cash-for-MiG offer caused "any variation in Communist air activity."

As the war wound down, there were no Communist takers for America's money. As General Clark writes, "After the armistice was signed we forgot all about the offer."

No Kum Sok did not read or hear about Operation Moolah. Its leaflets and radio broadcasts never reached him in Manchuria. Commanders in the North Korean and Soviet air forces never mentioned it. Nothing was said about it in the rumor mill on the flight line or during gossipy dinners with Russian pilots. What General Clark described as "our most spectacular psychological warfare exploit" meant absolutely nothing in No's world—or so it seemed.

CHAPTER 10

Uncle Yoo

I

After Stalin died, Uncle Yoo paid a surprise visit to his nephew's air base in Manchuria.

He was now Major Yoo, leader of a supply regiment in the North Korean air force. He had had a relatively good war. He was healthy, as was his wife, as were three of his four children. (American bombing killed his fourth child.) He stayed in his hometown of Hungnam when the war started, working as a supervisor in a factory there until the city was overrun in late 1950 by UN forces. Unlike many North Koreans whose political loyalties swung back and forth with invading and withdrawing armies, Yoo remained true to his Great Leader, joining guerrillas fighting against the Americans and the South Koreans. When the Chinese pushed UN forces south in early 1951, Yoo joined the air force and began rising as an officer.

He visited his nephew at Dongfeng airfield, a base about fifty miles north of the Korean border. In the months before No Kum Sok's uncle showed up, his morale had hit rock bottom. He had been passed over for promotion to battalion commander. The officer who got the job, No believed, was a poor pilot and an inferior orator at party meetings. No's pride was hurt, and the urgency of his desire to defect had grown.

All the while, the risks of dying in a MiG were rising. Sabres were everywhere, and No's commanders were increasingly inept. On March 21, 1953, they encouraged him and fifteen other MiG pilots to fly head-on into a trap. At thirty-three thousand feet over the Yalu, a clear blue sky was streaked with chalky vapor trails from a swarm of fighter jets flying at higher altitude. No's regimental commander radioed for help. Were they friend or foe? he asked.

"Don't worry about them," replied ground control, adding that they were either Russian or Chinese MiGs. "Keep climbing."

The fighters were Sabres, and No's unit flew up into an ambush. One of No's friends, Lieutenant Kim Lee Joo, was hit and lost control of his MiG. He shouted over the radio that his ejection seat had failed. No watched him free himself from the cockpit. His parachute failed to open.

As North Korean losses increased, as American pilots became more aggressive in picking off MiGs in Manchuria, North Korean air force commanders began telling increasingly ludicrous untruths about success in the air war. After a day in which Sabres shot down several MiGs, No heard General Wang Yong, the air force commander, announce with joyous enthusiasm that another five or six Sabres had been destroyed. No's regimental commander, Colonel Tae Kuk Sung, claimed to have shot down two Sabres in one dogfight, which brought his claimed total of American kills to five and made him an ace. For his achievements, Tae was personally congratulated by Kim Il Sung and given a hero's medal in Pyongyang. Five red stars were painted on his MiG. No believed Tae was a liar. He had flown with the colonel on the day he supposedly became an ace, and no Sabres were shot down.

The visit with Uncle Yoo was brief, lasting no more than a few minutes. But for a despondent young pilot who had not heard anything about his family for years, the conversation was emotionally crushing—and confusing. No's mother was dead, Yoo said, killed in an American bombing. Yet he was vague about the details. No suspected Yoo was lying and wondered why he would do that about something so painful.

No would never see Uncle Yoo again. But before the summer of 1953 was over, he would learn that his uncle had indeed lied to him.

A week before the war ended, No Kum Sok joined hundreds of North Korean pilots and mechanics at Dandong airfield to listen to a speech that explained the terms of the armistice that would go into effect at midnight on July 27, 1953.

Once the truce began, it would be illegal to bring weapons or soldiers back into North Korea, said General Kim Han Jun, the top political commander of the North Korean air force. So everything—the entire air force and all its aircraft—had to be moved across the border before then. The general said it would be sent to Uiju, the airfield where No was nearly killed by Sabre strafing in the fall of 1951. The Chinese were again repairing the runway there and making it ready for returning MiGs.

No waited respectfully until General Kim had finished speaking, then asked a question: "What about night raids before the truce goes into effect? Won't they destroy our MiGs on the ground?"

The general said they would probably try but that the "Soviet Union can always supply us with more MiGs."

The general also made it clear to No and the other airmen that North Korea intended to cheat on the terms of the armistice in every possible way. "The border between China and Korea is long and the Neutral Commission cannot be everywhere," the general said, referring to the Neutral Nations Supervisory Commission, which had been created during truce talks and had ten mobile teams from Sweden, Switzerland, Czechoslovakia, and Poland patrolling the borders.

For the next four days, No and five other pilots shuttled two dozen MiGs from Dandong to Uiju, returning each time on a truck. As soon as a MiG landed, it was pushed south into nearby hills and covered with camouflage. Soon, though, the Americans spotted the transfers. In what one U.S. Air Force general described as a final "blaze of glory," waves of bombers dropped five-hundred-pound bombs on Uiju and six other North Korean airfields.

With the truce fast approaching and North Korea's strategy switching from fighting the war to cheating the peace, No began to believe his dogfighting days were done. He had survived more than a hundred combat missions during which he encountered American fighters. He did not want to press his luck. In the final days of a war he despised, he feared being the last pilot to die.

Yet on July 24, three days before the truce, he and fifteen other pilots were ordered to climb into the cockpits of MiGs parked at the Dandong runway and start their engines. Scanning the sky before takeoff, No saw six Sabres at low altitude above the airfield. He had never felt more vulnerable.

The MiGs took off two by two, with No flying as wingman to Captain Kim Jung Sup, his battalion's vice-commander. As wingman, No's responsibility was to stick with Captain Kim throughout the mission and guard his back. Seconds after takeoff, Captain Kim announced a problem.

"My landing gear is not retracting," he shouted over the radio to ground control. "What shall I do?"

Before ground control could answer, No jumped at the chance to save his skin—and Captain Kim's.

"If your landing gear is not retracting," No said over the radio, "get down and land at once!"

Captain Kim returned to base and landed safely, with No, his relieved wingman, following him down. They taxied off the runway as the other fourteen MiGs climbed up into the jaws of a Sabre attack.

As No turned his MiG over to mechanics, he saw two fighters—a Sabre chasing a MiG—hurtling toward the airfield. When the American opened fire, No saw tracers tear open the fuselage of the MiG. Its pilot was Lieutenant Su Chul Ha, who had been No's teenage classmate at Hungnam Chemical College and had traveled by train with him to enroll at the naval academy, then to Manchuria for flight training.

The badly damaged MiG flew too low for Su to eject. He tried to crash-land on the runway but overshot it. As the Sabre pulled up and away, the MiG exploded in a ball of orange flames. No felt the heat on his face. Su Chul Ha was the last MiG pilot killed in the Korean War.

With two days left in the war and the Americans still bombing airfields, the North Korean air force decided it would be wiser to dismantle its MiGs, put them in crates, and transport them across the Yalu in barges. Then they could be reassembled in North Korea after the truce forced the Americans to stop dropping bombs. As the armistice began on the night of July 27, No crossed the river in a barge carrying five crated MiGs. It docked about nine hours after the truce deadline. MiGs in crates would continue to arrive in North Korea—in violation of the truce—for several months.

After the armistice, there was no housing for pilots near Uiju's bomb-shattered airport, so the air force found barracks for them in nearby Uiju town, which had been spared from American carpet bombing. A couple of days after No arrived, he discovered he had family in the town. Out walking on a dirt road, he encountered his aunt, Ko Kye Sook, his mother's sister and the wife of his Uncle Yoo.

No had wanted to avoid her and her entire family, but having seen her in the road, he had no choice except to say hello and act polite. After his uncle's disturbing visit to his air base in Manchuria in the spring, he had received a letter from his fourteen-year-old cousin, Yoo San Yeol, the eldest son of his aunt and uncle. The letter said—just as Uncle Yoo had said back in March—that No's mother was dead, killed in the war. It did not explain how or when; No believed his uncle was behind the letter.

Aunt Ko seemed delighted—and overwhelmed—to see her nephew. She cried about the many North Korean airplanes that had come crashing down in flames during the war and how she had worried that No had been burned to death in one of them. With the war ended, she told him, he should find a nice girl to marry and have some children. She offered to help him find a wife and invited him to her house for supper.

No felt ill—and trapped. But he did not want to be rude, so he accepted her invitation. After returning to his barracks to fetch chocolate bars for her three sons, he walked over to the house the government had given his aunt and uncle. Uncle Yoo was away, apparently on air force business.

As soon as No arrived, his aunt began cooking—and talking. Her eldest son, the one who had written the letter, said nothing. The two younger cousins were also silent.

The war—and her fanatical husband—had transformed Aunt Ko

into an emotionally committed Communist. At considerable length, she criticized the members of No's extended family who were not Reds. No interrupted her to ask how his mother had died.

"Your mother is not dead," she replied. "She went to South Korea."

Before No could reply, his aunt criticized his mother for abandoning Kim Il Sung.

"Why would she want to go to South Korea?" his aunt asked.

No was not completely surprised to learn that his mother was alive, because he had suspected his uncle and cousin lied to him.

"How did she reach the South?" he asked.

"Don't ask me that kind of question," his aunt said. "Just believe me. She is there."

No asked why Uncle Yoo had lied.

"He did not want you to worry about your mother," she said.

Disgusted and depressed, No returned to his barracks, where he was in for an even greater shock.

"Since you have visited your aunt, you now know the whereabouts of your mother," said Lee Kun Il, a chief weaponry pilot and a comrade of No's since their days at the naval academy.

No's world was spinning out of control. Somehow, this pilot knew where No's mother had gone. No suspected that Uncle Yoo, perhaps while visiting the air base in Manchuria, had spread word that No's mother was a traitor living in South Korea. If so, in a country that enforced collective guilt, No was now at risk.

"My mother is dead," No said coldly.

More than ever, he hated the police state that surrounded him. He needed to escape and find his mother.

As No later learned, she had found her way to South Korea thanks to a North Korean army truck and a U.S. Navy boat lift. Shortly before the outbreak of war, as she was walking on a road near her home in Hungnam, the truck hit her and badly injured her leg. The driver stopped and took her to a hospital in Hungnam, where she remained a patient as UN troops stormed north in the fall of 1950 and occupied the port city.

By December of that year, Chinese troops were forcing their way into the city. American and South Korean soldiers were ordered to flee by ship. Before leaving, as the U.S. Army X Corps blew up the city's infrastructure, the U.S. Navy organized a "Christmas Evacuation" of ninety-one thousand North Korean refugees.

A hundred thousand would-be refugees were left behind on the docks. But on crutches and with the help of friends, No's mother squeezed aboard the last navy ship to leave Hungnam.

II

When Kim Il Sung's war was finally over and his country lay in ruins, he turned catastrophe at home into leverage over fraternal Communist countries. He expertly milked the Soviet Union, China, and the Communist Eastern bloc for aid that would rebuild North Korea and secure his dictatorship for generations to come. In the process, he demonstrated, yet again, a genius for gathering strength from failure.

Kim never paid a price for the prewar judgments and wartime strategies that beggared and killed his people. His phoenixlike rebirth after the war was nothing short of astounding. But it would not have been possible without the unwitting assistance of the United States and the unbridled passion of air force generals for dropping bombs and napalm on civilian targets. Three years of American saturation bombing generated revulsion and outrage in socialist countries. By burning down cities, blowing up irrigation dams, and laying waste to the capacity of North Koreans to feed, clothe, and shelter themselves, the United States made Kim and his government seem pitiable and deserving—at least as seen from Moscow, Beijing, and other Communist capitals.

The Great Leader exploited this sympathy for all it was worth, demanding that the Soviet Union, China, and Eastern Europe pay to reconstruct what the Americans had razed. It helped immensely that Stalin—the principal prolonger of the war and of North Korea's suffering—had died. It also helped that new leaders in Moscow were rushing to undo Stalin's excesses.

Kim shrewdly played to the post-Stalinist zeitgeist.

"[He] believed his allies owed him whatever was required to rebuild his country, since much of the destruction had resulted from their insistence on continuing the war for the benefit of the entire socialist camp," according to the historian Kathryn Weathersby. "The Korean War left Moscow, Beijing, and the other fraternal states with a badly damaged, resentful ally they were compelled to support."

Kim's demands produced a singularly generous moment in the history of global Communism. North Korea vacuumed up more short- and long-term aid from socialist countries than any country before or since. In what became known as the "North Korean miracle," economic growth expanded rapidly for more than a decade and remained ahead of South Korea's until the early 1970s. Much less publicized was Kim's decision in the late 1950s to build a gulag of political prison camps to eliminate his perceived enemies and scare potential malcontents into silence.

The reconstruction "miracle" would have been impossible without buckets of other people's money: several decades of fraternal aid, credits, expertise, and hardware, most of which was never repaid.

For the size of its economy, China was inordinately generous. Thirty-four divisions of the Chinese army stayed on in North Korea for five years after the war ended, providing free labor for reconstruction projects. China's no-strings aid to the North in 1954 amounted to more than 3 percent of its annual budget—and was a third more than the combined aid that year from the Soviet Union and Eastern Europe. A few months after the war ended, Mao, who viewed Kim as an egotist and a second-rater, explained at a Beijing banquet in Kim's honor why the North deserved so much help: "The Korean people are brave. They can handle suffering. [They are] courageous, disciplined, not afraid of hardship. They have paid a heavy price in both manpower and material, but the result of their struggle has greatly aided us . . . Had the enemy not been beaten back away from the Yalu River, China's development would not be secure."

As important as China was in rebuilding North Korea, Kim focused his postwar importuning on Moscow.

Only four days after the armistice, he outlined with impressive specificity the Soviet Union's responsibility: sixty-two specialists must come at once to North Korea, he told the Soviet embassy. Within six months, he said, they must draw up plans to rebuild nearly all the industrial plants that the Americans had destroyed. The Soviet chargé d'affaires in Pyongyang, in passing along Kim's demands, noted that the "fundamental calculations are based not on the maximal use of domestic resources but on receipt of maximum aid from the Soviet Union and the people's democracies."

To maximize aid before socialist guilt petered out, Kim organized and led a six-member delegation that rushed to Moscow in mid-September, less than two months after the war ended. It proved to be a singularly lucrative nineteen-day trip, securing funds for reconstructing old factories and building new ones. He made contacts that would allow his government to tap into a steady stream of concessional trade, technology transfer, and military equipment over several decades. Kim also negotiated delays in repayments of loans.

There was, however, a hiccup in the Great Leader's harvest, one that embarrassed him and his Soviet patrons. While Kim was in Moscow, a late-model MiG-15 disappeared without explanation from North Korean airspace.

In the cockpit was the youngest pilot in the North Korean air force.

PART III

FLIGHT

CHAPTER 11

Flying Clear

I

"I'm going to defect."

No spoke these words quietly—and in deadly earnest—to his best friend and fellow MiG pilot, Lieutenant Kun Soo Sung.

No had been close to Kun since their first year together at the naval academy. They rode the same train to Manchuria to learn how to fly. They were both pretend Communists who during flight training had written and illustrated the *Battle Gazette,* the newspaper that flattered their commanders. Kun was a sponsor and key supporter when No joined the Workers' Party. They survived nearly two years of dogfights over MiG Alley. Although they did not serve in the same unit, their commanders and fellow pilots viewed them as the closest of friends. If No defected, everyone would point a finger at Kun.

It was a warm, sun-washed afternoon in early September, five weeks after the end of the war. They were out for a walk together in the countryside, well away from the bomb-cratered airfield at Kusong, a small town where they had been transferred.

No had quietly teased his friend for years, telling him that someday he would fly away to South Korea. They understood it as a secret boast between young pilots who trusted each other—a rarity in the North Korean military.

This time, though, Kun knew that No was not teasing, and he was frightened. North Korea enforced collective punishment for family and friends of wrongdoers. Nothing could be more wrong—more infuriating to the Great Leader and his enforcers—than stealing a MiG.

"Don't go," Kun warned. "If you go, I am in trouble."

Now No felt scared. He should have kept his mouth shut. What if Kun reported him?

As they walked together, No tried to switch gears, to make it seem as if he had been kidding. Breezily, he asked Kun to steal a MiG and escape with him. Just as casually, Kun said he would. They were clearly kidding each other now, and Kun sounded relieved. They knew they could never pull it off. They were assigned to different air force units, No to the Sixtieth Aviation Regiment, Kun to the Fifty-ninth. Coordinating a simultaneous escape in MiGs during peacetime was fantasy.

The conversation wandered. Kun was obsessed with sex and his lack thereof. He asked No to walk with him to some nearby farmhouses. They could knock on doors, he said, and find girls eager to satisfy the heroic needs of fighter pilots. No let his friend go on alone.

Back at the airfield, No convinced himself that Kun would not betray him; he was too good a friend. But No also realized that an awful price would be paid for what he was determined to do. Kun would be executed, perhaps along with many others. Still, there was no other way. It was not possible to run from North Korea with a clear conscience, not even for a young pilot with a dead father, no siblings, and a mother who was already safely out of the country.

No put the consequences out of his mind. He had to think of himself. He was so set on escaping by this point that he had begun to dream about it nearly every night. In most of the dreams, he made it successfully to South Korea. In one he saw his mother. In another, he stood on a sidewalk in New York City gazing up at the Empire State Building, the top of which was enveloped in clouds.

Though the war was over, the government was as paranoid as ever about its perceived enemies, and much of its paranoia was directed at veterans who had fought in the war on the North Korean side. In Kusong, while out walking with an air force security officer, No came across an old factory building packed with newly returned North Korean prisoners of war. They were filthy, emaciated, and sitting dejectedly on the floor. The security officer told No that there were South Korean spies among the returning POWs and the government could not be too careful. All of the former prisoners, he said, would be reeducated to cleanse their minds of what they had seen and learned in the South. Spies would be found and punished. Careful to show his devotion, No congratulated the security officer for his perceptiveness and agreed spies must be everywhere.

II

Kim Il Sung needed to put on a show. He needed to find, expose, and destroy a "wicked spy clique" working inside North Korea that would serve as a sensational and sustained distraction from his failed war. He also needed to excite a war-weary public by revealing new threats from a devious external enemy—the United States.

The plot to overthrow him—the one supposedly finalized in the fall of 1952 in the living room of North Korea's foreign minister, Pak Hon Yong—suited his needs.

Kim knew early on about the plot being hatched by the so-called domestic faction within his government. Whether there was ever any real armed threat to his government has not been well documented, although it is clear that Pak Hon Yong and his supporters were genuinely sick of Kim's leadership, and Kim feared they might be able to get rid of him. At a party plenum in December 1952, Kim delivered a long rant against the intrigues being cooked up by "factional elements."

His speech set in motion a trial for treason that began a week after the Korean War ended and lasted four memorable days. It would become an international media extravaganza. Inside the Supreme Court of North Korea, a few foreign reporters would be allowed to listen to astonishing confessions from recently arrested government and party officials. Their confessions implicated Eisenhower in fantastic schemes "to topple the Party and the State by means of armed revolt and sell the Korean people as colonial slaves to U.S. imperialism." The confessions struck many observers as rehearsed, ridiculous, and coerced.

"We must bear deeply in mind that if these factional elements are left alone, they will ultimately degrade themselves in enemy espionage," Kim said. "All our Party members should further heighten their revolutionary vigilance and Party spirit, strictly keep watch over the actions of these elements and see that the factional elements did not move one step within our Party."

Arrests of "anti-party traitors" had begun in March of 1953, eleven days after Stalin died. Twelve members of the domestic faction were arrested, including Yi Sung Yop, minister of justice, who was said to be the coup's chief organizer. Pak Hon Yong, who would have replaced Kim as leader had the coup succeeded, was also arrested and expelled from the party. But he was not among the twelve prosecuted so publicly in 1953.

Before the trial began in August, Kim and his aides had done their homework, with the apparent coaching of Soviet advisers. The proceedings replicated the highly orchestrated pageantry of a mid-1930s Soviet show trial, when Stalin manipulated the levers of justice—judges, prosecutors, defense lawyers, witnesses, and mass media—to convict and execute aging Bolsheviks who were getting in his way. Though Stalin was dead, the trial was proof that Kim Il Sung remained his eager and attentive disciple.

The twelve were charged with planning a coup, sabotaging the underground Communist movement in South Korea, colluding with the Japanese, and spying for the United States. All twelve defendants pleaded guilty to everything.

The coup's purported mastermind, Yi Sung Yop, confessed he had a meeting in Seoul on June 26, 1950, with Harold Noble, a senior American political adviser to the U.S. military command. At the meeting, Yi said, Noble informed him of America's plan for an amphibious assault on

Inchon and instructed him to organize an uprising in Pyongyang. As foreign observers at the trial quickly established, however, Noble was not in Seoul on June 26. He was on vacation in Tokyo. The claim that Mac-Arthur could have devised and circulated his Inchon plan one day after North Korea invaded to start the war was hard to swallow, as was the contention that an American political adviser would share a top secret plan with a Korean Communist.

"Any notion of plausibility seems to have deserted the scriptwriters of the show trial," writes the historian Andrei Lankov. All the defendants "played their roles obediently" with the persuasive assistance of "torture, blackmail, and false promises."

The trial unfolded like a Monty Python skit, with defendants enthusiastically explaining their crimes and welcoming the privilege of being executed.

"I am a running dog of American imperialism," said Yi Kang Guk, the former president of the General Commodities Importing Company at the Ministry of Trade, as he began his confession. He pleaded guilty to the absurd charge that in 1935, a decade before Kim Il Sung's rise to power in North Korea, he had been hired in New York as an American spy.

On the trial's final day, all the defense lawyers took the stand to solemnly proclaim the guilt of their clients. The lawyer for Yi Sung Yop said, "Although he called himself a Communist, he has been an adherent of a petty bourgeois ideology, a person who could never overcome the influence of backward and reactionary bourgeois nationalism."

Yi himself took the stand to affirm the fairness of the trial. "I am grateful for having been provided with an advocate and for the opportunity to speak freely during the four days of the trial," he said. "Whatever punishment I am given by the trial, I will accept with gratitude. Had I two lives, to take them both would have been too little."

All twelve defendants were found guilty of all the crimes the prosecutor (a pal of Kim's from their time in Manchuria) had charged them with. Ten were sentenced to death; two received long prison terms. All their property was confiscated by the state. Several of the men facing death were not executed until two years later, when the supposed coup leader, Pak Hon Yong, was finally tried. Kim may have waited to dispose of Pak, whose populist support remained potent, until he had consolidated enough power to do as he pleased without challenge.

For Pak's trial, the Great Leader rolled back the ridiculous theatrics. Full-blown Stalinist show trials required months of planning, scriptwriting, and backstage preparation. International news coverage made them look farcical, which reflected badly on Kim's judgment and smudged his desired image as a globally significant Communist leader. Pak's trial lasted just one day. Press coverage was limited to summary accounts in government newspapers. He had no defense lawyer, having turned down the one offered by the government. Yet he confessed to all charges, including a ludicrous one that he had been an American stooge since 1919.

Pak, though, was not as effusive a confessor as his supporters had been during their show trial. He told the court he did not know the details of the plot to overthrow the government, yet because the plotters were his close friends, he said he was responsible for what they had done. Pak was immediately sentenced to death, and his property was confiscated. This quick and not-so-showy method of eliminating enemies—while publicly connecting them to spy rings operated by the United States, Japan, and South Korea—would become a template for coming purges.

In the years ahead, Kim's propaganda machine cited "evidence" from the 1953 show trial. It was used to dramatize the Great Leader's courage and cleverness in fighting and defeating Americans in the Korean War—even as traitors and spies surrounded him. As his official biographer enthused, "To have successfully fought U.S. imperialism, the strongest enemy, while spy cliques were entrenched in the Party and carrying out their intrigues! How great is Comrade Kim Il Sung!"

III

New orders in September 1953 sent No south by train to another bombed-out airfield. This one was at Sunan, a village on the northwest outskirts of Pyongyang. From Sunan, it was only ninety miles—less than ten minutes in a MiG—to the thirty-eighth parallel. He had never been stationed so close to South Korea.

He reported to officers' quarters inside a large stone church that stood oddly alone and undamaged amid a wasteland of bomb craters, rubble, and burned-out buildings. (American bombers had tried to avoid direct hits on churches.) In the days after No arrived at Sunan, mechanics and other air base workers pitched tents around the church.

The concrete runway at Sunan was long enough for a MiG. It had been built a year earlier, though never used because of near-constant American bombing. With the war over, the concrete had been patched. Supposedly, it would safely accommodate jet fighters, but as No studied the runway, he was not so sure. It seemed too bumpy.

Eighty MiGs in wooden crates had been smuggled into North Korea since the armistice, with at least sixteen arriving by train in Sunan before No did. The North Korean mechanics who had taken them apart in Manchuria and who put them back together had not been well trained for their work. They had done their work hurriedly, and they made mistakes. They removed wings before disconnecting fuel and hydraulic lines, which bent and flattened rubber tubing, increasing the risk of blocked fuel lines and faulty landing gear. The condition and maintenance of the reassembled MiGs were poor. Tires were bald, with cords showing through rubber. One of these planes was later described as "ridden hard and put away wet."

The reassembled MiGs sat on a dirt apron next to the runway at Sunan, which would later become Pyongyang Sunan International Airport, the country's primary aviation facility.

During the war, the latest-model MiGs were almost always flown by Soviet pilots, especially in the first two years. But in late 1952, after the Russian honchos had gone home, No and several other North Korean pilots were assigned the most advanced fighter, the MiG-15bis. It had a significantly more powerful engine than the model No initially flew. More important, it had an intuitive layout of instrument panel switches and a hydraulic control system, both of which made the plane much easier and safer to fly. On Sunday morning, September 20, base commanders at Sunan told No that Kim Il Sung had given orders for immediate combat readiness of the entire military. MiG flights, they said, would begin the following morning. They also said that because he was the most experienced pilot on the base, he would be the first to take off. He would fly alone, not in formation. He would not follow a lead pilot or have a wingman at his tail.

These orders were far better than he had dared hope for. At the very least, he had expected to shake loose a wingman. He had a plan to do so. He would perform an aerobatic maneuver called an Immelmann, a high-speed, high-g, 180-degree change of direction. While flying due north, No intended to climb suddenly, execute half a loop, and fly upside down in the opposite direction. After uprighting his MiG, he would open up the throttle and hightail it for the thirty-eighth parallel.

But now, it seemed, he needed only to take off and turn toward South Korea.

From his training in Manchuria a year earlier, when his commanders planned and then aborted an attack inside South Korea, No had learned how to approach the American air base at Kimpo. He also knew exactly how much fuel he would need in a gas-guzzling MiG. To make sure he remembered, he had taken the extraordinary risk of scribbling down map coordinates on note cards that he carried with him.

The North Korean air force was in organizational disarray. Responding to the Great Leader's orders, its commanders were frantic to get MiGs in the air. They had not yet developed flight protocols to make sure that pilots monitored each other in the air. But his commanders were not fools. Soon, No thought, his window of opportunity would close.

In the morning, he would go.

No had the remainder of one more day. He strolled with another pilot into a part of Sunan the Americans had failed to flatten. A few one- and two-story buildings remained standing, though their windows were broken and covered by tattered newspapers. Mules and oxen pulled wooden-wheeled wagons through narrow dusty streets. Residents dressed in rags and looked hungry. But on a warm and lazy Sunday, they were welcoming. Having heard no bombs in nearly two months, they seemed to believe the war was over. The two pilots found a restaurant made of unpainted plywood and ordered *naengmyeon,* a famous Pyongyang cold noodle dish made of buckwheat noodles, potatoes, sweet potatoes, boiled egg, vinegar, and mustard. As they ate, a middle-aged shoeshine man repaired and polished No's lace-up leather flight boots.

Captain Han Hak Soo, the officer eating noodles with No, was another classmate from the naval academy and a fellow MiG pilot but not a friend. Han had built his reputation on lies about how many American warplanes he had shot down. During a mission over MiG Alley, his fighter had come under heavy attack. Forty-six .50-caliber bullets punched holes in his MiG-15. After he managed to land safely, Han said that during a wild dogfight he had shot down three Sabres. No one believed his incredible claim except his commanders, who were desperate enough to dress up their dismal combat reports with American kills. For his bold lie, Han had been promoted to captain, named a battalion commander, and given a medal. As Han ate his noodles, he told No he was expecting another promotion soon.

After lunch, the two men walked to a nearby river, took a swim, and swapped stories about the miseries of cadet life at the naval academy. No was talkative but careful. Han was more careerist than Communist, but he was a known liar who would have relished the chance to snitch. No did not intend to tell anyone else about his plans.

On his way back to the airfield, No noticed an elderly woman arguing with a merchant who was selling toiletries out of the back of a wagon. The old woman reminded him of his grandmother, who was killed by an American bomb. The woman noticed No's stare and, after losing her argument with the merchant, approached the pilot. The merchant would not take her cash, she complained, because the bills were old and soiled. No had a pocketful of crisp paper money that he would never need. He gave her 5,000 won (worth about $10). She thanked him profusely, begged to know his name, and tried to give him her tattered currency in exchange. He waved off the money, telling her to spend it somewhere else.

That night, inside the stone church near the runway, No ate what he intended to be his last meal in North Korea. Meat, vegetables, rice, and tea—all excellent. Along with fifty other officers, he bedded down in the church's sanctuary and surprised himself by sleeping well.

On Monday, September 21, the weather across the Korean Peninsula was perfect for flying, a clear, cool autumn morning with a moderate wind out of the north. No needed good weather. He did not know how to take off or land using instruments. He had never landed on a runway blanketed in fog.

Dressed in his blue flight suit, newly shined boots, and leather jacket, he skipped breakfast and walked out to the runway, carrying his leather flight helmet. There, he was startled to see General Lee Whal, vice-commander of the North Korean air force.

Lee was an odd duck among North Korean generals, and not just because he stood six feet tall and sported a handlebar mustache. The son of a rich landowner, he had flown military aircraft for the Japanese during World War II. Under Kim Il Sung, who rose to power dispossessing land-owners and demonizing Japanese collaborators, Lee's background would normally have qualified him for exile, prison, or death. But his sins were forgiven because the infant North Korean government needed an air force and Lee was eager to help build it. He trained pilots and donated several buildings for classrooms, dining halls, and dormitories. At air-fields back in Manchuria, Lee had impressed No as a high-spirited, well-spoken, and decent man. Unlike other senior officers, he did not shout Communist slogans at the men.

Out on the runway ramp, the general remembered No's name and gave him a fatherly pat on the shoulder. He cautioned No to be careful of craters and ruts on the runway.

"Oh yes," the good-natured general added, "don't get lost."

Waiting for his 9:05 takeoff slot, No sat on the edge of the runway apron. He felt confident enough to glance at note cards scribbled with Kimpo landing information. Seated nearby was Senior Lieutenant Chae Byung Zae, the pilot scheduled to take off after No.

"I feel like flying a bit longer today than normal," No said, trying to sound casual.

Chae then volunteered that he felt like flying near the South Korean border.

No was silent.

"Why not land on the other side?" Chae asked.

Sensing now that Chae was joking, No smiled. But at the same time he was flabbergasted that any North Korean air force pilot would dare make such a joke. For a moment, he was too muddled to say anything. Then he offered Chae the honor of taking off first.

"You will make history," No said. "You will inaugurate Sunan airfield."

Delighted by the offer, the pilot accepted.

In training exercises, the first MiG to take off was always the first to land. As Chae headed off for his MiG, No told him, "Don't land too soon. As soon as you do, they'll tell me to land."

No took off to the north, toward China and into a wind that was beginning to kick up dust. The runway was even bumpier than it looked. As he advanced the throttle and released the brakes, his MiG bounced and shuddered. This must be one of the worst runways in the world, he thought. But as he rose into the sky and retracted the landing gear, the airfield was no longer his problem.

On the instrument panel of his MiG, No saw the photograph of Kim Il Sung. It was standard-issue on all North Korean aircraft. The picture frame also held an inspirational slogan for fighter pilots. In red letters, it said, "Aim and fire this vindictive ammunition at the damn Yankees."

Halfway to China, No veered left toward the Yellow Sea, then left again to follow the Korean coastline south. With another quick left he was back over the interior of North Korea, where down below he could see the ruins of Pyongyang. Even at nineteen thousand feet it looked like a bombed-out hell.

Here he had to make an irrevocable decision. If he made another left, he would complete his training loop and could land on schedule at Sunan. If he turned right and flew south over the thirty-eighth parallel, he would be a traitor.

He took a final inventory: Yes, the North Korean government had treated him fairly, trained him to be a jet pilot, and kept him from being butchered as an infantryman in the war. He was a decorated veteran, relatively well paid, and extremely well fed, especially compared with his country's skeletal peasants. He could perhaps become one of the elite in a postwar order. North Korea, after all, was his home.

But what about his mother's defection to South Korea? Uncle Yoo had been blabbing about it. Sooner or later the air force command would have to react. And even if they did not execute him, imprison him, or kick him out of the air force, what would his life be like in North Korea? He envisioned years of living as a pretend Communist, attending boring meetings, betraying friends, never trusting anyone.

He turned south.

Increasing his airspeed to 620 miles an hour, he became uncomfortably aware of his heart. It was slamming around inside his chest. He feared it might burst. Holding the control stick with his right hand and rubbing his chest with his left, he tried to calm himself down.

Fast approaching the border, he craned his neck right and left in the MiG's cramped cockpit, straining at his oxygen-hose tether to scan the sky for MiGs or Sabres or puffs of smoke from antiaircraft guns. There was nothing.

Over the radio, he heard the voice of the pilot who had taken off first that morning. Lieutenant Chae was asking the control tower for clearance to land. He had not taken any extra time in the air.

"Jesus Christ," No said to himself, "they'll expect me next."

The control tower barked at him. His code number was eighty-seven.

"Where are you, eighty-seven?"

The control tower repeated the coded question again and again at five-second intervals.

Beyond a range of rugged mountains, seemingly floating on the southern horizon, No glimpsed the runway at Kimpo.

He was certain that by now he had been spotted by American radar. He expected at any moment to see Sabres rising to challenge him. When they came, he planned to wag his wings as a sign of friendly intentions while firing colored flares as a signal of distress.

Yet the Americans paid him no mind, even as he violated their airspace and flew directly toward the busiest military airfield on the Korean Peninsula. Since the end of the war, Kimpo had become home base for two fighter wings (each with three thousand airmen) and a squadron of mixed propeller and jet aircraft. It was so busy during daylight hours that there was almost never a moment when an aircraft was not landing.

Although the war was over, fighter pilots continued to train for combat. Nearly every day there were mock dogfights pitting a senior Sabre pilot and his wingman against two other Sabres. John Lowery, then a pilot at Kimpo, flew with a cloth target attached to the tail of his Sabre. Other Sabre pilots would practice shooting at it. "The perceived threat after the war had not changed," Lowery said. "Everybody that I was associated with was just hot to tangle with a MiG. We were spring-loaded to the fire position."

And yet, as far as No could tell, the Americans were ignoring his MiG. To keep it that way and to get on the ground as quickly as possible, he decided to make a straight-on approach—from the wrong direction. Every other aircraft was landing against the northerly wind. No decided to land with the wind, heading south. The approach would increase his landing speed, increase the distance he would need to come to a stop, and increase his risk of a high-speed, head-on collision on the runway.

He had been trained for such risky business in Manchuria, where MiGs often landed simultaneously from opposite directions. As No approached, he caught sight of a Sabre about to land. Not sure that the pilot would spot him on the runway and steer away, No quickly considered his options. To the right of the runway, there was no place to put down. Taxiways snaked through rough ground to ramps where about thirty American fighters were parked. There were wooden barracks, tents, and a large hangar. On the left of the runway, there was a small dirt landing strip and an open field. To avoid a collision, No decided to land there.

The approaching Sabre, though, came in faster than No anticipated.

It landed smoothly and taxied off the main runway, allowing him what seemed to be clear access to the main runway.

Nearing touchdown, he pulled back on the throttle, lowered the wing flaps, and pressed a switch that extended air brakes on the flanks of the MiG's fuselage. Locking down the landing gear, he worried again about antiaircraft gunners, expecting that by now they had him in their sights. So he rocked his wings and fired his flares—red, green, white, and yellow—to indicate an emergency landing. He hoped the flares would not be perceived as rockets.

Then he saw another Sabre, landing at the far end of the runway. They were going to touch down at the same moment.

No came in much faster than he intended. He believed for a moment that he might overshoot the airfield. His wheels hit midway down the seven-thousand-foot-long runway. Straining the brakes, he was struggling for control when he spotted the Sabre dead ahead. Its pilot did not seem to see him. No steered as far to his right as he could and prayed.

The Sabre pilot, Captain Dave Williams, had seen No's plane.

"There is somebody landing the wrong way," Williams shouted over the radio, seconds before his Sabre touched the runway.

With inches to spare, Williams veered right. As the two planes roared past each other, both traveling at about 140 miles an hour, Williams shouted over the radio a second time.

"It's a goddamn MiG!"

Williams stopped at the end of the runway, climbed out of the cockpit, and crouched under a wing to steady his nerves. Sabre pilots in the landing pattern above Kimpo, having heard that a MiG was on the runway, unlocked their guns and prepared to fire. They later judged No's decision to come in fast and land the wrong way as a smart play.

"If he had made a go-around, I would have got him," said Jim Sutton, a pilot who was circling over Kimpo that morning.

No's escape planning had taken five years and eight months, dating from the day he first saw the Great Leader in the fertilizer warehouse. His escape flight took seventeen minutes. He took off from North Korea at 9:07 and landed at Kimpo at 9:24.

After his much-too-exciting landing, No smiled under his oxygen mask and talked to himself.

"I'm safe. I made it. I'm free."

The Americans would not shoot him now, he told himself.

He was premature in coming to that conclusion.

American airmen were watching him with their fingers on the triggers of antiaircraft guns. Inside gun emplacements on both sides of Kimpo's runway, they were trying to decide whether they should shoot at the taxiing MiG. In the end, they decided against it. Had they gone ahead, they would also have been shooting at each other.

Neither trucks nor troops rushed out to surround No's plane. The runway was empty except for Dave Williams, the shaken Sabre pilot. No could not tell if anyone else at Kimpo had even noticed his MiG.

Unsure how to proceed, he taxied off the runway and followed a ramp that took him toward a row of parked Sabres. They had been on runway alert all morning. Pilots sat in their cockpits, ready, if called upon, to start their engines and take off.

Captain Cipriano Guerra was one of them. That morning he was reading *Astounding Stories*, a science fiction magazine, but happened to look up as No landed from the north. "I saw this jet coming in upwind," Guerra said. "I figured one of our guys had goofed."

Guerra watched slack-jawed as the fighter touched down, narrowly avoided a collision, and turned in his direction. Only then did he recognize it as a MiG and begin to worry that it might start firing at point-blank range. He was "petrified" and considered preemptively spraying the MiG with .50-caliber machine-gun fire.

As Guerra nervously eyed him, No eased his fighter into an empty slot between two parked Sabres. He released the clamps that secured the cockpit canopy and rolled it back. Removing his oxygen mask and unfastening straps that connected him to his seat and parachute, he reached out to the instrument panel, grabbed the framed photograph of Kim Il Sung, and ripped it loose.

He urgently needed to destroy that picture. Climbing out of the cockpit and jumping to the ground, he threw it to the tarmac, smashed the frame, and ripped the photograph in small pieces. A Sabre pilot who watched him concluded that No was saying a bitter good-bye to his girlfriend. "The flier pulled out the picture of a girl from a pocket of his flying suit, ripped it up and threw it away," he told the Associated Press.

Standing next to his MiG, No began shouting the only English word he could remember from middle school.

"Motorcar! Motorcar!"

Watching all this, Guerra decided it would be inappropriate to shoot the MiG pilot. He jumped down from his plane and jogged over to say hello.

No saluted Guerra, smiled, and shook the American's hand.

They stared at each other and at each other's aircraft. Without a common language, neither was sure what to do. Within seconds, the confusion increased. Half a dozen other pilots climbed out of their fighters and rushed over to the MiG. No shook more hands.

Although he was trying to seem friendly, he was increasingly uncomfortable. He wanted somebody to take him to headquarters, where he could explain himself to someone who spoke Korean or Japanese or Russian. But he could think of no way to make this request other than by continuing to shout for a motorcar. As he did so, he sensed that some pilots were beginning to wonder if he was nuts.

"About then, I decided that I'd better do something with the guy," recalled Guerra. "So I loaded him in a vehicle and took him to HQ."

Within minutes, Sabres at Kimpo were scrambled to intercept any North Korean aircraft that might be dispatched to destroy No's airplane before it could be examined. None came. Armored cars and soldiers with M1 rifles surrounded the MiG. It was towed to a hangar where it could be hidden from view. That day, mechanics began taking the MiG apart and crating the pieces for transport off the Korean Peninsula.

Just before Guerra's jeep reached the office of Lieutenant General Samuel E. Anderson, commander of the Fifth Air Force, a pilot in the front passenger seat turned around and gestured for No to surrender his service pistol. It was the weapon he had considered using for a brief moment to shoot the Great Leader. He handed it over.

IV

When the stolen MiG touched down, it was 4:24 a.m. in Moscow, where Kim Il Sung had just completed nine successful days of extracting money and aid from Stalin's successors.

The night before, at a sumptuous Kremlin dinner in Kim's honor, the Soviets announced a record package of reconstruction grants for North Korea, including postponement of loan payments and gifts of heavy equipment and consumer goods. At dinner, the Soviet prime minister, Malenkov, compared Kim's struggles for independence to those of the thirteen American colonies.

"The glorious Korean people have written a new and wonderful page in the history of the liberation struggle, and this page teaches us that there is no force in the world capable of breaking people who have taken the fate of the country into their own hands," Malenkov said.

In response, Kim thanked the Soviets and said that with their help North Korea had "upheld its freedom and independence, thwarted the aggressive plans of the American imperialists, and forced them to sign a truce."

When Malenkov and Kim woke up the next morning, the triumphalism of that dinner turned sour. On that day and for the rest of the week, photographs of a dashing young North Korean pilot and a gleaming silver MiG-15 were splashed across the front pages of newspapers in most world capitals, except Moscow, Pyongyang, and Beijing.

Never before and never since has one North Korean defector stirred up such a global hoo-ha. The *Washington Post* celebrated No's heist with a banner headline across its front page, "Red MiG-15 Brought to Seoul." The *New York Times* also made No's defection its lead story, with a front-page headline attributing the theft of the MiG to the American offer of $100,000. Wire service, radio, and television news accounts throughout the week said that the pilot was chockablock with cold war secrets. They recounted how he had handed over the latest model of a battle-ready combat jet the Americans had been trying for years to get their hands on.

Kim Il Sung never spoke publicly about the loss of the MiG or about No's defection. But he did retaliate, according to Captain Lee Un Yong, a North Korean air force flight instructor who defected to South Korea two years after No. General Wang Yong, the top commander of the North Korean air force, was demoted, and five of No's air force comrades and commanders were executed, Lee said. Although he did not know the names of all five, Lee said one of those killed was Lieutenant Kun Soo Sung, No's best friend.

As for Uncle Yoo, there was never any information about his fate or that of his wife and children.

V

The Americans did not see him coming, although they insisted that they did.

Soon after No shut down the engine on his MiG, an air force spokesman claimed that the control tower had guided the plane to a safe landing. The Associated Press reported that an "Allied officer revealed that a flight of Sabre jets met the Communist jet at the southern border of the demilitarized zone . . . and escorted it to Kimpo." The report added that the plane had "apparently" been picked up by Allied radar and Sabres were dispatched to meet it. A MiG certainly would not approach the vital air base "without our knowing about it," one officer told the AP.

In truth, the Americans had been caught with their pants down and eyes closed.

Just as No took off that morning from North Korea, the radar at Kimpo was turned off for maintenance. The Americans made no attempt to escort No's MiG, intercept it, or shoot it down. Even the few American pilots in the flight pattern over Kimpo who caught sight of the distinctively snub-nosed, swept-wing interloper as it descended from the north did not recognize it as an enemy aircraft. None of them altered flight plans or alerted flight control. They did not realize what was in their midst until after No had landed and Dave Williams howled over the radio about a goddamn wrong-way MiG.

Only then did the air base spring into action. As the MiG was towed, pilots and other airmen ducked into their hootches to grab cameras and swarmed the taxiway for photographs. They complained riotously when military police refused to allow them inside the hangar. With orders to make sure that No's defection and his purloined MiG were kept secret, MPs demanded that pilots and airmen stop taking photographs. They confiscated cameras and exposed film. One officious security official charged up into the control tower, where "he warned us that we were to say nothing to anyone concerning the incident, practically threatening us with death if we did mention it," recalled Wilfred M. Husted, an air-traffic supervisor.

Efforts to keep the lid on failed almost immediately. After lunch that Monday, Husted returned to his tent, where airmen asked him what all the hubbub was about. Dutifully, Husted said nothing. He tried to change the subject by turning on the radio, which was tuned to Kilroy, the local Armed Forces Radio station. As soon as the radio warmed up, Kilroy told the world that a MiG-15 had landed at a U.S. Air Force base in South Korea.

Inside the headquarters of the Fifth Air Force, a medical officer poked and prodded No for fifteen minutes, sampling his blood and impressing him by using a brand-new needle to do the job. No was then escorted to the commander's office for an amiably empty encounter with General Anderson, who did not speak Korean and had no interpreter. After exchanging hellos, the general sat behind his desk while the pilot sat stiffly on a wooden chair. For half an hour, they wordlessly eyed each other as Anderson's aides made an urgent call to Tokyo for interrogators and translators. Within an hour, ten of them were on a plane bound for Kimpo. Back in the general's office, the silence was finally shattered when

Major Donald Nichols, head of intelligence for the Fifth Air Force, burst into the room and introduced himself to No, using his pretty good Korean.

Nichols was the T. E. Lawrence of Korea. One of his commanders, General Earle E. Partridge, called him "a one-man war" and "the most amazing and unusual man" he had ever met. Nichols, then thirty, drank too much, never wore a proper uniform, and was overweight. He was also the most effective American intelligence operative of the Korean War era. He had arrived in Korea in 1946 with less than three months of schooling as a spy. Before that he had been a motor-pool sergeant. Before that he had grown up on welfare in Florida, stealing farm equipment from neighbors and dropping out of school in seventh grade. Yet by traveling in disguise through North Korea and by using payoffs, extortion, torture, and an extraordinarily close relationship with President Syngman Rhee of South Korea and many other senior South Korean officials, he built a covert network of informers, guerrilla fighters, and high-level political contacts that operated throughout the war in both Koreas. Before the war started, his warnings were the first to predict Kim's invasion of the South, although they were ignored at MacArthur's headquarters. He controlled more than six hundred agents on both sides of the border, and his sources were often better than those of the Central Intelligence Agency or army intelligence.

Russian warplanes were one of his passions. Nichols lured—and later interrogated—the North Korean air force pilot who defected in 1950 in an Ilyushin Il-10 airplane. Nichols risked his life and won the Distinguished Service Cross in 1951 by leading a mission behind enemy lines that photographed and brought home parts from a wrecked MiG-15. The following year he organized an even more successful mission that brought back the entire wreckage of another MiG.

Now a North Korean pilot—fresh from delivering a battle-ready MiG, an item Nichols had been lusting after for years—was eager to talk. Nichols could hardly contain his excitement. He shot the breeze with the general for about ten minutes before saying to No, "Let's go to my place."

They flew in Nichols's helicopter to the compound of the 6004th Air Intelligence Service Squadron on the western edge of Seoul. There, Nichols ran the show. Like Santa Claus, he handed out hundred-pound bags of rice on paydays.

When they entered his office, a pack of mixed-breed dogs (No counted ten, including several huskies) got up and wagged their tails. The questioning could not officially begin until the interrogation team arrived from Tokyo. So they waited in Nichols's office, where No petted the dogs and Nichols kept being called away for meetings. Nichols's Korean assistant served No an ice-cold bottle of Coca-Cola, a beverage he had never heard of. He loved it at first taste. Years later, he would buy stock in Coca-Cola.

Drinking his Coke, No heard, for the first time, about his $100,000.

The major's assistant mentioned that the U.S. government, in return for delivery of the MiG, would soon give No enough money to buy thirty-three brand-new American cars. No understood that this was an impressive sum of money, but he did not understand why the Americans would want to compensate him for an aircraft that happened to be his ticket to freedom. The Korean assistant did not explain. Like everyone else whom No would meet in the hours and days ahead, he assumed that the North Korean pilot had been lured to South Korea by Operation Moolah.

Later in the morning, as the wait continued for the interrogators from Tokyo, Nichols sat down with No and informally questioned him. During their conversation, which was not recorded, the major casually declared, "You are a rich man now."

Nichols did not elaborate, also assuming that No had come for the money and knew the particulars of Operation Moolah. No was deeply confused by this talk of his being a rich man. He did not know what to say.

On a completely different subject, Nichols asked him about an important general in North Korea.

"Have you seen General Lee Whal?"

No had indeed seen him—that very morning in North Korea.

General Lee was the tall, wellborn, mustachioed officer who patted No's shoulder and joked with him about not getting lost.

Suppressing his wonderment about the reasons behind Nichols's question, No related the details of their encounter.

Nichols was delighted. He clapped his hands, described Lee as "my friend," and said that he had sent him two letters.

It would be many years before No understood the scale of Nichols's spying operation in North Korea, but this claim that the vice-commander of the North Korean air force was a friend of an American major did not come as a complete shock to No. Back in Manchuria, No had suspicions about the general. More than once, No had watched Lee elbow his way into the daily logistics of the air war, ordering MiGs to fly into airspace where Sabres were waiting to pounce.

As No continued waiting for his interrogators, air force photographers insisted that he pose for propaganda photographs. For some pictures, he put on his Snoopy-style helmet, bulbous black oxygen mask, leather gloves, and parachute. For others, he gazed soulfully into the middle distance with his leather flight jacket partly unzipped. For still others, he was photographed from behind as he looked over his MiG.

No looked like a defector from central casting. He was lean and handsome, with high cheekbones and a full head of thick black hair. He was twenty-one but looked younger.

After the photographers finished, No's flight suit was confiscated. He was issued air force fatigues and escorted to lunch at the officers' mess, where he found the food to be inedible—bland and greasy. He could not help but compare it with the gourmet meals he had enjoyed in Manchuria with the honchos. The American pilots, though, were wolfing it down. At the officers' mess, No could not even find water to drink, just tasteless powdered milk and coffee that was much too bitter to drink. American military food shocked his system; it took about a week before he could eat enough of it to make a dent in his hunger.

After lunch, the intelligence officers arrived from Tokyo, and No's interrogation began in a conference room at Nichols's compound. Most of his questioners were college-educated Japanese Americans. Only one, a Korean American, spoke Korean. So the interrogation was conducted mostly in Japanese, which No still spoke fluently. The men asking questions were not like North Korean military officers or any Asians he had met. They were informal, plainspoken, compassionate, and direct. The one he liked best, Shigeo Morisato, later taught him English and became a close friend.

For all their friendliness, his interrogators were relentless. Over two days, they grilled No about his personal life, the circumstances of his escape, the placement of North Korean air force units, the leadership and command structure of the air force, the location of airfields in North Korea and Manchuria, and on and on.

Nichols personally wrote the report on No's initial interrogation. The fifty-five-page document was a rush job: finished in three days, stamped "SECRET," and kept secret for sixty years. It is, however, a remarkably thorough account of the equipment, leadership, training, and strategies of North Korean and Soviet air operations in Manchuria and North Korea during the war. As judged by his interrogators, No was a lucid, precise, and cooperative source. "He was able to recall," the report says, "air units, personnel strength, structure, and number of aircraft assigned to respective units."

No explained the tormented mind-set of North Korean pilots, many of whom were undertrained in Manchuria and overwhelmed in combat.

"Even after becoming full-fledged MiG-15 pilots," Nichols's report says, "they were kept under constant watch under a system of intra-unit surveillance whereby every pilot was required to report any suspicious speech or action of their own pilot friends."

No also explained the odd, erratic, and seemingly cowardly behavior of MiG pilots in the last years of the war, after the honchos had gone home.

Question: "When a Sabre is attacking MiGs from the rear and there are two more MiGs behind and above the Sabre, why don't those MiGs jump the Sabre?"

Answer: "The reason for that is that they are afraid that, in turn, they will be jumped from the rear by other Sabres."

No was asked why a lone MiG pilot, when fleeing from Sabre fire, would "fire into the air without reason." Drawing on his own experience, he answered, "Possibly to shoot up the ammo so that they could claim participation in combat, or maybe because of excitement the pilots 'froze' on the trigger and fired the guns involuntarily."

His interrogators were curious about what No knew about American fighter pilots preying on MiGs inside Manchuria—in violation of UN rules and orders from Washington.

Question: "Did you ever hear about U.N. aircraft across the Manchurian border?"

Answer: (*Laughs*) "Not only have I heard about it, but I have actually observed them personally."

As No tired, his interrogators gave him American cigarettes, which they said would help him think. No was impressed by the cigarettes, which were not rotten like the Chinese and Russian brands he had become addicted to. Before his first round of interrogation ended, a transcript shows that No was asked about the American offer of cash for his MiG. The interrogator seemed surprised by No's ignorance.

Question: "Did you know that the U.N. has offered a reward for MiG pilots escaping to U.N. airfields with their MiGs?"

Answer: "I have never heard about it."

Question: "Didn't you read the leaflets we dropped regarding the reward?"

Answer: "No, I have never seen them."

In his report on the interrogation, Nichols seemed dubious that No had never heard about the reward.

"Refugee stated, apparently in all sincerity, that all North Korean pilots had been prohibited from tuning in on South Korea radio broadcasts," Nichols wrote. "He also declared emphatically that he had never seen any propaganda leaflet guaranteeing him any monetary compensation for a delivery intact of a MiG into U.N. hands. Therefore, refugee was ignorant, ostensibly, of the standing monetary offer made by the U.S."

When the interrogation ended at two in the morning, Nichols's assistant escorted No to a small apartment where a futon had been placed on the floor for him. Bleary-eyed but jubilant, No lay down and reviewed all that he had accomplished in one day: flying clear of Kim Il Sung, escaping a dead-end future in North Korea, and finding safety in the West. As an unexpected bonus, the Americans had been kind to him, even complimentary. One interrogator told him that someday he could become president of South Korea.

The Americans, though, had pestered him about reward money—what he knew and when he knew it—and they did not seem to believe his answers. It was irritating and confusing.

When No awoke at 7:00 a.m., a morning newspaper had been placed next to his futon. He read a story about himself on the front page. In describing his escape, it explained what his interrogators had assumed he already knew: for nearly half a year, the Americans had been dangling dollars as bait for a MiG pilot to land at Kimpo—and a North Korean named No Kum Sok was the first to bite.

No deeply resented the implication that he was more interested in money than in freedom. But at least now he could make sense of his interrogators' questions. In No's view, Operation Moolah had never tempted a single North Korean, Chinese, or Soviet pilot. To start with, the Americans had dropped their leaflets in the wrong place. They should have dropped them in Manchuria, where MiG pilots were based. Even if pilots had read the leaflets or heard the radio broadcasts, No believed, they would never have trusted the Americans enough to risk being shot down.

Finally, he knew that Communist pilots did not understand how much $100,000 was worth. The reward would have been much more tempting, he thought, if the Americans had promised a good job in America.

No also realized that it did not matter what he thought. His life—and his befuddling future as "Moolah Man"—was now in the hands of the U.S. government.

CHAPTER 12

Squeezing the Moolah

I

Thirteen time zones away from No and the MiG, the president of the United States was ticked off by Operation Moolah and its vulgar financial inducements.

Eisenhower did not want the fighter jet and worried that its theft might undermine the fragile armistice in Korea. He believed the Russian-made aircraft should be returned to its rightful owner as soon as possible, and to discourage other pilots from coming in from the cold, he wanted to cancel Operation Moolah. He also wanted to make sure that the North Korean pilot, whose name Eisenhower had yet to learn, would not blow the $100,000 on booze and broads. Better yet, he wanted to find a way to pressure the pilot to turn down the moolah altogether.

Eisenhower never made these views public. But they echoed long and loud in the White House, the Pentagon, and the State Department, where subordinates spent the next year trying to thread a needle: keeping the president happy while keeping reporters from learning that Ike, the outwardly genial general, wanted to pay out the reward money very slowly or not at all.

Eisenhower had flown out of Washington early on Monday morning, September 21, before reports about the MiG and the defector reached the White House. While he was giving speeches that day in Massachusetts, his national security team met and decided that even though the Korean War had ended, the United States must honor the commitment made in Operation Moolah. They authorized the air force to announce in Washington that afternoon that the reward would be paid. Air force headquarters also sent a message to its Far East Command saying that Operation Moolah remained in effect and cash rewards for additional MiGs would be paid in the future.

Eisenhower hurriedly approved his security team's decision during a busy day of glad-handing in New England, but that night in Boston he had second thoughts.

"I am sorry that I was not in Washington today to discuss the MiG incident with the entire staff," he dictated in a personal and confidential four-page letter to his longtime adviser and confidant, Walter Bedell Smith. Smith, who had served Ike during World War II, was then undersecretary of state and had participated in the meeting at which No's reward was authorized.

"I realize that the recommendations sent to me had the unanimous support of my shrewdest and most knowledgeable advisers on such matters; however, I must confess I was not convinced," Eisenhower wrote.

What upset him was "the ethics of the case." He fretted in his letter that keeping the MiG, paying the reward, and continuing to promise cash for MiGs would violate terms of the truce that ended the fighting. He also viewed the payment of bribes for aircraft as a tired old warfare trick that was beneath the dignity of the United States—and not likely to lure in any more MiGs.

"If we are to win the propaganda war—and I think it most important that we do—we have to be alert for every opportunity to produce *unusual* results," he wrote. "The normal and the routine are not good enough, and I do not for a moment believe the defection of this one North Korean will encourage any others to come in."

During World War II, when he was supreme Allied commander,

General Eisenhower had had personal experience with defectors absconding in airplanes. His command gave the French several American-made P-40 ground-attack aircraft, and two French pilots flew them to German-occupied France. In his letter to Smith, Eisenhower mentioned the irksome matter of the P-40s, noting that "these incidents are so scattered and so infrequent as to have little significance."

The president wrote that if MiGs "start coming in to us by the hundreds, I will eat crow, but knowing the Communists I would gamble that there will be little if any more of this. Their methods of punishing people through torturing families are too well known and too effective to give rise to any great hope that we are going to wreck the Communist Air Force in this fashion."

Eisenhower, who came from a poor Kansas farm family and had always lived on his military salary, was not pleased to authorize a large payment of taxpayer money for property stolen from a foreign government. Still, he reluctantly agreed in the letter he wrote from Boston "that we had to pay the $100,000 in this case."

Keeping the MiG was another matter. "We are not anxious to have this one," Eisenhower wrote. "And certainly I cannot see why we want any more of them." He also suggested that Operation Moolah be "withdrawn" and that the "Communists [be notified] that we had no interest in the MiG plane, and if they wanted to send a pilot down and take it back, that would be all right with us."

The advantages of these actions, he wrote, would be that the United States could "stand before the world as very honorable people, maintaining that while we had not been guilty of real violation of the Armistice, we were anxious to avoid any implication of violating its spirit . . . If we get accused of violating the spirit of the Armistice, and this argument makes any headway with neutrals and even some of our friends, I think we will experience a defeat in this so-called psychological warfare."

The president closed by telling Smith, "This note is for no official action whatsoever. I am merely trying to put my personal thoughts before you."

That no-action proviso would be ignored in the coming days and months. The president had put his druthers down on paper, and the president's men were eager to please.

On No's second morning in South Korea, the U.S. Far East Command had not yet been apprised of Eisenhower's views. This was largely a function of time zones. When the president dictated his letter on Monday night in Boston, it was already Tuesday morning in Korea.

Having heard nothing to the contrary from Washington, air force officers in Seoul were of the opinion that the stolen MiG and its pilot constituted a great victory in America's propaganda war against Communism. They decided to put No on immediate public display—at a press conference in Seoul.

But before they showed him off to reporters, they decided he needed some coaching. On one especially touchy subject, they coached him to lie. A well-dressed American in civilian clothes (whose name No never heard) asked if he had ever seen American fighter jets in Chinese airspace. Of course, No replied, he had seen many Sabres shoot down MiGs on takeoff and landing from Manchurian airfields. The well-dressed man said that if a reporter asked about these incursions in Manchuria, No must say he had seen nothing.

II

In Pyongyang, Kim Il Sung knew exactly how he was going to transform his wrecked country into "a glorious socialist power." He would follow Stalin's strategy from the 1930s and bet the future on heavy industry. To that end, the money he had extracted from his Communist brethren was spent on iron, steel, and chemical production. As Kim imposed his will, the largest single branch of North Korean industry became machine building. New factories, many of them turnkey imports from countries like Poland, Hungary, and Czechoslovakia, began churning out diesel motors, electrical instruments, and machine tools.

"Comrade Kim Il Sung, with his unbounded love for the country and the people, could no longer tolerate a continuation of Korean backwardness," his official biographer wrote. "Why should not the people, who endured so many sufferings and fought so heroically, live in a country more developed and more advanced than others? The Great Leader made up his mind to give the Korean people . . . a first-rate culture which would be the envy of the world's people."

He wanted it done fast, a blitzkrieg to industrial modernity. Visiting a bombed-out brick factory soon after the cease-fire, Kim said that rebuilding the site using "ordinary methods of construction" would take five years, "but if you think of factory reconstruction as a battle and attack it, you can get it completed within two months."

Some of North Korea's extraordinary growth in the 1950s was due to Kim's ability to inspire—and compel—sustained unpaid labor from his people. Every able-bodied citizen, soldier and civilian alike, was forced to repair streets and remove debris. "Reconstruction was, in a sense, war by other means," writes Charles K. Armstrong, a historian of the era, noting that Kim and his Manchurian partisans understood governance only through the prism of their own blood-soaked lives: guerrilla war, conventional war, and Stalinist control.

Yet the imperious wrongheadedness that defined Kim's command of the Korean War soon reappeared in his leadership of the reconstruction war. In his rush to build heavy industry, the consumer economy—food, clothing, and household goods—was largely an afterthought. He tended to ignore basic infrastructure and worker training. His first three-year plan made no mention of building paved roads. His government neglected maintenance and improvements to hydroelectric dams and the Japanese-built power grid, a mistake that in decades to come would leave much of North Korea in the dark. As new factories were built, the top-down planning system did not make provision for training enough young technicians to operate or maintain them.

The most misbegotten of Kim's early postwar planning schemes was for agriculture. The war had killed a high percentage of the country's male farmers; about three-quarters of postwar farmworkers were women and children. "It is a quite common scene that 6–8 women are dragging the plow in the knee-deep water of the rice stubble," a Hungarian diplomat reported. The Great Leader made a bad situation worse by hurriedly collectivizing nearly all the country's farms. Rice and grain production stalled and then declined.

Within a year of the war's end, bad weather, farm collectivization, and a policy of forcibly confiscating rice from farmers led to severe food shortages, which the government tried to hide. In a foretaste of what would become North Korea's chronic "eating problem," Kim had to ask China and the Soviet Union for emergency food aid.

III

Lies were nothing new to No Kum Sok. Had he not been an experienced and convincing liar, he would never have been in a position to steal a MiG. Moreover, the Korean War, as he witnessed it unfold, was made of lies. The Soviet Union lied about its pilots fighting over MiG Alley. Kim Il Sung lied about who started the war and then lied about who won it. If anyone dared tell the truth about how catastrophically Kim managed the war, he was imprisoned or killed.

So when the Americans at Kimpo instructed him to lie about the Sabres he had seen in Manchuria, No understood what they wanted. In any case, he felt he had no choice.

Just before he left the American intelligence compound to travel to the press conference in central Seoul, No had another talk with Major Nichols. The spymaster told him to get out of South Korea and settle in the United States. Learn English, go to college, and become somebody, Nichols said.

Ever since he was a boy studying his father's picture books about America, No had wanted to do as Nichols advised. During his first day of interrogation, he had been unable to think of a way to ask how or if he could travel to the United States. Now, with a green light from the intelligence chief, he decided to insist at every opportunity on going to America.

No had never witnessed a Western-style press conference, yet he was not particularly worried about what it would be like to star in one. He assumed it would be an orderly affair: a handful of friendly newsmen chatting with him in an office, as he had done with air force interrogators. But as he sat between two security guards in the backseat of a light blue Chevrolet sedan, with sirens blaring and lights flashing while his motorcade pushed through crowds in the war-shattered streets of Seoul, he began to get nervous.

Though the Korean War had ended, news from Korea—about freed prisoners of war, truce violations, and unearthed bodies from secret mass killings—continued to dominate foreign news dispatches in American and European newspapers. A large American and international press contingent remained in Seoul. For these reporters, the defection of a Communist MiG pilot was the juiciest story in weeks. It had military, diplomatic, and strategic implications—and a wonderful human-interest core. More than two hundred journalists wanted to photograph the North Korean and find out why he had swiped a MiG. They packed the press conference, which was held in a building where many correspondents lived. When No was ushered into the room by a large African American air force sergeant holding a submachine gun, row upon row of television lights stunned him. Wearing U.S. Air Force fatigues, a peaked fatigue cap that was several sizes too small, and North Korean underwear, he stood at a table loaded with microphones. He spoke slowly through an interpreter, choosing his words carefully and struggling to contain his fear.

For an hour and a half he answered questions and made global news. He was the first defector since the end of the war and the first eyewitness to explain publicly that Soviet pilots had trained North Koreans like himself to fly MiGs. He described how legions of Soviet pilots had participated in air-to-air jet combat against Americans throughout the Korean War. He also explained, again as the first eyewitness to speak to the Western press, that North Korea was currently bringing in warplanes from Manchuria in violation of the armistice.

Asked if North Korean leaders believed war would start again, No replied, "Yes, they do, and they are preparing for it." He also said Kim Il Sung's government continued to tell his people that the Korean War was not over "in order to keep them working hard."

What "startled reporters" most at the press conference, according to a United Press dispatch, was No's statement that he had heard nothing about Operation Moolah. While he said that he was "very glad" to learn about the reward money, he found it impossible to say how he planned to spend it.

"After a pause and alternately grinning and wetting his dry lips, casting his eyes downward at his shifting feet, he said, 'I don't know,'" the *New York Times* reported.

No was much more eager to talk about where he hoped to live and study. Echoing the advice he had just received from the spymaster Nichols, he told reporters that he hoped to go soon to the United States and attend college.

Asked about his family back in North Korea, he said he had none except for his mother. "She is somewhere in South Korea. But I don't know where and I don't know how to find her."

Another reporter asked about the photograph that No destroyed after jumping down from his MiG. "Was it your girlfriend?" the reporter asked.

It was a photograph of Great Leader Kim Il Sung, No said. His answer was apparently not what reporters were interested in. The girlfriend angle was better copy, and most news accounts of the press conference omitted any mention of Kim Il Sung.

As instructed by his American handlers, No did lie.

In response to a question about American warplanes north of the Yalu, he said he had not seen any.

If he had told the truth, if he had detailed the extraordinary frequency and relative ease with which Sabres shot down MiGs over

Manchuria in the last year of the war, his press conference would not have been a propaganda coup for the United States. Reporters would have written about American pilots ignoring United Nations rules and disobeying direct orders from Washington.

Instead, No's performance was a propaganda home run. Reporters focused on North Korea's smuggling of warplanes. "Reds Breaking Truce," said a front-page headline in the *New York Times*. Nearly every story around the world focused on how shocking it was that the North Korean pilot did not know—or claimed not to know—about the reward money.

No returned by motorcade to Nichols's compound for another marathon interrogation. In the days, weeks, and months to come, there would be hundreds of these sessions, and in all of them No impressed his interrogators, according to air force documents.

"He was most cooperative and in no way obnoxious," wrote Colonel Jack H. Bristow, an air force staff surgeon who questioned No. "He was not sullen and at the same time not boisterous. He did not appear to be bored with the interview, but on the other hand seemed to derive a certain amount of satisfaction from answering the questions put to him. During the interview he appeared to be quite relaxed and smiled and laughed occasionally as the situation dictated. He showed no signs of nervousness or apprehension, but rather gave one the impression that he felt secure in his present position."

Before the questions ended on that second day, again at 2:00 a.m., No learned that he would be granted political asylum. If he wanted, he could live in the United States. He also learned that he would be leaving Korea in the morning.

The day after No defected, the air force announced in Seoul that his MiG had been dismantled and loaded on a cargo plane and was bound for the United States. The *New York Times* reported that it would be subjected to an "exhaustive technical study" at Wright-Patterson Air Force Base in Dayton, Ohio.

The air force told No, just before he boarded a military plane at Kimpo, that he was headed for Tokyo for more interrogation.

Neither statement was true. On September 23, the MiG and its pilot were transported separately and secretly to Kadena Air Force Base on Okinawa, the American-controlled Japanese island about a thousand miles south of Tokyo.

Also in secret, the air force urgently located and immediately dispatched two of America's best pilots to Okinawa. Major Chuck Yeager, the first man to break the sound barrier and the legendary test pilot who would become the hero of *The Right Stuff* (Tom Wolfe's book and the Oscar-winning movie), was called away from Edwards Air Force Base in California. Captain Tom Collins, a test pilot who had just set a new world speed record in a Sabre, was plucked from Wright-Patterson, along with his boss, Major General Albert Boyd, also a test pilot.

General Boyd waited until they were over the Pacific before telling Yeager and Collins why they had been ordered to take a very long, hush-hush flight in a C-124 transport aircraft.

"Boys," he said, "we are going out to fly a MiG-15."

Boyd's briefing covered these points: The truce that ended the Korean War is shaky. If fighting starts back up, Americans could duel again against MiGs. So your orders are to test-fly this stolen fighter as if it were a brand-new aircraft and learn everything possible about its speed, handling, strengths, weaknesses, and fighting capabilities. You'll have to work fast because if the Commies say they want the MiG back, we have to return it within forty-eight hours.

Before he finished, Boyd had bad news for Yeager.

"I want Tom to be the first one to fly it," Boyd said, "because, Chuck, you have had enough firsts."

Yeager, who hated to be second at anything, groaned.

The cargo plane bound for Okinawa was loaded with instruments and testing equipment from the Air Technical Intelligence Center at Wright-Patterson. Besides Boyd, Yeager, and Collins, the passengers included engine experts, hydraulic specialists, aerodynamicists, and intelligence analysts who had been waiting for years to examine a combat-ready MiG.

All of this had been set in motion by the reactions and overreactions of advisers scrambling to please Eisenhower. It would have been easier, safer, and far cheaper to transport the MiG back to the Air Technical Intel Center in Ohio. But Ike wanted to return the MiG to its rightful owner in a timely fashion, so the Pentagon opted for field-testing during the rainy season on a semitropical island whose only advantage was a location six thousand miles closer to North Korea than Dayton, Ohio.

No went to Okinawa (rather than Tokyo, where his interrogators were based) to be available, when needed, to help Yeager and Collins understand how to fly a MiG.

Back in Washington, Walter Bedell Smith seemed stung by the president's criticism of his initial decision in "the matter of the MiG." In a memorandum for the president, Smith tried to explain his thinking and then proposed a face-saving way for the administration to get out of paying No.

"So that you will not think too ill of my judgment," Smith wrote, "I was consulted and expressed an opinion only in the matter of the payment of the $100,000, which, as you know, I felt should be paid, as the good faith of the United States was involved."

Having said that, Smith explained that he would "try to arrange to have the pilot reject the $100,000 on the basis that his action was because of his own convictions and not for money." To keep the pilot from grumbling, Smith said the government could make him a "ward" of the National Committee for a Free Asia, which was secretly funded by the CIA. Smith said the committee "will give him the technical education he wishes and provide for his future to the extent of the reward which he would otherwise have received . . . I feel that there is real propaganda value in this."

This was precisely what Eisenhower wanted to hear. When he read Smith's memo, Eisenhower scribbled at the bottom, "Now we're clicking."

The CIA took over management of No Kum Sok when he flew away from Seoul. His agency handler, dressed in a light brown suit with a red tie, sat near No on the plane leaving Kimpo but did not introduce himself until they landed on Okinawa. The reason for the unannounced change of destination was safety, said the CIA man, who spoke Korean with a Russian accent and called himself Andy Brown. This, of course, was not true. The reason was Eisenhower.

After landing at Kadena Air Force Base, No and Brown rode in another Chevrolet to a guarded compound on the south end of Okinawa. The compound included about forty newly built bungalows. The one that became No's for his first nine days on the island was the most luxurious house he had ever slept in. It was painted bright yellow and had two bedrooms—one for No, one for Brown. There was a living room, a family room, and a spacious kitchen. The refrigerator was stocked with eggs, bacon, milk, ham, and soft drinks. When he first saw the bungalow from the Chevy, No saw what seemed to be thin horizontal bars on its windows and began to worry that he was about to be locked up. They turned out to be venetian blinds.

No's handler called himself Andy Brown. But his real name was Arseny Yankovsky, and, as the CIA later concluded, he might have played on both sides of the Korean War. Born in Vladivostok in 1914 to a rich, landed, and aristocratic family, Yankovsky had led a life shaped by revolution and war. The Bolshevik Revolution forced his family out of the Russian Far East into Japanese-occupied northern Korea, where White Russians hunted tigers and took their holidays on the seacoast. In the mid-1940s, the defeat of Japan and the Soviet occupation of North Korea again uprooted the family. Many family members were arrested, and some were sent to Siberia, where they died. But Yankovsky escaped south in 1948, walking across the thirty-eighth parallel and finding his way to Seoul. American intelligence was eager to hire a savvy operative who had contacts in the North and spoke Korean, Russian, Japanese, and English. As a Tokyo-based employee of the CIA, Yankovsky metamorphosed into Andy Brown and built a network of Korean agents. When the war began, he sent them to North Korea by air, land, and sea to gather military intelligence.

Most of his agents, however, were caught and executed. So many died so quickly that Brown came under suspicion as a Soviet double agent. As part of the CIA's mole hunt in the late 1950s, when Brown had moved to Washington, he was quietly fired by the agency, which then helped find him a job in the Far East as a public relations man for TRW, the aerospace firm. He lived in Tokyo and San Francisco until his death in 1978. His family has insisted that the CIA betrayed him, that he hated Communism, and that he was never a Soviet agent.

It would be several years before No learned Yankovsky's secrets. On Okinawa, he only knew what Andy Brown told him. On their second day together on the island, Brown told No to take a lie-detector test and never tell anyone that he had been ordered to take it. No agreed and was hooked up to the wires of a mysterious machine. Brown apologized for the unpleasant questions he was about to ask. They included the following.

"Have you ever had sex with a man?"

No truthfully answered that he had not.

"Do you drink alcohol?"

Trying to make a good impression, No lied. The machine caught him.

Brown laughed and congratulated No.

"Men are supposed to drink," he said. "If they don't, they're not men."

The rest of the test seemed to please Brown, as well as the other intelligence people who reviewed its results. No kept silent for forty-three years about the lie-detector test because of Brown's warning, and because he felt honor-bound to protect America's secrets.

Brown suggested that No change his name to Kenneth so that Americans would not have to call him Kum Sok. He agreed and learned to answer when people called him Ken and Kenny.

After the polygraph, he settled into a grueling routine of interrogation and language training. Four hours a day, five days a week, for six months he answered questions from a rotating cast of specialists serving in the air force, army, and navy. He tried his best to help the people he hoped would soon be his countrymen, but as the interrogations dragged on, his patience ran thin, especially when he was asked niggling questions that he could not answer, such as the thickness of runway concrete at airfields across North Korea and Manchuria. When the day's interrogations ended, English lessons began, also four hours a day, five days a week.

Some interrogations became field trips, as when an air force instructor-pilot went up seven times with No in a two-seat Lockheed T-33 Thunderbird jet trainer to find out how good a pilot the North Korean was.

His control of the throttle "was very smooth," and he was "capable of flying the aircraft in a satisfactory manner," the instructor found. But No was "an extremely cautious pilot, taking great care to keep from situations that might get him in any unusual attitude such as stalls . . . or that might lead to flight in bad weather." The air force concluded that his training was "definitely inferior" to that of the American pilots he had fought against. As a combat dogfighter, the air force concluded, No had received training that was "entirely inadequate for a strong offensive or defensive air force . . . That No could have destroyed any [enemy aircraft] the test pilot considered doubtful." This secret assessment was never passed on to No, but it more or less squared with his own evaluation of his chances when engaged in aerial combat with an American pilot flying a Sabre.

No became depressed on Okinawa. Partly, it was the long hours of interrogation; the Americans were nice but unremitting. Mostly, it was post-traumatic stress. Though he had stopped pretending to be a Communist, he still feared he would be found out as a faker and executed. He knew his fear was irrational, but it would not go away. He lost his appetite. He lost weight. He became anxious, especially about English. He was afraid he would never learn it, and furious that his best chance to master the language as a schoolboy in North Korea had been thwarted by Soviets and Kim Il Sung. Although he would eventually learn to speak English much better than Korean, his anger at being denied the language as a boy never went away.

Days after No and Brown moved into the yellow bungalow, they heard on Armed Forces Radio that No's mother was alive and looking for her son. Andy Brown translated the English broadcast: She had turned up at a South Korean army base in the southeastern city of Daegu, where she had been living for nearly three years. She had seen her son's photograph in the newspaper and wanted to be reunited with him. As proof, she showed the army officers a childhood photograph of No. She had lots of them. Among the few possessions she had managed to take with her as she fled North Korea was a family photo album.

No was overjoyed, as were U.S. Air Force intelligence officials. They soon turned No's reunification with his mother into another anti-Communist propaganda triumph, complete with a press conference in Seoul; a photo op with the South Korean president, Rhee, at his presidential mansion; and a custom-made navy blue double-breasted suit for No.

An air force transport plane flew No back to South Korea. But instead of taking him straight to his mother, the air force took him to the press conference.

The first question came from a South Korean reporter. He asked where No had found such a fine and fancy blue suit. Feeling vaguely ashamed, No said the Americans bought it for him.

After a few more questions, during which No again emphasized his eagerness to move to the United States, the air force sprang a made-for-media surprise. No's mother walked onstage. She was dressed for the press in traditional Korean garb, with a white blouse and a long white skirt. Cameras rolled as mother and son saw each other for the first time in four years. She was forty-two years old. No thought she looked older. He refrained from embracing her in front of the press. He would always resent how the American government milked publicity from what should have been a private moment. As for his mother, she seemed, at first, not to recognize the young man in the blue suit. She turned away for a moment, then studied his face and said, "My prayers have been answered."

When the press conference ended, No assured his mother that they would have dinner together that night. Then he was whisked away in a limousine to meet President Rhee, who told No that if he moved to the United States, he must return to South Korea and fight for Korean reunification. That night, in a private dinner at a hotel, No talked with his mother for about four hours and gave her $200 worth of South Korean currency. The Americans had given him the cash, with instructions that he give it to her.

Following orders, he left Seoul—and his mother—the next morning, boarded a transport plane back to Okinawa, and resumed his routine of interrogation and English lessons.

CHAPTER 13

Right Stuff and Fake Stuff

I

It was late evening inside the big hangar at Kadena Air Force Base on Okinawa, where American mechanics had put the MiG-15 back together. The test pilot Tom Collins, fresh from Ohio, sat in the cockpit. No leaned in toward Collins while standing on the fighter's left wing and explained the function of each switch and gauge on the instrument panel. Because No was speaking Korean, Andy Brown leaned into the cockpit while standing on the right wing, translating No's instructions into English. At least he tried to. His grasp of airplane lingo was not good. When Collins was finally satisfied that he understood what a gauge was for, he wrote down its functions in English on a strip of white tape and stuck it to the instrument panel. It was slow work.

As the three men labored on past midnight, they heard footsteps on the hangar's concrete floor. Chuck Yeager, dressed in his flight suit, had come to say hello. He jumped up on the MiG's right wing.

"Does he know who I am?" Yeager asked Collins, pointing at No.

"I don't know," Collins replied.

"Well, ask him," Yeager snapped.

"You ask him," Collins snapped back.

Yeager spoke to Brown.

"Will you tell him that I am Major Yeager and I am the first man to fly faster than the speed of sound?"

Brown tried his best, but he mangled it.

No had no awareness of Yeager's remarkable achievements as a World War II fighter ace or test pilot. He had never heard of the man. His CIA handler was of little help. Brown had never heard of Yeager either.

Yeager leaned into the cockpit and pointed to the Mach indicator on the instrument panel.

"Tell him I am the first man to fly faster than Mach 1."

Brown again did his best to translate terminology and concepts that he did not really understand. This time, though, a clear meaning jumped the gap between English and Korean. No's face lit up.

"Oh," he exclaimed, "you are Dr. Mach!"

Ernst Mach, an Austrian physicist and philosopher, first predicted and described the shock waves generated when a projectile reaches supersonic speed. No had learned about Dr. Mach in Manchuria during flight training. It slipped his mind that Dr. Mach, as of 1953, had been dead for thirty-seven years.

When the translation of No's excitement at meeting the great Austrian professor reached the great American test pilot, Yeager's face flushed. In his frustration, he, too, forgot that Mach was dead.

"No!" Yeager said. "Dr. Mach is very old and has a beard."

Again, No was puzzled.

Yeager then laughed, jumped off the wing, and walked away.

Collins, No, and Brown returned to the painstaking work of translating a MiG instrument panel into English.

After that awkward encounter, Yeager proved himself in No's eyes to be a gracious and curious man, not at all cocky or full of himself, exceedingly hardworking, and brave beyond belief. He and Collins both listened carefully to No's advice on how to fly the MiG. The pilots were under strict orders to steer clear of politics when talking to No. They could only ask him questions about technical and practical matters related to flying the MiG. As far as the world knew, No was not on Okinawa. He had "been taken under the wing of the top-secret Central Intelligence Agency at an undisclosed location," said a story in the *New York Times*.

Sometimes Yeager took No's advice, as when the North Korean explained the suicidal risk of intentionally putting the MiG into a spin. No told Yeager and Collins that in the event of a spin, they should push the control stick as far forward as possible toward a white line painted on the instrument panel. No warned that that alone would probably not be enough to save their lives. If the MiG does not recover after three spins, No told them, eject.

Perhaps because they had only one MiG, both pilots refrained from spinning it. "The Koreans probably lost more pilots spinning than from American guns," Yeager wrote. "So, spin testing was a big no-no." Collins put it this way: "Frankly, we lost our guts and didn't spin it."

But goosing the MiG to make it fly faster than the speed of sound— which No told them could not be done and which he advised against because the plane would be uncontrollable as it approached Mach 1— was irresistible to Yeager. He took the fighter up to fifty-five thousand feet for what he intended to be its first supersonic flight. From previous tests, Yeager knew that the plane pitched up its nose as it approached Mach 1. So he flipped the plane upside down and descended full throttle at a forty-five-degree angle. The MiG's aerodynamic tics wrenched it down into a nearly vertical dive.

The ride, as No had warned, was awful.

"The airplane was buffeting very bad," Yeager said in a postflight report that the air force kept secret for decades. None of the controls functioned, except for the throttle. "I was just riding; I couldn't any more guide it than I could a house. I kept going down. I didn't bother to use the dive brakes and kept full power on it."

At thirty thousand feet, the bucking MiG reached Mach .98, believed to be the fastest speed any MiG-15 had ever been flown.

Collins, flying a Sabre, had gone up with Yeager that day and was following him down. Seeing Yeager helpless, Collins managed to catch his eye and motioned with his right thumb, a signal for his colleague to eject.

Yeager ignored him.

At eighteen thousand feet, the MiG hit denser air. Suddenly it was shrouded in condensation. Yeager could not see anything when the MiG "started pulling out [of the dive] slowly by itself." At twelve thousand feet, it disappeared into storm clouds. At three thousand feet, Yeager was finally flying level, and he followed Collins back to Okinawa, where they landed in a blinding rain.

After eleven test flights, the verdict from Collins and Yeager was that the MiG-15 accelerated very nicely and had a high rate of climb, which made it a "usable weapon for high-altitude interception of bomber aircraft"—precisely what the honchos had done while shooting down B-29s.

But the test pilots also found that the plane's "handling qualities and Mach number limitations make it an inferior fighter-to-fighter weapon."

No had told the air force as much before Yeager and Collins began risking their lives. Forty-one years after that test, Collins and No met for an Operation Moolah reunion. Collins said then that No "gave me confidence . . . I always felt he was trying to do his very best to tell me about the airplane."

When the flight tests finished on Okinawa, air force mechanics again took the MiG apart and engineers studied its components in granular detail. Just in case the North Koreans or the Soviets asked for the plane back, the disassembled fighter was kept on Okinawa for five months. Having heard nothing from the "rightful owners," the air force brought the MiG to Wright-Patterson in early 1954 for two more years of test flights, many of them flown by Collins. After it was damaged in a hard landing in 1956, the fighter was donated to the National Museum of the U.S. Air Force near Dayton, where it remains on display next to a Sabre.

II

While Americans were testing the MiG that North Korea never acknowledged losing and did not want back, the Great Leader made public what his mythobiographers would later describe as his "immortal work of genius": the *juche* idea.

In a speech to party propagandists on December 28, 1955, Kim introduced the term *juche,* which means self-reliance. At the time, he was trying to distance North Korea from Soviet and Chinese influence. He needed nationalist window dressing for his continuing efforts to isolate and destroy Korean politicians with Soviet and Chinese backgrounds.

"We are not engaged in the revolution of another country but in our Korean revolution," Kim said. "Therefore, all ideological work without exception must be subordinated to the interests of the Korean revolution."

The Great Leader claimed in his memoirs that he first came up with the *juche* idea when he was seventeen and being held in prison in Manchuria by the Japanese. At times, he could be quite specific about what *juche* meant, saying that it means "solving one's problems for oneself on one's own responsibility under all circumstances."

But what was most brilliant about the *juche* idea was its ambiguity. The meaning seemed deliberately muddy. It was an infinitely adjustable ideological instrument that could be tuned and retuned over time to suit the Great Leader's autocratic needs. *Juche* reassured Koreans that they had once and for all overcome the humiliations of Japanese colonialism. *Juche* told the world North Korea would never again be a plaything of the great powers. As the cult of Kim grew more solipsistic and delusional, *juche* became an "assumption that Korea is the center of the world."

The *juche* idea, as it mutated, became what the Korea scholar Brian Myers has called a "jumble of banalities" that is dull, evasive, and hard to understand: "It recalls a college student trying both to stretch a term paper to a respectable length and to discourage anyone from reading it through." As such, *juche* became a decoy designed by Pyongyang to prevent the outside world from seeing the Kim family's true ruling ideology, which Myers describes as "paranoid nationalism" built on "an implacably xenophobic, race-based worldview."

Whatever conceptual mush *juche* would turn into, its literal meaning as self-reliance was spectacularly belied by the facts on the ground in

North Korea in the mid-1950s. At that time, aid and loans from socialist countries financed more than 80 percent of the country's imports. *Juche* notwithstanding, the Great Leader was a beggar. And he remained a beggar for decades because his priorities kept North Korea from building a sustainable economy. The country rarely generated enough growth to pay its bills. For nearly four decades, about half of the output from North Korean heavy industry was made possible by aid from Moscow. When the Soviet Union collapsed in the early 1990s, so did the handouts and so did North Korea's economy.

The *juche* idea, as implemented by Kim Il Sung, guaranteed that North Korea could never be self-reliant.

III

While No was helping Yeager and Collins test the MiG on Okinawa, the American government kept searching for ways *not* to pay the reward from Operation Moolah. In November 1953, as No began his second month of interrogations, Andy Brown asked No to star in another press conference in Seoul, where he would tell reporters that he did not want the $100,000. Brown vaguely explained that there had been some bureaucratic complications in arranging payment. He promised that the government would take good care of No once he moved to the United States.

"This doesn't mean you don't get the money," Brown said. "They will buy you a car and whatever you need."

No felt powerless to object. He had been sworn in on Okinawa as a U.S. government employee and was being paid $300 a month, which to him seemed like a fortune. With shopping privileges at the base exchange in Kadena, he could buy more clothes, food, and gadgets than he had ever imagined possible. He spent $250 on a fancy German-made Contax camera. He opened a savings account at the American Express office on the base. As for the reward money, No believed he was entitled to what the government had promised. But the Americans had taken charge of his life, and he felt they were taking good care of him. Compared with what it had been like in North Korea, life was great. But even if he had wanted to, he could not complain to the press. His whereabouts remained secret.

Two days after No landed the MiG at Kimpo, Eisenhower told his secretary of state, John Foster Dulles, to pay the reward "under some sort of trusteeship." The Departments of State and Defense chewed over that order for sixteen days. Then Dulles received a telephone call from Secretary of Defense Charles Wilson, who was worried that the Eisenhower administration would be "in trouble" if it did not pay the reward.

Dulles replied that Eisenhower had become concerned about the embarrassing possibilities of giving so much money to a Red defector. The president, Dulles said, "hoped that it would be paid in some kind of trust so that it would not be blown on 'wine, women and song.'"

Wilson feared something much worse: bad media coverage.

"The press has displayed continued interest in the payment of the reward," he told Dulles. "Once secrecy is removed [about No's whereabouts on Okinawa] it will not be practical or desirable to keep him from the press . . . [Reporters] might point out that his mother is a poor refugee . . . [The money] must be paid on a basis that can stand inspection by the press."

Dulles conceded the point. The two cabinet secretaries agreed that they would come up with "some kind of a thing that can be completely disclosed to the press." By the time it reached No in Okinawa, that "thing" was Andy Brown's request that No tell the world he did not want the money.

After No agreed to do exactly that, he heard nothing for several weeks. Brown finished his temporary assignment as No's handler and returned to his CIA office in Tokyo. In his absence, a revolving cast of U.S. government employees, civilian and military, American-born and foreign nationals, took turns teaching No how to think, speak, and eat like an American. He learned how to drive a jeep, write a personal check, and shop in a supermarket. He dined regularly at the homes of American families on the island. His stomach was trained to tolerate hot dogs and other American delicacies. At his first Thanksgiving dinner, he worried about the turkey, expecting it to taste like a tough old eagle, but discovered he liked it.

Nearly all his hosts and handlers advised him to attend an American university, although they hotly disagreed about which one would be best. No learned of the surpassing excellence of Brigham Young University from Lieutenant Reid Clark, a Mormon Sabre pilot from Utah. Clark strongly urged No to stop drinking coffee, give up Coke, and go to church.

No's social circle included Larry Wu-Tai Chin, a Chinese-born translator and analyst who worked on Okinawa for the Foreign Broadcast Information Service, a CIA-funded group that translated shortwave radio broadcasts. Chin often invited No to his home for dinner and questioned him about his life in North Korea, his ongoing interrogation, and his living conditions on Okinawa. No liked Chin, whose English was excellent, but found him a bit too curious and thought he seemed more Chinese than American. His doubts proved prescient. Chin was convicted in 1986 of having spied for more than three decades for the Chinese government, and he committed suicide in an American jail cell. He was apparently spying for China when No dined at his house.

For several weeks, No worried about the press conference at which he was supposed to reject the money. Brown then returned to Okinawa and told No that the generals in Tokyo had changed their minds, deciding that the U.S. government would look cheap if the press reported that No had been pressured to give up the $100,000.

Brown, though, did not clarify how—or if—the reward would be paid.

About a week later, No received a surprise crash course in money management, courtesy of the State Department, which dispatched a personal investment specialist from Foggy Bottom to Okinawa. The man, whose name No never caught, lectured No for several hours over three days. Through a translator, he told No that the reward was a once-in-a-lifetime opportunity that he should not waste. The financial adviser did not mention Eisenhower or his concerns, but insisted that No be cautious in his investment decisions. Stocks, bonds, and interest rates were, at the time, a complete mystery to No; he had no idea what the State Department man was talking about.

The headquarters of the Far East Command in Tokyo told the world on November 28, 1953, that No had been paid for Operation Moolah. A press release said he deposited his reward check in the American Express Bank on Okinawa. The military released a photograph of No standing at the bank's counter in his blue suit, signing a deposit slip as an attractive young woman, identified as bank clerk Flora Swinford, looked on approvingly.

"Lieutenant No has requested that the U.S. Air Force assist him in establishing a trust fund with the reward money for his education in the United States and for the care of his mother who is still in Korea," the release said.

No had made no such request. He did not know what a trust fund was. The air force had distributed the photograph and the press release in an attempt to stop reporters in Tokyo and Seoul—who still had no access to No on Okinawa—from asking any more questions about why the government had not paid the money.

The check No deposited that day was given to him by his handler at the time, Lieutenant Clark, the Mormon who was working for the 6002nd Air Intelligence Service Group. The check, though, was a phony. After his trip to the bank, the balance in No's account did not change. The air force never told him that his photo-op deposit was a sham.

By the late spring of 1954, No had spent half a year under interrogation. The Americans were running out of questions, and he was itching to go to the United States.

"His reading and writing ability in English was good," according to an air force report, "with comprehension and speaking ability fair."

But he could not travel. The Americans had not offered him citizenship, and he did not have a passport. Under South Korean law, all defectors from North Korea are automatically citizens of the South and entitled to a passport. The government in Seoul, though, refused to give one to No. It insisted that the headline-making young pilot come back to South Korea and go to work for its air force.

This was unacceptable to No. More than ever, he was obsessed with going to America. The Eisenhower administration, too, wanted him in the States, where it intended to parade him around as an anti-Communist hero. The Pentagon was negotiating an exclusive two-part, as-told-to story that would run in the *Saturday Evening Post* in October 1954 under the headline "I Flew My MiG to Freedom." The CIA, meanwhile, had secured No's admission in the fall as a freshman at the University of Delaware.

South Korea, which depended on American aid for postwar reconstruction, was pressured to back down on the passport, and it did. No arrived in San Francisco on May 4, 1954, where he held a press conference and Universal Pictures featured him in a newsreel that was shown in movie houses across the United States. In the newsreel, the narrator said that No would return to South Korea after a year of studying in the United States.

"Looking like an American Joe College in sports clothes and a pork-pie hat, he smiled broadly and spoke to newsmen in fairly good English," the Associated Press reported. "He said he would spend part of his reward money to study political science at the University of Delaware, part to support his mother who escaped to South Korea in 1950 and the rest to help rebuild South Korea."

But in San Francisco, No did not actually say the words reporters and the newsreel attributed to him. When he landed in the United States, he did not know how, when, or if he would get the reward money or what he would do with it. At the press conference in San Francisco, it was his official escort and translator, the army captain James Kim, who explained No's supposed plans. Without No's knowledge or approval, Kim answered reporters' questions in ways that suited the public relations interests of the Eisenhower administration. No never intended to move back to South Korea or send money to help rebuild that country, and he never told the press that he would do so.

CHAPTER 14

Learning and Purging

I

A week after coming to the United States—more than eight months after he stole the MiG—No finally learned what the Eisenhower administration was going to do with his moolah.

A bank vice president laid it out for him in the main office of Riggs National Bank on Pennsylvania Avenue in Washington. At the time, Riggs was the leading bank in the nation's capital. Eisenhower banked there, as did Vice President Richard Nixon, more than twenty previous presidents, and most of the city's embassies and diplomats. Riggs later marketed itself as "the most important bank in the most important city in the world." Its luster was eventually lost to scandals, mismanagement, and CIA-managed ties to unsavory governments, including that of the Chilean dictator Augusto Pinochet. Riggs disappeared in 2005 after a bank merger.

If No would sign the papers on the table in front of him, the banker said, then $100,000, tax-free, would be deposited in his name. There were a number of conditions. The money would go into a trust, and No would not have access to the principal, because the government worried he might spend it too fast and too frivolously. He would receive a onetime payment of $5,000 to help get him started in a new life, cover his housing, and pay school fees at the Newark campus of the University of Delaware. He would receive a monthly stipend of $250. The trust fund and its restrictions would remain in place for five years, with automatic renewal every five years unless No revoked it.

No still did not understand what a trust fund was. As he listened to the banker, he concluded that the Americans were trying to chisel him. Confused, suspicious, and seething, he refused to sign, walked out of the world's most important bank, and went back to his hotel room.

No had gone to Riggs with a three-man entourage. They included Arvin E. Upton, managing partner of the Washington office of a prestigious New York–based law firm, LeBoeuf, Lamb, Leiby & MacRae. Without No's knowledge or consent, the CIA had hired Upton as his personal lawyer and financial adviser. No later had to pay for the services of the lawyer the CIA had hired. The government also billed him for his hotel stay in Washington and his first-class transpacific flight to San Francisco. The second man at the bank was a CIA agent named Tony Chaikowski. He came to the bank carrying a check for $100,000 to be deposited—if No signed the trust agreement.

The third man was Captain Kim, the army escort and translator who had been with No since they left Okinawa. No had become friends with Kim, a gregarious Korean American who grew up in Los Angeles. Kim had come along when No flew from Okinawa to Seoul to see his mother in the fall of 1953. On their journey to San Francisco six months later, they stopped off in Guam, Wake Island, Manila, and Honolulu, where they had eaten well, visited tourist sites, and enjoyed each other's company.

Kim was someone No believed he could trust. He was not aware that the army captain had, during press conferences in San Francisco and again in Washington, put words in his mouth. In the Washington office of the U.S. Information Agency, where reporters were summoned when No arrived in the capital, Kim told reporters that No had "asked for a lawyer to set up a trust fund for the $100,000 he received for turning over the MiG." No denies this. Kim also told the press that whatever money remained after No had paid for his college education and provided for his mother "would go to the Korean people," which was not No's intention.

After arriving in Washington but before the meeting at Riggs National Bank, Kim had taken No up to Capitol Hill to introduce him to his high school classmate, House representative Joseph Holt, a Republican from Los Angeles and a longtime friend of Vice President Nixon's. After shaking hands, Holt announced that they would visit Nixon at his office in the Capitol. No had not been expecting to meet someone so important. He was ashamed of how he was dressed: corduroy jacket, skinny tie, brown plaid pants.

Nixon did not mind. He and No chatted amiably for ten minutes and had their picture taken together. No found Nixon to be friendly, dynamic, well-spoken, and surprisingly youthful, given that he was supposedly the second most important official in America. Nixon, then forty-one, asked what No planned to study in college. When No said political science, Nixon told him, "I hope you win all the elections," and sent him on his way. Two decades later, when Nixon was impeached and resigned from the presidency, No felt sorry for him.

While touring Capitol Hill, No was formally introduced at a House session and had a brief meeting with Speaker Joseph Martin, a Republican. He did not talk to Eisenhower that day or ever. For all his micromanaging of No's reward money or perhaps because of it, the president never asked to meet with No.

On the day of his unhappy encounter at Riggs National Bank, No went back to his hotel to brood about whether the U.S. government was trying to cheat him. He was free to grumble and complain. But he had very few, if any, options, other than to do what he was told. Cut off from his mother, he had no one to give him independent counsel. His friends, such as they were, were military officers and CIA agents. They were pleasant enough, but their loyalties were not to him. The only person No could talk to was Captain Kim, and Kim followed the government script.

After two days, No was persuaded that the trust fund was not a trick, and he walked back to the bank. Kim came along, as did the lawyer hired by the CIA and the CIA agent with the check. No signed the papers. In the fall of 1954, after he began classes at the University of Delaware, reporters continued to ask about the reward money and suggested in news stories that it had not been paid, which irritated the CIA. Agents told No to make it clear to newsmen that he had the money and he was happy about how it had all turned out. The Associated Press, the *New York Times*, and the *Saturday Evening Post* all reported—without qualification—that No was richer by $100,000.

No also began Americanizing his name, a process that would end with his becoming Kenneth H. Rowe. As a freshman at the University of Delaware, he was Kenny No. On the advice of the CIA, he briefly stopped talking to reporters, perhaps because the government had negotiated an exclusive with the *Saturday Evening Post* and it had not yet been published.

"He lived up well to the 'No' part of his name," said an Associated Press feature story that appeared in the *New York Times* in September 1954. "No pictures, no story, no comment."

II

Kim Il Sung spent a lot of time on the road in the 1950s.

North Korea's economy and food supply depended on aid. To keep it coming, Kim had to travel to Communist capitals, flash his big smile, and remind comrades of the wartime suffering inflicted on North Korea by the Americans. By far the longest such trip was in 1956, when he traveled to eight Eastern bloc countries and visited Moscow twice. He was away for seven weeks, from the beginning of June to July 19.

Dictators take a risk when they travel. Fear melts away. Discipline flags. Underlings get ideas. For Kim, the risk was particularly high in 1956, a time of food shortages and hunger in North Korea and of ideological ferment and political unrest across the Communist world. Stalin was three years dead, and Stalinism had become an embarrassment to nearly everyone except the Great Leader, who needed Stalinist repression as a shark needs teeth.

Khrushchev had energized reformers with his famous February screed against Stalin's "crimes" at a party congress in Moscow. Kim shrewdly declined to attend that meeting, but he could not (at that time) prevent many of his countrymen from noticing profound changes under way in the Soviet Union. The Kremlin was emptying the Soviet gulag, easing censorship, exploring "peaceful coexistence" with capitalists, experimenting with a consumer-led economy, and reinventing leadership as a collective enterprise. The cult of personality was passé. There would be no more godlike Stalins in Moscow. "Little Stalins" were being elbowed out of power in Bulgaria, Hungary, and Poland. In every Eastern bloc country except Albania (which would become a special friend to North Korea), political prisoners had been released.

It was a nerve-racking year for Kim. Before he arrived in Moscow, his own ambassador to the Soviet Union, Li Sang Jo, sabotaged Kim's trip by meeting with Soviet Foreign Ministry officials, dishing dirt about Kim's out-of-control cult of personality, and suggesting it be passed on to Khrushchev.

"Everything is decided by Kim Il Sung alone," Li complained. "The people around Kim Il Sung fawn over him."

Kim's government was giving propaganda a bad name, the ambassador added.

"Day after day this propaganda tries to convince the people of the considerable increase in their standard of living, which in reality isn't there," Li said. "As a result, the people might stop believing such propaganda, which is divorced from reality, and it can cause irritation and unrest."

Reality was indeed grim. Hungry North Koreans had been leaving farms in search of food; hospitals were treating malnourished people for eating grass.

One thing that particularly irked Li—and which he repeatedly complained about to the Soviets—was Kim's fantasy rewrite of history, which had turned a national museum on the history of the Communist revolution in Korea into a museum on the mostly made-up history of the Great Leader.

"When the participants of the revolutionary movement in Korea see that all the efforts are ascribed to one man, Kim Il Sung, they have a feeling of bewilderment," Li said.

When Kim arrived in Moscow two months later, his ambassador had poisoned the Communist well. The party's Central Committee scolded Kim for "improper behavior." Soviet officials, including Khrushchev, ordered him to roll back his cult of personality. Having come to Moscow for handouts, Kim was in no position to push back. He conceded the "correctness of the comradely advice in the presence of fraternal leaders."

When he returned home in July, de-Stalinization had spread, infecting the Central Committee of the North Korean Workers' Party. North Korea had not yet been sealed off from the outside world. Foreign newspapers were on sale. News about anti-Communist uprisings in Eastern Europe was printed in the Korean-language press. Government officials in Pyongyang met relatively freely with diplomats from the Soviet Union and China, and Koreans who had lived in those countries were particularly attuned to reforms going on elsewhere. Some of them could no longer bear the Great Leader, and they thought even less of his thuggish and ill-educated partisan buddies, who, they complained, were taking all the best government jobs.

"Kim Il Sung's personality cult has obtained an intolerable character," said Yi Pil Gyu, head of the Department of Construction in Kim's cabinet and a former fighter in China for Mao. It was July 20, 1956, a day after Kim returned from Europe, and Yi was sitting inside the Soviet embassy in Pyongyang, telling the acting Soviet chargé d'affaires, A. M. Petrov, that he and other Central Committee members "consider it necessary" to force Kim to change his ways. Yi said that he and other disgruntled cadre members would use "sharp and decisive criticism within the party" or, if need be, "forcible upheaval."

Petrov was a sympathetic listener, having watched as Kim's farm policies caused the food crisis. The Soviet diplomat had told a Hungarian colleague that Kim "is surrounded by bootlickers and careerists . . . Whatever is said by the leader, they accept it without any dispute." Petrov believed that Kim's cult of personality was "a primary and decisive factor in every mistake" made by the government.

Yi and other malcontents—several of whom had briefed Soviet diplomats on what they were up to—decided to take on the Great Leader at a plenum of the Central Committee in August. Nothing so brazen had been attempted before. They accused Kim of concentrating too much power in his own hands. They denounced the incompetence of his guerrilla cronies and charged that his policies were starving the masses.

Kim had excellent spies and was not taken by surprise. The majority of members on the Central Committee were his loyalists and had been prepped to vote against whatever the critics might propose. By most accounts, the challenge amounted to little more than harsh words and never came remotely close to using or even advocating the use of violence to implement change. Nonetheless, Kim crushed those who dared grumble. Some were expelled from the party; others were arrested. In weeks, months, and years to come, nearly everyone who participated in the "August group" (along with anyone suspected of anti-Kim thoughts or sympathies) was purged from the government and, in many cases, executed without trial. To save their necks, many Koreans with Chinese and Soviet backgrounds fled the country.

As Kim's official biographer explained, the events of August 1956 "failed to disturb Comrade Kim Il Sung . . . Rather, it was the traitors to the revolution who had reason to be terrified . . . Foolishly enough, treacherous people were frantically engaged in efforts to organize clandestine intrigues in order to destroy the Party and the revolution."

Moscow and Beijing were not happy when they learned that Kim had not kept his promise to behave more "correctly." They particularly did not approve of his persecution of Soviet- and China-born Koreans for advocating reforms that were being pursued across the Communist world.

In a move without precedent, the Soviet Union and China sent a joint delegation to Pyongyang to straighten Kim out. It was Mao's idea, according to one Soviet official. Mao "began to complain about Kim Il Sung, saying that he was such and such a person, that he had launched that idiotic war, that he was a mediocrity, and that it was necessary to dismiss him."

The two men leading the delegation were, by any measure, formidable.

From Moscow came Anastas Mikoyan, a wily Bolshevik who had managed to thrive under Lenin and Stalin and then helped Khrushchev write the fiery speech that branded Stalin as a murderer. Mikoyan had become a post-Stalinist fixer, the go-to guy for dealing with big egos in small countries. Over the summer he had been in Budapest, where he helped remove from power a presumptuous "Little Stalin" named Matyas Rakosi. He had also been to Warsaw with Khrushchev to push Stalinists out of power and install a leader more suitable to the Kremlin. Mikoyan had close blood ties to the Soviet military-industrial complex. His brother helped design the MiG.

From Beijing came Peng Dehuai, the famous Chinese general who loathed Kim and whose army had saved North Korea from the Americans. Throughout the Korean War, Peng had shown contempt for what he saw as Kim's incompetence and childish behavior.

When they arrived at the train station in Pyongyang, Kim did not come to meet them. He knew they were trouble. As he later told an Albanian diplomat, "Mikoyan and Peng Dehuai, etc. [arrived] with bad intentions to meddle in our internal affairs."

That meddling compelled Kim to de-Stalinize himself and North Korea—or so it seemed for a short time.

Under the watchful eyes of Mikoyan and Peng, Kim was pressured to convene another plenum of the Central Committee in September, at which he agreed to un-purge the people he had just purged in August. He also agreed to refrain from wholesale purges in the future.

For a few months, Kim kept his word. Many of his harshest critics got their jobs back. There was a noticeable thaw in censorship. But Kim reneged on a promise to publish an account of his incorrect behavior as it had been exposed at the party plenum in September. He never allowed the North Korean people to know that two powerful men had come to Pyongyang from Moscow and Beijing to put him in his place—or that he had agreed to do as he was told.

The Soviet and Chinese archives have not yet revealed why Mikoyan and Peng did not simply sack Kim and replace him with someone more malleable and less Stalin-like. Historians disagree as to whether the delegation was ever authorized to do so. A reason for the delegation's indecision seems to have been Mikoyan's unfamiliarity with East Asia and Korea. He had no understanding of the country and no connections in Pyongyang. Unlike in Hungary, there were no street demonstrations by which to gauge the unpopularity of Kim's government. The North Korean People's Army had made sure of that.

Kim was also lucky.

He was bailed out in October 1956 by a bloody revolution in Hungary, where protesters took de-Stalinization to its logical conclusion. In a spontaneous nationwide uprising, the Hungarians toppled the Soviet-imposed government, organized themselves into militias, and tried to force Soviet troops out of the country. This was not the kind of reform Khrushchev had in mind. After hesitating briefly, he and other Kremlin leaders crushed the uprising. Soviet forces killed more than twenty-five hundred Hungarians. A new chill gripped the cold war, and reform froze across the Communist world.

The Great Leader could not have been more pleased. He now had the perfect excuse for sticking with Stalinism. There would be no risky "revisionism" on his watch. By the end of 1956, Kim's Propaganda Department boasted, in effect, "I told you so." The Hungarian government fell, it said, because naive comrades had foolishly followed the Soviets' reform agenda off a cliff, rather than wielding the tried-and-true tools of Stalinism, including a cult of personality.

As important to his survival was the widening split between China and the Soviet Union. Kim's patrons in Moscow and Beijing had begun to bicker and would continue to do so for decades. The Soviet Union and China still gave Kim loans and weapons, food and fuel, and they still bought his country's shoddy goods. But never again would they work together to try to roll back his appetite for cruelty, vengeance, and murder. As he later explained to a visiting Albanian, "Those who [had] the intention of cutting off my head . . . were forced to leave empty-handed and the right remains with us."

III

In a photograph taken on the steps of a campus building at the University of Delaware, Kenny No is a twenty-two-year-old freshman, impeccably dressed in a white shirt and tie, sitting with four other students. He looks younger than the others, and he looks happy. But the picture is not representative of his first years in the United States, which were lonely and difficult. He found it all but impossible to reconcile the trauma of his wartime past with the calm of his on-campus present. His placid days of study ended with fitful nights of dreaming about betrayal and death.

He also worried constantly that he would flunk out and be forced to leave the United States. He had told Richard Nixon he would study political science, but that was a fib. The calculus and physics he had studied back in Hungnam Chemical College—combined with his facility for mathematics and his experience as a pilot—made engineering much easier than political theory. Back in the naval academy in North Korea, he had been allowed only two hours a day for study, which was never enough time to master his course work. But at the University of Delaware, he could study as many hours as his dark moods would allow.

He struggled mightily with American English. To nail down slang, he memorized by rote the meaning of phrases that made no logical sense: "throw the book at him," "get a kick out of it," and "look up a girl."

During his third year of college, after he had more or less conquered English, No accepted an invitation to travel to Niagara Falls to deliver a speech to the Aero Club of Buffalo. There, he ran into the air force captain Cipriano Guerra, the Sabre pilot who watched No land his MiG the wrong way at Kimpo and who was the first American to shake his hand. After their speeches, No learned that Guerra—fearing MiG guns—almost killed him with .50-caliber machine-gun fire. The fighter pilots laughed about the misunderstanding and talked on and on about flying, fighting, and war. The trip to Buffalo launched a lifelong avocation for No and introduced him to a group of American peers who understood what it meant to go to war at six hundred miles an hour. He met air force fighter pilots all over the United States for dinners, conferences, and visits to flight museums (especially the one in Ohio that houses his MiG). The pilots embraced him as one of their own, and they became close friends.

Having enjoyed his velvety rides in a Chevrolet on Okinawa, No bought a new two-door turquoise Chevy from a Delaware dealer for $2,250. He haggled over the price for two weeks. CIA agents, who kept watch over him at college, congratulated him for getting a good buy. No became friends with several of these agents, who tended to be older men in their forties and fifties with wives and kids. They invited him to their homes and introduced him to their families. He stayed in touch with many of them after they retired from the agency, and he attended their funerals.

While agents from the CIA were good to him, the agency itself refused to help No secure permanent residence status in the United States or become a citizen. The agency told him that the federal government did not want to upset the South Korean government, which wanted No to come back there to live. So every six months he had to renew his visitor visa. After nearly two years of wrestling with red tape at the immigration office, No went to the home of a favorite professor, Dr. John Munroe, head of the history department, to ask for help. Delaware is a small state, and the professor was friendly with the politicians who ran it. He picked up the phone and called the U.S. senator J. Allen Frear Jr., who a week later introduced a bill that said, "No Kum Sok (also known as Kenneth No) shall be held and considered to have been lawfully admitted to the United States for permanent residence." The Senate and the House quickly approved the bill, Eisenhower signed it, and No's visa problems were over.

Becoming an American citizen was not as easy. No had spent half a year telling his life story to American intelligence agencies, but immigration examiners insisted on rehashing much of it, including why he had joined the North Korean Workers' Party. The long, mind-numbing process dragged on for six years. In 1962, he finally became a citizen.

Before he had sorted out his own immigration status, No began trying to bring his mother to the United States. Her request for a visa was denied because she was poor and could not prove that she intended to return to South Korea. Two attempts by Delaware lawmakers in the

House and the Senate to pass bills to bring No's mother to the States failed.

Her dilemma was resolved by the Hungarian Revolution, the same uprising that helped Kim Il Sung keep his Stalinist teeth.

By gunning down people in the streets, the Soviet crackdown in Hungary triggered a refugee crisis in central Europe. To help out, Congress passed the Refugee-Escapee Act of 1957, which admitted twenty-nine thousand refugees who had faced persecution in Communist countries. Most were Hungarians, but North Korean refugees also qualified. With the help of the State Department and congressmen from Delaware, No's mother was the first person to arrive in the United States under the new law, and her reunion with her son was deemed newsworthy enough to be filmed and shown in a newsreel in American movie houses. No met her in Seattle, escorted her to a welcoming ceremony in Washington, and then brought her back to Delaware, where he was about to graduate with a degree in engineering and go to work for the DuPont company in Wilmington.

Not long after No's mother arrived, she began searching—as Korean mothers compulsively do—for a suitable wife for her son. With the help of two Korean-born Catholic priests, she found a young South Korean woman who would soon become Clara Rowe. She was born in Kaesong, a city near the border that separates the two Koreas. During the war, her family was trapped in Seoul for three months under North Korean army occupation. Her older brother was taken to the North and never heard from again. But she, her mother, and two younger siblings were liberated by American marines and taken to Pusan, where they lived until the end of the war. There, she found a job with Catholic Relief Services, an American charity, which provided her with connections that allowed her family to emigrate to New York City in 1958. She was working for Catholic Relief Services in an office on the sixty-fifth floor of the Empire State Building—the skyscraper No had seen in his pre-escape dreams—when she was introduced to her future husband.

While making wedding plans in 1959, No heard from Andy Brown (a.k.a. Arseny Yankovsky), the translator and CIA agent he met on

Okinawa. Brown had moved to Washington and was still working for the CIA, although he would soon be fired on suspicion of being a Soviet double agent. He invited No to come down to Washington for the weekend, where they met on a Saturday morning at the Lincoln Memorial.

At lunch, Brown congratulated No for being such a successful defector. Then Brown uncorked his own incredible life story as a White Russian on the run, which No was hearing for the first time. He described his flight from the Reds in the Russian Far East and again from North Korea after Soviet troops marched in. He told No that he killed a Russian soldier with a hammer and changed into the dead man's uniform as part of his escape to South Korea.

When Brown finished his tale, he asked No about the reward money from Operation Moolah and invited him to travel to Taiwan, where No could invest in several surefire business opportunities. As he listened, No remembered the advice Brown had given him back on Okinawa: beware of Americans who could be thieves. Brown seemed not to know that the reward money was in a trust account and would remain there for years. Kenny No politely ignored the offer and never again saw Andy Brown.

EPILOGUE

I

When Kim Il Sung outmaneuvered his would-be overseers from Moscow and Beijing in the autumn of 1956, he was still a youngish dictator, just forty-four. He enjoyed another four decades of vigorous good health, during which leaders in China and the Soviet Union (later Russia) did nothing to contain his increasingly preposterous cult of personality or stop him from using Stalin's tool kit of repression. After the Korean War, the United States maintained a large military presence in South Korea, about twenty-eight thousand troops in 2014, as deterrence against another attack from the North. Washington tried and mostly failed to restrain Pyongyang's development of long-range missiles and nuclear weapons. But the U.S. government paid little attention to what Kim did to his own people.

In the late 1950s, Kim expanded the scope and severity of his Stalinist purges, punishing about a hundred thousand ordinary people suspected of being "hostile and reactionary elements." Some were executed without a trial. As the world has learned in recent years from defectors and satellite photographs, he also built a vast network of labor camps for political prisoners. Hundreds of thousands of "wrong thinkers" and their families have perished in this gulag, which continues to operate, cleansing society of those who pose a risk to "Kim Il Sung nation." In the camps, guards breed prisoners like farm animals and then raise the resulting children to be slaves and snitches unaware of the outside world. Guards have license to murder, rape, starve, and torture prisoners without consequence.

Kim also created a caste system that ranked the entire population based on perceived political reliability. The "core" class lived close to him in the capital, Pyongyang, where they had access to government jobs and plenty to eat. They and their heirs became the elite. The "wavering" and "hostile" classes were shipped off to the countryside, where access to food was unreliable.

Kim borrowed, too, from the madness of Mao, imitating the Great Leap Forward and forcing the entire population to do unpaid labor. By the end of 1958, the Chollima movement (named for a flying horse of Korean legend) required North Koreans to do up to five hours of work a day, pulling weeds, digging ditches, and building roads. This forced labor was tacked on at the end of an eight-hour workday. These "campaigns" continue up to the present day, with urban residents sent every year to the countryside to plant seed, spread fertilizer (often human excrement, as chemical fertilizer is frequently in short supply), and harvest crops on cooperative farms.

As the Great Leader expanded the machinery of repression, he narrowed his intellectual base, closed his circle of advisers, and supercharged his cult of personality. Cartoonish histories of Kim and his partisans in Manchuria became required texts for indoctrination sessions in the late 1950s. In a country that then had about ten million residents, nearly a hundred million of these books were printed. As the status of the "guerrilla state" grew, the role of the Soviet Union and China in creating, arming, and defending the country was excised from public memory.

The reality was that Kim had entered North Korea in 1945 with only about 130 guerrilla comrades who had fought with him in Manchuria. Having come of age in a murderous civil war, these men were unschooled, conspiratorial, and ruthless. Outside his family, they were the only people the Great Leader ever trusted. Starting in the late 1950s and continuing until their deaths, they dominated the party's ruling Central Committee and held the most important jobs in the government. After they died, their children and grandchildren took over, as the government became increasingly inbred, caste based, xenophobic, Kim-centric, and corrupt.

The guerrillas and their children were largely incompetent as stewards of the economy, presiding with the Kim family over a collapse of the country's industrial base (excepting weapons production), the deterioration of infrastructure, and a declining ability to grow food or buy it from the outside. In the late 1990s, after the old Soviet Union disappeared and Russia cut off subsidies, about a million North Koreans starved to death. It was a rare peacetime famine in an industrialized state.

In the final four decades of his life, Kim's self-glorification and taste for luxury grew rapidly, like an untreated and aggressive tumor. An estimated thirty-four thousand monuments to his wonderfulness had been erected by the 1980s. He had at least five palaces. His birthday became the most important public holiday. When he traveled, his aides brought along a special toilet equipped to analyze the character of his stool. On penalty of being sent to the labor camps, all North Koreans were required by his government to celebrate his genius. Adults were obligated to wear his picture on their lapels, hang his portrait in their houses, and build (or at least pretend to build) their emotional and intellectual lives around "burning loyalty to the Leader."

For all his egotism, cruelty, and incompetence, Kim's populist touch lasted as long as he did. He traveled frequently around North Korea, giving guidance at factories, posing with children, and smiling his fatherly smile—and being photographed while doing so. These photographs never showed an unsightly, baseball-sized, inoperable calcium growth visible on the right back of his neck since the 1970s. The growth, called a *hok* in Korean, is often caused by poor childhood nutrition. Photographs also failed to capture what eyewitnesses said was his eye-popping obesity. Sidney Rittenberg, an American who worked as a translator in Mao's China, recalls being "astounded by the sight" of Kim in the Great Hall of the People in Beijing. "I have never seen a public figure so fat, his vast round stomach blending seamlessly into a thick jowly neck. He looked nothing like his pictures."

When he died peacefully in 1994, at age eighty-two, millions of North Koreans wept for weeks. His corpse, like those of Lenin, Mao, and Ho Chi Minh, was specially embalmed and put on public display under glass. By the time he died, North Korea was on the brink of collapse, with mass starvation soon to sweep the country. The Great Leader's competition with South Korea had been lost: an average South Korean salaryman lived a more comfortable life than all but a few of the elite in Pyongyang.

Yet if greatness is measured by a leader's enduring stamp on a country, Kim is perhaps the greatest of the past century. No totalitarian state has survived as long as the one he invented, and only his became a family dynasty. In a sense, he and his heirs have succeeded in stopping time itself.

Kim's grandson Kim Jong Un, in an attempt to legitimize his rule, has gone to extraordinary lengths to look like the Great Leader, with a porcine physique, a Mao suit, and a military haircut with no sideburns. His uncanny facial resemblance to his grandfather is widely attributed to plastic surgery. Even Kim Jong Un's wife bears a resemblance to his grandfather's first wife.

Kim Jong Un also has the family knack for purging. He ordered the killing of his uncle Jang Song Thaek for "dreaming different dreams and involving himself in double-dealing behind the scenes." Since he took over from his father in 2011, Kim Jong Un's speeches have echoed classic Great Leader themes, calling for "absolute trust, single-minded unity, and monolithic leadership." His denunciations of his enemies sound as if they had fallen from the lips of his grandfather: "The United States and other hostile forces, ignoring our magnanimity and goodwill, are viciously stepping up their maneuvers in order to annihilate our republic politically, isolate it economically, and crush it militarily."

Kim Jong Un was not yet thirty when he became leader, but he quickly mastered the family recipe for wielding power. It blends Stalinism with militarism that frightens the masses with warnings that American bombers will return unless North Korea arms itself to the teeth and citizens prepare for the worst.

When Kim Il Sung died—and again in 2011 when Kim Jong Il died—outside experts predicted that the Kim family would lose its grip. Yet as Kim Jong Un steps into his grandfather's shoes, the foundations of the family dynasty remain in place. China supports and subsidizes North Korea as a buffer between itself and a South Korea closely allied with the United States. Pyongyang continues to develop potent military capabilities—nuclear weapons, intercontinental ballistic missiles, legions of special forces—that make it a formidable enemy, especially as viewed from South Korea and Japan, where any conflict could produce hundreds of thousands of casualties. Finally, the Kim family has lost none of its capacity for cruelty to its own people. The border with China has become harder to cross since Kim Jong Un came to power. Recent satellite photographs show new construction in the political labor camps.

Americans, meanwhile, remain largely ignorant of the mass death and vast devastation that their air force caused during the Korean War—and of the bogeyman role that they continue to play inside North Korea. As a forgetful superpower, the United States often gives the Kim family exactly what it needs to whip up anti-American hysteria and legitimize itself. When Kim Jong Un was making noisy but empty threats to bomb the United States in the spring of 2013, the U.S. Air Force responded by flying nuclear-capable B-2 stealth bombers over the Korean Peninsula.

II

Ken and Clara Rowe were married in New York City in 1960. They soon had three children, two boys and a girl. Their daughter, Bonnie, became a lawyer, concert musician, and music teacher in Toledo, Ohio. Their elder son, Raymond, is mentally handicapped and works at a rehabilitation center in Daytona Beach, Florida. Their younger son, Edmund, became an aerospace engineer, like his father.

In raising his family and organizing his life, Rowe has been profoundly influenced by what he learned during his first six months on Okinawa. His interrogators and minders told him to immerse himself in American culture and not to associate with Korean people. It was easy advice to follow when he arrived in the United States, as there were few Koreans to associate with. But after immigration law changed in the mid-1960s, South Korea became one of the top five countries of origin for immigrants coming to America. The number of people of Korean descent surged to 1.7 million, making the United States second only to China as a destination for Koreans living outside the Korean Peninsula.

By then, living apart from Koreans had become a habit for Rowe, influencing his choice of friends, employment, and housing. He stayed away from big Korean communities and did not read Korean newspapers or books, and his children did not grow up speaking Korean in the house or anywhere else. They do not understand the language, which Rowe rarely speaks to his wife. Neither he nor his wife eats much Korean food. Rowe has no regrets for moving so far away from his language and culture. He thought and dreamed about escaping to America almost from the moment the Soviet army marched into Korea, and he regards his distance from all things Korean as a measure of his success.

A notable exception to all this is television. South Korean soap operas have hooked Rowe's wife and his daughter, and he watches South Korean historical dramas. The programs, which are well made and wildly popular across East Asia, showcase impossibly beautiful Korean women and handsome Korean men. In the soaps, nearly everyone is rich, adulterous, driving fast cars, and living in fabulous houses. To understand the plots, the Rowes watch programs that have English subtitles.

Rowe had a long, successful, and peripatetic career. After DuPont, he found jobs at Boeing and General Dynamics. After becoming an American citizen in 1962, he obtained a security clearance for work on government weapons systems. Then, as a contract engineer, a position that allowed him to make considerably more money, he worked at General Electric, General Motors, Lockheed, Grumman, Westinghouse, and Pan American Airways. He moved often and lived everywhere from San

Diego to Seattle to Saudi Arabia. Near the beginning of his career, he taught engineering for two years at the University of North Dakota in Grand Forks. At the end, he taught thermodynamics for seventeen years at Embry-Riddle Aeronautical University in Daytona Beach, a school that *Time* magazine has called the "Harvard of the sky." He retired there at age sixty-eight, six years after the Great Leader died.

To keep fit in his eighties, Rowe gets up at 5:15 every morning, walks a mile, and does calisthenics, including sixty push-ups. He cut back to sixty when he was in his seventies, after having done a hundred push-ups every day since his time at the North Korean Naval Academy. Rowe keeps his hands and forearms strong with the help of a pair of spring-loaded hand grippers, squeezing each one a hundred times a day. Over the years he has worn out these grippers while they were still under warranty. When he returned them to a sporting goods store for free replacements, a clerk told him it had never happened before.

Rowe's mother, who came to America in 1957, lived with her son until his marriage to Clara. Then she followed Ken as he and his family moved from city to city, renting a nearby apartment and visiting them two or three times a week for the rest of her life. She never learned much English and spent several months a year back in South Korea visiting friends. Rowe and his mother got along well, except when they talked about religion. His mother was a devout Catholic, especially later in life. Rowe had turned away from religion in middle school in North Korea; it was the only Communist teaching that ever stuck. Rowe's mother died in Daytona Beach in 2004 at age ninety-three, having spent more than half her life in the United States.

After settling in America, Rowe was reluctant to return to South Korea; he worried about safety. In 1968, thirty-one North Korean commandos attacked the presidential residence in Seoul, killing sixty-eight South Koreans before they were all tracked down. Pyongyang has also sent assassins to Seoul to try to kill prominent defectors. Rowe waited until 1970 to travel to Seoul for the first of half a dozen visits. On that first trip, with the help of the South Korean air force, he met four other defectors who had escaped North Korea in military aircraft. It was from one of them that he learned—seventeen years after the fact—of the vengeance that the North Korean government had taken for his escape. His best friend, Lieutenant Kun Soo Sung, was executed in 1953, along with four other air force officers.

Rowe had often dreamed about Kun before he returned to Korea. In those dreams, the two young pilots looked at each other but never spoke. When Rowe learned that his friend was dead, he was saddened and angry. But seventeen years had gone by, too much time for him to be overwhelmed by guilt. After he learned of the execution, he stopped dreaming about Kun. He never dreamed about Uncle Yoo.

Twenty years after he first went to Riggs National Bank in Washington, Rowe revoked the trust fund from Operation Moolah. He wanted to invest his money a bit more aggressively than Riggs had done. Since 1974, his investments of the original $100,000 reward—combined with savings from his earnings as an engineer—have made him a multimillionaire. Although he keeps most of his money in conservative mutual funds, he enjoys playing the stock market and every year makes a few trades.

It took sixty-one years before Rowe learned—from the author of this book—of the presidential fingerprints on Operation Moolah. Rowe now believes the trust fund that Eisenhower insisted on helped keep his windfall safe while he learned how to manage money. Still, there was never a risk he would squander it. He is not a frivolous spender. He and his wife have lived for thirty years in a modest three-bedroom Daytona Beach tract house. For decades he mowed his own lawn, pruned his shrubs, and sharpened the blades on his lawn equipment. In 2014, he finally hired a lawn service because of his age.

Rowe is grateful for the U.S. government's help in making him rich. But it still irritates him that he was called Moolah Man. More maddening was the assumption that he stole the MiG out of a desire for money. As a free man in the land of his childhood dreams, he believes he needed no one's help to become successful.

In the fall of 2008, Rowe received devastating news about his son Edmund, who had worked for nineteen years as an engineer at Robins

Air Force Base in Georgia. Edmund shot his wife with a .45-caliber revolver and then shot himself. The shootings occurred on September 21, the anniversary of his father's escape from North Korea.

When a Georgia newspaper reporter telephoned Rowe to ask about the deaths, he said he was so shocked he could not think straight. His forty-two-year-old son was newly married. "I thought everything was going well," he said.

Since the shootings, Rowe and his wife have continued to grieve. They did not approve of their son's marriage to a thirty-five-year-old base secretary who was less educated than Edmund. The wedding took place four months before the shooting, and they did not attend. Edmund, who was an avid gun collector, left no note to explain what happened or why. Rowe does not know the significance, if any, of the date of the shootings. He thinks it is probably a coincidence that his son died fifty-five years to the day after his escape.

During his first decades in the United States, Rowe never imagined that the land of his birth would become a Stalinist kingdom. When Kim Il Sung died, Rowe expected the regime to die with him. It seemed possible that the Korean Peninsula could be united under a democratic government, which he hoped to be able to visit. Like most expert outside observers of North Korea, he assumed that at the very least the North's political system would evolve in some fundamental way. It had happened in the Soviet Union after Stalin and in China after Mao. So when Kim's son Kim Jong Il became the leader in 1994 and North Korea stumbled on as a totalitarian state, Rowe was sick with disappointment.

When Kim Jong Un took over in 2011 and began imitating the Great Leader, Rowe's disappointment turned to disgust. He believes Kim Jong Un is worse than his father or grandfather—and much less intelligent. Nothing will change, Rowe has concluded, until the North Korean people find a way to rise up. But he knows, too, that the Kim family will imprison or kill all those who try.

If Rowe had stayed on, he believes, he would have been executed by the government for his mother's flight to South Korea or died of starvation in the 1990s famine. He has never regretted his decision to fly away.

ACKNOWLEDGMENTS

Out of the blue, Kenneth Rowe telephoned me at my home in Seattle in November 2012. He said he had just read my book about a North Korean prison camp escapee, and asked if I had ever heard of No Kum Sok and the MiG he stole from North Korea in 1953. I had not and told him so. He laughed a little and suggested I should be better informed.

After a few weeks of remedial education, which included reading his 1996 memoir, *A MiG-15 to Freedom*, I called him back and apologized. I asked if he would allow me to tell the story of his defection in a book that also chronicled the rise of Kim Il Sung and explained the ferociousness of U.S. Air Force bombing during the Korean War. He liked the idea and agreed to help. Rowe is a patient man with a phenomenal memory. Both traits were sorely tested in writing this book, and I am grateful for his constant support.

A few months before Rowe contacted me, the U.S. government decided to declassify a large cache of air force intelligence reports on No Kum Sok. They had been kept secret for fifty-nine years. Rowe did not know that they existed. It is good to be lucky. The documents proved essential in jogging his memory, unearthing new details, and confirming his story.

ACKNOWLEDGMENTS

Luck would have meant nothing, though, without an assist from the National Archives in College Park, Maryland. The reports were in two dusty boxes, part of a huge and sketchily catalogued series of air force intelligence records from the Korean War. Timothy K. Nenninger, chief of the textual records reference branch at the archives, and reference archivist Eric van Slander found them and made them available to me. Before they did their detective work, Carl Gershman, president of the National Endowment for Democracy, put me in touch with the Archivist of the United States David S. Ferriero, who manages the National Archives. Ferriero expedited my request. Also invaluable was the help of Joseph S. Bermudez, who made available his collection of declassified air force documents about No Kum Sok, his flying skills, and air force testing of the purloined MiG.

The fog of lies, disinformation, and propaganda surrounding Kim Il Sung's rise to power has lifted in recent years because of work by scholars and researchers with access to government archives in Moscow and Beijing. They have found (and translated into English) diplomatic cables and transcripts of personal conversations that detail the role of Stalin and Mao in enabling Kim's invasion of South Korea and in saving him from his incompetence. I am deeply indebted to this scholarship, much of which is available online from the Cold War International History Project at the Woodrow Wilson International Center for Scholars in Washington. My primary guide to these sources has been Kathryn Weathersby, who has done groundbreaking research on the Korean War in the Soviet archives and is a visiting scholar at the U.S.-Korea Institute at the Johns Hopkins School of Advanced International Studies. She generously shared her papers (published and not-yet published), her expertise, and her time. Adam Cathcart, a lecturer at the University of Leeds and expert in many things Chinese and Korean, jump-started this book by telling me where to look for sources and scholars, giving me a box of books that turned out to be essential, and offering encouragement. In trying to understand Kim Il Sung, I am deeply indebted to the research, analyses, and clear writing of a legion of eminent experts on

Korea, including Andrei Lankov, Shen Zhihau, Evgenijy P. Bajanov, Natalia Bajanova, Balázs Szalontai, Bradley K. Martin, Sheila Miyoshi Jager, Sergei N. Goncharov, John W. Lewis, Xue Litai, James F. Person, Charles K. Armstrong, Bruce Cumings, Alexandre Y. Mansourov, Robert A. Scalapino, Chong-Sik Lee, Adrian Buzo, Sydney A. Seiler, Dae-Sook Suh, Hongkoo Han, William Stueck, and B. R. Myers. I had access to the work of these scholars thanks to the University of Washington Library and its extraordinary collection of books on North Korea. I also want to thank Sidney Rittenberg for telling me what Mao thought of Kim Il Sung.

To understand the air war in Korea, I am indebted to the work of Robert Frank Futrell, Conrad C. Crane, Douglas C. Dildy, Warren E. Thompson, Xiaoming Zhang, Igor Seidov, James Salter, John Darrell Sherwood, and Kenneth Werrell. Also helpful were U.S. Air Force veterans from the Korean War, including John Lowery, Jim Sutton, and James K. Thompson.

At the Dwight D. Eisenhower Presidential Library, the archivist Valoise Armstrong located presidential memoranda that astonished Rowe by informing him of Eisenhower's role in Rowe's long struggle to secure his "moolah."

When I first traveled as a *Washington Post* reporter to South Korea, my guide and mentor in Seoul was Don Oberdorfer, a professor at the Paul H. Nitze School of Advanced International Studies at Johns Hopkins University and my former colleague at the *Post*. He took me under his wing, introduced me to important people, and encouraged me to dig into the story of North Korea.

It is also high time for me to thank David Maraniss, whose steady excellence has given me a model to try to follow. For the same reasons, I thank Tom Kizzia, Chip Brown, Bob Woodward, Ted Gup, Michael Getler, David Hoffman, Rick Atkinson, Bill Keller, Joe Lelyveld, Susan Chira, Stephen Engelberg, Ben Bradlee, Leonard Downie, Robert Kaiser, Phil Bennett, Fred Hiatt, Jackson Diehl, Glenn Frankel, Tom Wilkinson, Bill Hamilton, and Donald E. Graham. I also thank Sheila Kowal, an extraordinary reader.

243

ACKNOWLEDGMENTS

To my agent, Raphael Sagalyn, and my editors, Kathryn Court and Tara Singh Carlson, your support and wisdom have been essential.

And, of course, above all, thanks to Jessica, Lucinda, and Arno.

Seattle, 2014

TIME LINE

1905: Japan takes control of Korea

April 15, 1912: Kim Il Sung born near Pyongyang

1920: Kim's family moves to Manchuria to escape the Japanese

1929: Kim expelled from eighth grade and jailed in Manchuria for anti-Japanese activities

1930: After release, Kim, seventeen, joins guerrillas fighting the Japanese

January 10, 1932: No Kum Sok born near Hamhung in northeast Korea

February 18, 1932: Japan tightens grip in Manchuria, creating puppet state

1934: Kim arrested by Chinese Communist partisans in a bloody anti-Korean purge

June 4, 1937: Kim becomes a legend in Korea by leading a guerrilla raid against Japanese police in the Korean border town of Pochonbo

July 7, 1937: Japan declares war on China

1941: Hounded by the Japanese, Kim retreats to the Soviet Far East and joins the Soviet army

August 10, 1945: Japan offers surrender after A-bombs destroy Hiroshima and Nagasaki; Soviet troops enter Korea

August 11, 1945: The United States draws an arbitrary line dividing Korea along the thirty-eighth parallel, creating North and South Korea

August 28, 1945: Soviets stop invasion of Korea at thirty-eighth parallel as Stalin accepts a divided Korea

September 1945: Kim quietly slips back into Korea as a captain in the Soviet army

October 22, 1945: The Soviets introduce Kim in Pyongyang as the new leader of North Korea

February 22, 1948: Sixteen-year-old No attends a speech by Kim and decides to be a "No. 1 Communist" until he can flee the country

January 1949: No's father dies, and his mother becomes a street trader

March 7, 1949: In Moscow, Kim asks Stalin if he can invade South Korea

August 1949: No enrolls at the North Korean Naval Academy, hoping to avoid infantry service

April 1950: Stalin approves Kim's invasion plan and tells him to talk to Mao

June 25, 1950: North Korea invades South Korea

September 15, 1950: MacArthur launches Inchon invasion, cuts Kim's army to pieces

October 1, 1950: No starts flight training in Manchuria

October 13, 1950: For one day, Stalin orders Kim to abandon North Korea because Mao has opted not to fight the Americans; Mao then changes his mind and sends Chinese troops into Korea

October 19, 1950: UN forces occupy Pyongyang

November 1950: First clashes between Chinese and U.S. forces; Kim loses control of war to the Chinese general Peng Dehuai

December 1950: The Chinese push the Americans out of North Korea

January 4, 1951: The Americans flee Seoul for a second time

March 1951: The Americans retake Seoul and fight back to the thirty-eighth parallel

March 1951: No begins MiG training with Soviet pilots

July 8, 1951: Peace talks begin

October 1951: As a new MiG pilot, No encounters Kim at Uiju airfield

November 1951: With air war over MiG Alley raging, No enters combat against Americans, flying a MiG-15

April 1952: The Manchurian sanctuary for Communist aircraft collapses as U.S. fighters secretly cross border

March 5, 1953: Stalin dies, as does the Soviet and Chinese desire to prolong the Korean War

July 27, 1953: Armistice signed; uneasy peace begins

August 1953: Kim stages a show trial of his political enemies, consolidates power, and collects money from the Communist world

September 21, 1953: No Kum Sok takes off in a MiG-15 from North Korea

May 4, 1954: No Kum Sok arrives in San Francisco

NOTES

Introduction: Players and Game

2 **"the sun of mankind and the greatest man"**: Kim Il Sung, *With the Century* (Pyongyang: Foreign Languages Publishing House, 1996), 7:lv.

2 **Kim's government seized and redistributed farmland:** Large landowners held about 60 percent of land in North Korea in 1945. See Robert A. Scalapino and Chong-Sik Lee, *Communism in Korea* (Berkeley: University of California Press, 1972), 1:342n57.

3 **"Younger people throughout North Korea":** "Political Information: Public Opinion and Discontent in North Korea" (U.S. Central Intelligence Group Intelligence Report, Sept. 1947) (declassified Jan. 6, 2001).

3 **"All this proves that we can build":** Kim Il Sung, *Works* (Pyongyang: Foreign Languages Publishing House, 1984), 4:140–41.

4 **"The Americans," he said, "will not risk a big war":** Kathryn Weathersby, "Should We Fear This? Stalin and the Danger of War with America" (working paper 39, Cold War International History Project [CWIHP], Washington, D.C., July 2002), 9–11.

6 **By the end, about 1.2 million soldiers had been killed:** Bethany Lacina and Nils Petter Gleditsch, "Monitoring Trends in Global Combat: A New Dataset of Battle Deaths," *European Journal of Population* (Spring 2005): 154.

6 **"We were bombing with conventional weapons everything that moved":** Jon Halliday, "Air Operations in Korea," in *A Revolutionary War*, ed. William J. Williams (Chicago: Imprint Publications, 1993), 168n64.

6 **A Soviet postwar study of American bomb damage in the North:** Author interview with Kathryn Weathersby, who examined the study in the Soviet Archives in Moscow. Feb. 7, 2013.

6 **the official population of the country declined during the war by 1,311,000:** Nicholas Eberstadt and Judith Banister, *The Population of North Korea* (Berkeley: Institute of East Asian Studies, University of California, 1992), 32. The authors had access to statistics from the North Korean Central Statistics Bureau.

7 **"Over a period of three years or so, we killed off":** Quoted in Richard Rhodes, "Annals of the Cold War: The General and World War II," *New Yorker,* June 19, 1995, 53.

7 **But politicians in Washington found that to be "too horrible":** Quoted in Bruce Cumings, "Korea: Forgotten Nuclear Threats," *Le Monde Diplomatique,* Dec. 2004, citing Curtis LeMay oral history, April 28, 1966, John Foster Dulles oral history collection, Seeley G. Mudd Manuscript Library, Princeton University.

7 **In North Korea's version of history:** In 2013, a decade after historians found overwhelming documentary evidence in the Soviet Archives that Kim Il Sung and Stalin together orchestrated the invasion that started the Korean War, North Korea continued to insist otherwise. "All the facts go to prove the falsity of the U.S. assertion that the Korean War was started with 'southward invasion' by [North Korea]," concluded a dispatch in the official Korean Central News Agency. See "Remarks of Those Who Provoked Korean War Refute Rumor About 'Southward Invasion,'" Korean Central News Agency, June 27, 2013, http://www.kcna.co.jp/item/2013/201306/news27/20130627-18ee.html.

7 **A United Nations commission of inquiry has found that guards in the camps commit "unspeakable atrocities":** United Nations, "Report of the Commission of Inquiry on Human Rights in the Democratic People's Republic of Korea" (summary), Feb. 7, 2014, 12.

8 **"[Our people] have strong anti-U.S. sentiments because they suffered great damage":** *Pyongyang Times,* June 10, 1972, quoted in B. C. Koh, "The War's Impact on the Korean Peninsula," in Williams, *Revolutionary War,* 250.

8 **Schoolchildren are still trained to bayonet dummies of American soldiers:** Associated Press, "In Korea, Learning to Hate U.S. Starts with Children," *USA Today,* June 23, 2012, http://usatoday30.usatoday.com/news/world/story/2012-06-23/north-korea-teaching-hate-united-states/55784168/1.

8 **State media still lie about who invaded whom during the Korean War:** "True Stories About Korean War," *Rodong Sinmun,* July 3, 2013, http://www.rodong.rep.kp/en/index.php?strPageID=SF01_02_01&newsID=2013-07-03-0008&chAction=L.

9 **Outside the stadium on the day of the celebration, a book was on sale:** David Guttenfelder, Instagram image, July 22, 2013, http://instagram.com/p/cGOMm0Aw5l/?modal=true.

9 **"It is still the 1950s in North Korea":** Author interview with Weathersby.

Chapter I: Beginnings

15 **"heralded the dawn of the liberation of Korea":** Kim Il Sung, *With the Century*, 6:165.

15 **Stories spread about his wizardry:** Hongkoo Han, "Wounded Nationalism: The Minsaengdan Incident and Kim Il Sung in Eastern Manchuria" (Ph.D. diss., University of Washington, 1999), 365.

16 **"Looking round the crowd, I found their eyes":** Kim Il Sung, *With the Century*, 6:163.

17 **A confidential American intelligence biography:** "Biographical Sketches of Key Personalities" (Allied Translator and Interpreter Service report, 1952), 90.

17 **"[He] developed very early a preference for the company of people":** Bradley K. Martin, *Under the Loving Care of the Fatherly Leader* (New York: Thomas Dunne Books, 2004), 46.

17 **"Here he was busy running away":** Choe Hyon, quoted in Sydney A. Seiler, *Kim Il Song, 1941–1948: The Creation of a Legend, the Building of a Regime* (Lanham, Md.: University Press of America, 1994), 26.

18 **the Jerusalem of the East:** Donald N. Clark, *Living Dangerously in Korea: The Western Experience, 1900–1950* (Norwalk, Conn.: EastBridge, 2003), 121–22.

18 **the United States, despite a late-nineteenth-century treaty of "amity and commerce":** See Bruce Cumings, *Korea's Place in the Sun* (New York: W. W. Norton, 1997), 142; William Stueck, *The Korean War: An International History* (Princeton, N.J.: Princeton University Press, 1995), 13, 16.

18 **Manchuria became a fertile recruiting ground:** Han, "Wounded Nationalism," 9.

18 **Three years later, he was expelled from middle school:** Dae-Sook Suh, *Kim Il Sung: The North Korean Leader* (New York: Columbia University Press, 1988), 7.

19 **"I believed that revolution in my country would emerge victorious":** Kim Il Sung, *With the Century*, 1:366–7.

19 **"It is his persistence and obstinate will":** Dae-Sook Suh, *Kim Il Sung*, 30, 54.

20 **He was "upper-class," especially when compared with most Koreans:** Author interviews with Kenneth H. Rowe, a.k.a. No Kum Sok, 2013–14.

20 **Four out of five Koreans held menial and unskilled jobs:** Samuel Pao-San Ho, "Colonialism and Development: Korea, Taiwan, and Kwantung," in *The*

Japanese Colonial Empire, 1895–1945, ed. Ramon H. Myers and Mark R. Peattie (Princeton, N.J.: Princeton University Press, 1984), 377.

20 **Food production increased sharply:** Ibid., 379.

20 **most Koreans had none of these services:** Jun Uchida, *Brokers of Empire: Japanese Settler Colonialism in Korea, 1876–1945* (Cambridge, Mass.: Harvard University Asia Center, 2011), 66–74.

20 **On buses, the Japanese forced Koreans to give up their seats:** Ibid., 83.

20 **a "profound gratitude for the limitless benevolence of our Emperor":** Mark R. Peattie, "Japanese Attitudes Toward Colonialism, 1895–1945," in Myers and Peattie, *Japanese Colonial Empire*, 121.

20 **Japan attempted to "blot out an entire culture":** Ibid., 122.

21 **Korea entered the 1940s with the best-managed network of railways, roads, and ports:** Bruce Cumings, "The Legacy of Colonialism," in Myers and Peattie, *Japanese Colonial Empire*, 487.

21 **the "Entrepreneurial King of the Peninsula":** Barbara Molony, *Technology and Investment: The Prewar Japanese Chemical Industry* (Cambridge, Mass.: Council on East Asian Studies, Harvard University, 1990), 156–57.

22 **Baseball blossomed in Korean schools in the 1930s and 1940s:** Joseph A. Reaves, *Taking in a Game: A History of Baseball in Asia* (Lincoln: University of Nebraska Press, 2002), 114–17.

24 **The Japanese put a bounty on Kim Il Sung's head:** Dae-Sook Suh, *Kim Il Sung*, 52.

24 **This obscure racist purge on the eastern fringes of Manchuria—called the Minsaengdan incident:** The most recent source for information about and analysis of the Minsaengdan incident is Hongkoo Han, "Colonial Origins of Juche," in *Origins of North Korea's Juche*, ed. Jae-Jung Suh (Lanham, Md.: Lexington Books, 2013), 33–62. Also see Dae-Sook Suh, *Kim Il Sung*, 32–34; Scalapino and Lee, *Communism in Korea*, 1:168–70, 214–19.

24 **Kim called it a "mad wind":** Kim Il Sung, *With the Century*, 4:27–28.

24 **Chinese partisan leaders operated on the assumption that Koreans in eastern Manchuria were pro-Japanese:** Han, "Colonial Origins of Juche," 38.

25 **"Comrades, stop gambling on people's destinies":** Kim Il Sung, *With the Century*, 4:56–57.

25 **Kim became the preeminent Korean guerrilla leader:** Scalapino and Lee, *Communism in Korea*, 1:214; Dae-Sook Suh, *Kim Il Sung*, 34.

25 **"When the bundles of papers turned into flames":** Kim Il Sung, *With the Century*, 4:328.

25 **a "parental leader":** Han, "Colonial Origins of Juche," 54.

26 **They reportedly killed or captured twenty-seven Japanese officers and soldiers:** Dae-Sook Suh, *Kim Il Sung*, 37.

26 **Kim was indeed an idealistic leader:** Ibid., 46.

26 **"If you do not bring [money, food, and clothing]":** Dae-Sook Suh, *Documents of Korean Communism, 1918–1948* (Princeton, N.J.: Princeton University Press, 1970), 450–51.

27 **Terrorized women began dressing as men:** Scalapino and Lee, *Communism in Korea*, 1:315n4.

27 **Industrial-scale looting began:** Allan R. Millett, *The War for Korea, 1945–1950: A House Burning* (Lawrence: University Press of Kansas, 2005), 49.

29 **Stalin himself ordered the commander of Soviet occupation forces to "strictly observe discipline":** Kathryn Weathersby, "Soviet Policy Toward Korea, 1944–1950" (Ph.D. diss., Indiana University, 1990), 191, cited in Sheila Miyoshi Jager, *Brothers at War: The Unending Conflict in Korea* (New York: W. W. Norton, 2013), 20, 489n16.

Chapter 2: Poodle and Pretender

31 **"please make it so that it appears as though the anti-Japanese partisans participated in the war of liberation":** Quoted in Seiler, *Kim Il Song*, 46, from Lebedev testimony in *Chungang Ilbo*, Aug. 26, 1991.

31 **Kim might have been kept out on direct orders from Stalin:** Ibid.

32 **Kim and his men marked their first night in the fatherland with bowls of noodles:** Yu Song Chol's testimony, first printed in the Korean-language daily *Hanguk Ilbo* in a series that began Nov. 1, 1990, translated into English and available in an appendix to Seiler, *Kim Il Song*, 117.

32 **Kim "simply wanted to hide the truth of his shabby, humble return to Korea":** Ibid.

32 **"General Kim Il Sung returned home in triumph":** Baik Bong, *Kim Il Sung Biography* (Tokyo: Miraisha, 1969), 1:533.

32 **Stalin's investment in Kim began in 1941:** Sergei N. Goncharov, John W. Lewis, and Xue Litai, *Uncertain Partners: Stalin, Mao, and the Korean War* (Palo Alto, Calif.: Stanford University Press, 1993), 131.

33 **the First Battalion of the Eighty-eighth Sniper Brigade:** Kathryn Weathersby, "Dependence and Mistrust: North Korea's Relations with Moscow and the Evolution of Juche" (working paper 08-08, U.S.-Korean Institute, SAIS, Washington, D.C., Dec. 2008), 4.

33 **He was "lean and weak, and his mouth was always open":** Seiler, *Kim Il Song*, 97–98.

33 **He married Kim Jong Suk, a partisan fighter seven years his junior:** Dae-Sook Suh, *Kim Il Sung*, 51.

33 **An official North Korean biography of Kim Jong Il:** *Kim Jong Il Brief History* (Pyongyang: Foreign Languages Publishing House, 1998), 1. http://www.korea-dpr.com/lib/103.pdf.

33 **With the Soviets, Kim finally had time for political and military training:** Goncharov, Lewis, and Xue, *Uncertain Partners*, 131.

33 **At the military base, he was not the highest-ranking Korean:** Yu testimony, in Seiler, *Kim Il Song*, 105.

33 **"No one among us was thinking that Kim Il Sung would become the new leader":** Ibid., 116.

33 **They soon dominated every police and military organization in the North:** Dae-Sook Suh, *Kim Il Sung*, 69.

34 **To speed these appointments, Kim orchestrated boozy banquets for Russian generals:** Yu testimony, in Seiler, *Kim Il Song*, 124.

34 **refusing to change his name from Korean to Japanese:** Andrei Lankov, *From Stalin to Kim Il Sung: The Formation of North Korea, 1945–1960* (New Brunswick, N.J.: Rutgers University Press, 2002), 10–11.

34 **He was also proud and stubborn:** Ibid., 14.

34 **General Lebedev introduced Kim as a national hero and "outstanding guerrilla leader":** Ibid., 19.

35 **Kim had never worn a necktie:** Lim Un, *The Founding of a Dynasty in North Korea: An Authentic Biography of Kim Il-song* (Tokyo: Jiyu-sha, 1982), 144.

35 **"He looked like a callow young man":** Yu testimony, in Seiler, *Kim Il Song*, 124.

35 **"His complexion was slightly dark":** O Yong Jin, *An Eyewitness Report* (Pusan: Kungmin Sasang Chidowan, 1952), 141–43, translated in Scalapino and Lee, *Communism in Korea*, 1:324–25.

36 **Photographs were retouched:** See photographs of Kim Il Sung as reprinted in Scalapino and Lee, *Communism in Korea*, 1:plates 1–2.

36 **They "were dancing with joy and hugging each other":** Baik, *Kim Il Sung Biography*, 2:55–56.

38 **Kim constantly and effusively praised Stalin:** Weathersby, "Dependence and Mistrust," 8–9.

38 **Five weeks after his bumbling performance in Pyongyang:** This account relies on Adam Cathcart and Charles Kraus, "Peripheral Influence: The Sinuiju Student Incident of 1945 and the Impact of Soviet Occupation in North Korea," *Journal of Korean Studies* 13, no. 1 (Fall 2008): 1–28.

40 **"Shooting between our people is not only a disgrace":** Kim Il Sung, *Works*, 1:97.

40 **He told a citizens' assembly that "genuine Communists" could never have shot the young people:** Charles K. Armstrong, *The North Korean Revolution, 1945–1950* (Ithaca, N.Y.: Cornell University Press, 2003), 63.

41 **"Just as an army lacking iron discipline cannot win battles":** Kim Il Sung, *Works*, 2:18, quoted in Cathcart and Kraus, "Peripheral Influence."

41 **About ten thousand soldiers a year were sent to Siberia for training:** Dae-Sook Suh, *Kim Il Sung*, 102.

41 **according to American intelligence reports:** Cathcart and Kraus, "Peripheral Influence," 14, 26n103, citing declassified Central Intelligence Agency reports from 1947.

41 **In 1950, a student pilot taking MiG flight training suddenly disappeared:** Author interviews with No Kum Sok.

42 **The Soviets left behind all the armaments:** Goncharov, Lewis, and Xue, *Uncertain Partners*, 133.

Chapter 3: Sweet-Talking Stalin

48 **There was not a major event in the creation of North Korea that Shtykov did not influence:** See Armstrong, *North Korean Revolution*, 53; Andrei Lankov, "Russia and DPRK at the Beginning," *Korea Times*, Nov. 6, 2006; Jager, *Brothers at War*, 23.

48 **He deliberately downplayed efforts by the United States:** Weathersby, "Should We Fear This?," 5–6.

49 **Shtykov also supported Kim's belief:** Lankov, "Russia and DPRK at the Beginning."

49 **Kim told Shtykov of the personal toll:** Shtykov to Stalin, telegram, Jan. 19, 1950, cited in *CWIHP Bulletin*, no. 5 (Spring 1995): 8, trans. Kathryn Weathersby.

49 **"Lately, I've been feeling very frustrated":** Ibid., trans. Evgeniy P. Bajanov and Natalia Bajanova.

49 **"He thinks that he needs again to visit Comrade Stalin":** Ibid., trans. Weathersby.

49 **the "custodian-in-chief of the Soviet order":** Robert Service, *Stalin: A Biography* (Cambridge, Mass.: Belknap Press of Harvard University Press, 2005), 9.

50 **His principal opponent was the United States:** Robert Gellately, *Stalin's Curse: Battling for Communism in War and Cold War* (New York: Knopf, 2013), 13.

50 **Kim apparently had an outsized appetite:** Yu testimony, in Seiler, *Kim Il Song*, 130; Service, *Stalin*, 79–80, 107, 133. Also Lankov, *From Stalin to Kim Il Sung*, 72n32.

50 **"Comrade Stalin, we believe that the situation makes it necessary":** The quoted conversation between Kim and Stalin on March 7, 1949, is from Evgeniy P. Bajanov and Natalia Bajanova, "The Korean Conflict, 1950–1953: The Most Mysterious War of the 20th Century" (unpublished working paper, CWIHP), 17–19. The authors found the conversation in the Archives of the President of Russia.

52 **"It is impossible to view this operation other than as the beginning of a war":** Politburo message to Shtykov, Sept. 24, 1950, trans. in Kathryn

Weathersby, "To Attack, or Not to Attack? Stalin, Kim Il Sung, and the Prelude to War," *CWIHP Bulletin,* no. 5 (Spring 1995): 8.

52 **"the Americans will certainly move their troops into South Korea":** Weathersby, "Should We Fear This?," 8.

52 **"Such provocations are very dangerous for our interests":** Stalin to Shtykov, telegram, Oct. 30, 1949, cited and trans. in Bajanov and Bajanova, "Korean Conflict," 12.

52 **His pleas produced forty-eight telegrams to the Kremlin:** Kathryn Weathersby, "New Findings on the Korean War," *CWIHP Bulletin,* no. 3 (Fall 1993): 14.

52 **"I understand the unhappiness of Comrade Kim Il Sung":** Stalin to Shtykov, cable, Jan. 30, 1950, Archives of the President of Russia, trans. in Bajanov and Bajanova, "Korean Conflict," 36.

53 **"Explain to Comrade Kim Il Sung":** Stalin to Shtykov, telegram, Feb. 2, 1950, trans. in Bajanov and Bajanova, "Korean Conflict," 37.

53 **In early February, Stalin had approved North Korea's request:** William Stueck, *Rethinking the Korean War* (Princeton, N.J.: Princeton University Press, 2004), 73.

54 **North Korean reconnaissance teams had captured soldiers from the South:** Goncharov, Lewis, and Xue, *Uncertain Partners,* 143.

54 **The North was clearly superior:** Weathersby, "New Findings on the Korean War," 16.

54 **Stalin pledged delivery of more weapons:** The most detailed account of the conversations between Kim and Stalin in April 1950 is found in Bajanov and Bajanova, "Korean Conflict." Also see Shen Zhihua, *Mao, Stalin, and the Korean War: Trilateral Communist Relations in the 1950s,* trans. Neil Silver (London: Routledge, 2012), 122–23.

54 **He wanted to isolate China from any possible deals:** See Stueck, *Rethinking the Korean War,* 76; Shen, *Mao, Stalin, and the Korean War,* 125.

55 **"If you should get kicked in the teeth, I shall not lift a finger":** Goncharov, Lewis, and Xue, *Uncertain Partners,* 145. The quotation comes from the authors' 1992 interview with M. S. Kapitsa, a Soviet official at the meeting with Stalin and Kim.

55 **The American military had quietly pulled out of China:** Bajanov and Bajanova, "Korean Conflict," 40–42.

56 **The defensive perimeter of the United States in the Pacific:** See Weathersby, "Should We Fear This?," 11; Stueck, *Rethinking the Korean War,* 73.

56 **As a result, an estimated thirty-six million Chinese died:** See extensive account of the deaths under Mao in Yang Jisheng, *Tombstone: The Great Chinese Famine, 1958–1962* (New York: Farrar, Straus and Giroux, 2012).

57 **he made fun of the Soviet leader's "mechanical thinking":** Author interview with Sidney Rittenberg, Sept. 10, 2013.

57 **"Had Mao died [in the 1950s]":** Philip Short, *Mao: A Life* (New York: Henry Holt, 257), 629.

57 **"If the need arises, we can quietly send Chinese troops":** Quoted in Shen, *Mao, Stalin, and the Korean War,* 126.

57 **"a number-one pain in the butt":** Author interview with Rittenberg.

58 **Mao broke off the meeting with Kim:** This scene is drawn from ibid., 130; Weathersby, "Should We Fear This?," 12–13; Alexander V. Pantsov, *Mao: The Real Story,* with Steven I. Levine (New York: Simon & Schuster, 2012), 379.

58 **"Comrade Mao Zedong would like to have personal explanations from Comrade Filippov":** Roshchin to Stalin, cable, May 13, 1950, cited in Bajanov and Bajanova, "Korean Conflict," 51.

59 **"Instead of a local operation at Ongjin Peninsula":** Shtykov to Stalin, cable, June 21, 1950, cited in Bajanov and Bajanova, "Korean Conflict," 59–60.

59 **Stalin cabled back the same day:** Stalin's cable to Shtykov, June 21, 1950, cited in Bajanov and Bajanova, 60.

60 **"This war," Kim said on the radio, "is a war of righteousness":** Scalapino and Lee, *Communism in Korea,* 1:397–98n32.

Chapter 4: The Great Liberation Struggle

63 **Three days into the war, nearly 80 percent of the South's army was unaccounted for:** Jager, *Brothers at War,* 71.

64 **"Why heavens you'd see those fellows scuddle up to the Manchurian border":** Bruce Cumings, *Origins of the Korean War* (Princeton, N.J.: Princeton University Press, 1981), 2:692, citing John Allison oral history, April 20, 1969; William Sebald oral history, July 1965, in John Foster Dulles oral history collection, Seeley G. Mudd Manuscript Library, Princeton University.

64 **American soldiers believed officers:** Ibid., 693.

64 **"We've got to stop the sons of bitches":** Robert J. Dvorchak, *Battle for Korea: A History of the Korean Conflict* (Boston: Da Capo, 2003), 9.

64 **After two weeks in Korea, about half of them were dead, wounded, or missing:** Clay Blair, *The Forgotten War* (New York: Doubleday, 1987), 141.

65 **Stalin fretted when the Americans rushed into the war:** See Weathersby, "Should We Fear This?," 16.

65 **Stalin sent a cable in late August to Pyongyang:** Stalin to Kim Il Sung (via Shtykov), cable, Aug. 28, 1950, cited in ibid., 17.

65 **It was undone, in large measure, by Kim's impatience and incompetence as a war planner:** Analysis of Kim's war-planning failure is based on

research by Joseph S. Bermudez, chief analytics officer at AllSource Analysis Inc. Using classified and open source information, Bermudez has studied North Korea for thirty years. Interviewed by author, Nov. 11, 2013.

66 **Desperate for better battlefield leadership, Kim begged Stalin to send Soviet military advisers:** Jager, *Brothers at War*, 79–80, citing cables from Shtykov to Stalin.

66 **A North Korean pilot shot down on the second day of the invasion:** Robert Frank Futrell, *The United States Air Force in Korea, 1950–1953* (Washington, D.C.: U.S. Air Force, 1983), 98.

66 **"The air battle was short and sweet":** Ibid., 102–3.

67 **The purpose of the air campaign, according to Major General Emmett O'Donnell:** Ibid., 186.

67 **The official history of the air force campaign in Korea uses the word "leisurely":** Ibid., 192, 194.

67 **"We didn't have any opposition":** Ibid., 195.

67 **"Their memories of the war overwhelmingly focus on the performance of their aircraft":** Kathryn Weathersby, "Ending the Korean War: Considerations on the Role of History" (working paper 08-07, U.S.-Korean Institute, SAIS, Washington, D.C., Dec. 2008), 8.

67 **In the United Nations, the Soviet Union accused the Americans:** Conrad C. Crane, *American Airpower Strategy in Korea, 1950–1953* (Lawrence: University Press of Kansas, 2000), 43.

68 **The official history noted, too, that the air force always dropped leaflets:** Futrell, *The United States Air Force in Korea*, 198.

68 **"The Far East Air Force Bomber Command":** Futrell, *United States Air Force in Korea*, 195.

70 **After the war, an American bomb damage assessment:** Crane, *American Airpower Strategy*, 168.

72 **"He was a great thundering paradox of a man":** William Manchester, *American Caesar: Douglas MacArthur, 1880–1964* (Boston: Little, Brown, 1978), 3.

72 **During World War I, MacArthur wore riding breeches:** For a compelling description of MacArthur's invasion at Inchon, see David Halberstam, *The Coldest Winter* (New York: Hyperion, 2007), 293–315.

72 **He presented himself to the world, author William Styron wrote:** William Styron, "MacArthur," *New York Review of Books*, Oct. 8, 1964. http://www.nybooks.com/articles/archives/1964/oct/08/macarthur/.

72 **obsequious men who "catered to his peacockery":** Manchester, *American Caesar*, 6.

72 **"MacArthur's temperament was flawed by an egotism":** Ibid.

73 **He was "remarkably economical of human life":** Ibid., 4.

73 **"I can almost hear the ticking of the second hand of destiny":** Douglas MacArthur, *Reminiscences* (New York: McGraw-Hill, 1964), 350. Cited in Halberstam, *Coldest Winter,* 300.

74 **Mao specifically warned of an American attack at Inchon:** Shen Zhihua, "Sino–North Korean Conflict and Its Resolution During the Korean War," *CWIHP Bulletin,* no. 14/15 (Fall 2003–Spring 2004): 10. Also see Goncharov, Lewis, and Xue, *Uncertain Partners,* 171–72.

74 **"We estimate that presently, a U.S. counterattack is not possible":** Shen, "Sino–North Korean Conflict," 11.

74 **"I have never considered retreat":** Ibid.

75 **In late September, Shtykov reported to Stalin that Kim was confused:** Ibid.

75 **"We consider it necessary to report to you about extremely unfavorable conditions":** Bajanov and Bajanova, "Korean Conflict," 77.

75 **"At the moment that the enemy troops cross the thirty-eighth parallel":** Ibid., 78.

76 **To save Kim's government, Stalin told Mao that he should "without delay" dispatch:** Ibid., 97.

Chapter 5: Kicked in the Teeth

79 **As one of his commanders later wrote, the bombing "tormented" the Korean army:** Yu testimony, in Seiler, *Kim Il Song,* 153.

80 **"So what? Let the United States of America be our neighbors in the Far East":** Nikita S. Khrushchev, *The Korean War* (Moscow: Progress Publishing House, 1970), 28, quoted and trans. in Alexandre Y. Mansourov, "Stalin, Mao, Kim, and China's Decision to Enter the Korean War," *CWIHP Bulletin,* no. 6/7 (Winter 1995–96): 100.

80 **"If the American imperialists are victorious":** Shen, *Mao, Stalin, and the Korean War,* 140.

81 **"Well done!" he said. "Excellent!":** Ibid., 160; Goncharov, Lewis, and Xue, *Uncertain Partners,* 185, 279.

81 **Stalin had told Mao back in July that "we will do our best to provide air cover":** Shen, *Mao, Stalin, and the Korean War,* 167.

81 **He expected the Soviet air force to work with the Chinese infantry:** Ibid.

81 **"We asked, 'Can you help with your air force?'" Zhou said later:** Ibid., 165. There is some scholarly dispute about Chinese claims that Stalin refused to provide air cover. Mansourov argues that Stalin's betrayal of Mao was a fiction cooked up by Zhou's staff to make their boss look good. See Mansourov, "Stalin, Mao, Kim, and China's Decision to Enter the Korean War," 105.

81 **Mao's telegram weighed heavily on Stalin:** For a documented account of Kim's day of betrayal, see Mansourov, "Stalin, Mao, Kim, and China's Decision to Enter the Korean War"; Shen, *Mao, Stalin, and the Korean War*, 170–71; Kathryn Weathersby, "The Impact of the Wartime Alliance on Postwar North Korean Foreign Relations" (unpublished paper courtesy of author), 8–11.

82 **"The Chinese have again refused to send troops":** Stalin to Kim Il Sung, cable, Oct. 12, 1950, in Bajanov and Bajanova, "Korean Conflict," 102.

82 **Over the next few hours, Kim reportedly told his closest associates:** Mansourov, "Stalin, Mao, Kim, and China's Decision to Enter the Korean War," 104.

83 **Mao simply could not accept American domination of the entire Korean Peninsula:** Ibid., 104.

83 **"was glad that the final and favorable decision":** Ibid.

84 **Location defined safety in the Korean War:** For analysis of the international dimension of the Korean War, see Stueck, *Korean War*, 348–49.

87 **"There are no long-term plans, and adventurism is all one can see!":** Shen, "Sino–North Korean Conflict," 12.

87 **"He was the type of adventurer who left his fate to contingency and luck":** Lim Un, *Founding of a Dynasty in North Korea*, 183. A few Korea scholars, particularly Bruce Cumings, discount the work of the pseudonymous Lim Un as South Korean propaganda.

88 **Peng's judgment carried enormous weight in Beijing:** See Halberstam's incisive mini-biography of Peng in *Coldest Winter*, 356–59.

88 **"You are just hoping for a quick victory":** Shen, "Sino–North Korean Conflict," 15.

88 **North Korean tanks mistakenly attacked the Chinese:** Ibid., 12.

89 **China soon took control of roads, railways, ports, airports, food storage, and recruitment of men:** Weathersby, "Dependence and Mistrust," 9.

89 **the offensive would "get the boys home by Christmas":** Blair, *Forgotten War*, 433.

89 **the home-by-Christmas offensive "had turned into a bloody nightmare":** Ibid., 502.

90 **When Kim heard the news, he was silent for a moment:** Jager, *Brothers at War*, 127–28, citing An Sung-hwan, "Soviet Military Advisory Group Support to the NKPA, 1946–53," 456.

90 **Its importuning to Moscow was filtered through Beijing:** Ibid.

90 **In his memoirs, Khrushchev wrote that the Soviet ambassador in Pyongyang sent "very tragic reports":** Khrushchev, *Korean War*, 28. Quotation from Goncharov, Lewis, and Xue, *Uncertain Partners*, 191n127, which says the paragraph containing this quotation about Kim is missing from the English edition.

90 **He had been weaned, as the historian Adrian Buzo put it, "in a predatory, political subculture":** Adrian Buzo, *The Guerilla Dynasty* (Boulder, Colo.: Westview Press, 1999), 10.

91 **There, he "attacked almost everybody":** Dae-Sook Suh, *Kim Il Sung*, 122.

91 **When it came time to praise Stalin, he was less the lickspittle:** Weathersby, "Dependence and Mistrust," 8–9.

91 **His official biographer explained the new world according to Kim:** Baik, *Kim Il Sung Biography*, 2:332.

92 **The U.S. Air Force estimated it destroyed 75 percent of the capital:** Crane, *American Airpower Strategy in Korea*, 168n23, citing *Journal of Military History* 62 (April 1968): 366–69; 548th RTS, "Bomb Damage Assessment of Major North Korean Cities."

92 **the North Korean government said every modern building in the city was destroyed:** Charles Armstrong, "The Destruction and Reconstruction of North Korea, 1950–1960," *Asia-Pacific Journal* 8, issue 51, no. 2 (Dec. 20, 2010), http://www.japanfocus.org/-charles_k_-armstrong/3460#sthash.wp9QFc1Z.dpuf.

93 **Almost as soon as No arrived there by train on March 7, 1951:** Date of arrival found in No's declassified Air Intelligence Information Report, Oct. 28, 1953, 2.

93 **Unlike No, they failed to flaunt their dedication to the Great Leader:** Author interview with No and declassified transcript of No's post-defection interview with air force intelligence, Oct. 27, 1953, 22.

94 **In a coded message on November 20, 1950, Stalin promised Kim Il Sung:** Stalin to Kim Il Sung, coded message, Nov. 20, 1950, cited in Bajanov and Bajanova, "Korean Conflict," 84.

95 **ordered the air force "to destroy every means of communication":** Futrell, *United States Air Force in Korea*, 221.

95 **pilots smelled updrafts of "roasting human flesh":** Robert M. Neer, *Napalm: An American Biography* (Cambridge, Mass.: Belknap Press of Harvard University Press, 2013), 76–81.

95 **the stuff was "economical, efficient, and expeditious":** Futrell, *United States Air Force in Korea*, 187.

96 **Firestorms burned the city to the ground:** Xiaoming Zhang, *Red Wings over the Yalu: China, the Soviet Union, and the Air War in Korea* (College Station: Texas A&M University Press, 2002), 89.

96 **In the three devastating months that followed:** Crane, *American Airpower Strategy in Korea*, 65.

96 **"When you've hit a village and have seen it go up in flames":** Ibid.

96 **The Americans dropped more than thirty-two thousand tons of napalm on Korea:** Neer, *Napalm*, 99.

96 **"I have seen, I guess, as much blood and disaster as any living man":** Ibid., 99–100, citing MacArthur's testimony to Senate committees, May 3, 1951.

96 **these neophyte Soviet pilots "began evading and breaking off combat":** Zhang, *Red Wings over the Yalu*, 125.

Chapter 6: MiGs

100 **Two direct hits could bring down an American fighter jet:** Douglas C. Dildy and Warren E. Thompson, *F-86 Sabre vs MiG-15* (Oxford: Osprey, 2013), 27.

100 **MacArthur attributed the change to the murderous rise of the MiG:** Quoted in Crane, *American Airpower Strategy in Korea*, 50.

101 **American claims to the contrary, not a single MiG was lost:** Dildy and Thompson, *F-86 Sabre vs MiG-15*, 56.

101 **It was "one of the most savage and bloody" air battles of the Korean War:** Futrell, *United States Air Force in Korea*, 410–13.

101 **UN pilots counted more than twenty-five hundred of them in the Yalu River corridor:** Ibid., 411.

102 **Colonel Kozhedub's unit painted its MiGs with the colors of North Korea:** See Halliday, "Air Operations in Korea," 152; Zhang, *Red Wings over the Yalu*, 139; author interview with No.

102 **The orders from Stalin were part of a "carefully orchestrated ballet":** See Crane, *American Airpower Strategy in Korea*, 48, quoting Mark O'Neill, a researcher on the Soviet archives.

102 **"a curious case of double deniability":** Shen, *Mao, Stalin, and the Korean War*, 181.

102 **The Soviet air force contributed about seventy thousand pilots, artillery gunners, and technicians:** Weathersby, "Dependence and Mistrust," 10.

103 **"Almost overnight, Communist China has become one of the major air powers of the world":** Futrell, *United States Air Force in Korea*, 412.

103 **they made racist jokes about it:** Joke reported by Polish military attaché Pawel Monat and cited in Scalapino and Lee, *Communism in Korea*, 1:402–3n37.

103 **"We had to sit stewing in our cockpits for hours on end":** Halliday, "Air Operations in Korea," 153.

104 **American generals struggled in 1951 to keep tabs on the whereabouts of Chinese reinforcements:** Crane, *American Airpower Strategy in Korea*, 53.

104 **Chuck Yeager, the legendary American test pilot, called the MiG-15 "a flying booby trap":** Chuck Yeager and Leo Janos, *Yeager: An Autobiography* (New York: Bantam, 1985), 260, 259.

104 **Tom Collins, described it as "a little, light, peashooter machine":** "These U.S.A.F. Pilots Flew the MiG," *Air Intelligence Digest*, Dec. 1953, 8.

104 **Its instruction manual warned that flying for more than ten minutes:** No Kum Sok, *A MiG-15 to Freedom*, with J. Roger Osterholm (Jefferson, N.C.: McFarland, 1996), 102.

105 **The cockpit was an ergonomic horror:** Dildy and Thompson, *F-86 Sabre vs MiG-15*, 28.

105 **"At forty-five thousand feet":** "These U.S.A.F. Pilots Flew the MiG," 9.

106 **At the relatively low speed (for a MiG) of 130 miles an hour:** Ibid.

106 **they never learned about several MiG pilots who bailed out above thirty-three thousand feet:** Ben H. Thompson, "The Story of No Kum Sok," *Air Intelligence Digest*, Jan. 1955, 32.

106 **The majority of them, before coming to the Far East, had spent about three hundred hours:** Dildy and Thompson, *F-86 Sabre vs MiG-15*, 39.

107 **All of them had spent a year and a half with their fighters:** Larry Davis, *Air War over Korea* (Carrollton, Tex.: Squadron/Signal Publications, 1982), 35.

107 **He sent angry telegrams to his air force generals in Manchuria:** Zhang, *Red Wings over the Yalu*, 119.

107 **China's own air force regulations called for at least three hundred hours of flight time:** Ibid., 170.

108 **When the Chinese saw the enemy coming, they fled:** Ibid.

Chapter 7: Return to North Korea

111 **The total number of MiGs in the war:** Dildy and Thompson, *F-86 Sabre vs MiG-15*, 57.

115 **"We were driving Cadillacs while they had Fords":** John Darrell Sherwood, *Officers in Flight Suits* (New York: New York University Press, 1996), 75.

116 **"The best [pilots] from both sides sparred and dueled, fought and killed":** Dildy and Thompson, *F-86 Sabre vs MiG-15*, 5.

117 **It was quite a show, and each performance consisted of three acts:** Yu testimony, in Seiler, *Kim Il Song*, 168.

118 **He had become well known in the Soviet Far East:** Lankov, *From Stalin to Kim Il Sung*, 139. This section on Ho Kai draws heavily on Lankov's research.

118 **He was accomplished enough to become the second-ranking official:** Ibid., 141.

119 **Working with Kim, Ho was involved in early planning for the invasion of South Korea:** Ibid., 146–47.

119 **"Ho Kai was not only the closest cooperator of Kim Il Sung":** Lim, *Founding of a Dynasty in North Korea*, 215.

119 **He criticized Ho for denying membership to toiling pleasants:** Baik, *Kim Il Sung Biography*, 2:370.

119 **His crimes were called "closed-doorism":** Lankov, *From Stalin to Kim Il Sung*, 148.

120 **A politician who wanted Ho's job took the document directly to Kim:** The politician was Pak Chang Ok. See Yu testimony, in Seiler, *Kim Il Song*, 168.

120 **Kim accused him of "bureaucratism":** Lankov, *From Stalin to Kim Il Sung*, 149.

120 **he was being punished, in part, because he had been skeptical about "excessive praise":** Ibid., 150.

120 **"His body lay in the small bed of his son":** Ibid., 152.

121 **Ho's wife, who was outside Pyongyang:** Ibid.

121 **An air force reconnaissance aircraft reported on November 10, 1951:** Kenneth P. Werrell, *Sabres over MiG Alley* (Annapolis, Md.: Naval Institute Press, 2013), 210.

123 **The raid's toll, as measured by destroyed aircraft:** Futrell, *United States Air Force in Korea*, 415.

123 **More robust American efforts to wreck Uiju airfield and blow up its MiGs would soon begin:** Ibid., 416.

Chapter 8: An International Sporting Event

127 **A final accounting of the air war:** These numbers come from Dildy and Thompson, *F-86 Sabre vs MiG-15*, 62, 73.

128 **One pilot had a heart attack after landing:** Igor Seidov, *Red Devils over the Yalu: A Chronicle of Soviet Aerial Operations in the Korean War, 1950–53* (West Midlands, U.K.: Helion, 2014), 304–5.

129 **Many others refused to fly, claiming chronic battle fatigue:** Dildy and Thompson, *F-86 Sabre vs MiG-15*, 64.

129 **By the final year of the war, Sabre pilots could plainly see that many MiG pilots were "pitifully incompetent":** Futrell, *United States Air Force in Korea*, 654.

129 **An air force intelligence report noted:** Ibid.

131 **In the first six months of 1952:** Werrell, *Sabres over MiG Alley*, 130.

131 **"We shot them down in the landing pattern":** Walker M. Mahurin, *Honest John: The Autobiography of Walker M. Mahurin* (New York: Putnam, 1962), 84.

131 **"We just couldn't let anything incriminating get away":** Ibid.

131 **"The air war was a fluid encounter":** Walter J. Boyne, "The Forgotten War," *Air Force Magazine*, June 2000, http://www.airforcemag.com/Magazine Archive/Pages/2000/Jun%202000/0600korea.aspx.

132 **On this subject, MacArthur had been categorical:** Futrell, *United States Air Force in Korea*, 221.

132 **The air force commander in East Asia, General Stratemeyer:** Ibid., 377–78.

132 **"One day the six of us [pilots] were summoned to Fifth Air Force Headquarters":** Mahurin interview in 1997 with Secrets of War, http://acepilots .com/korea_mahurin.html; a similar version of this story is in Mahurin, *Honest John*, 88–89.

133 **"I'm determined to get a MiG as are most of the boys around here":** Letters of Major Thomas Sellers to his wife, quoted in Crane, *American Airpower Strategy in Korea*, 166–67.

133 **His posthumous Silver Star citation said he died inside North Korea:** Ibid.

133 **After interviewing fifty-four Sabre pilots who fought in the war:** Werrell, *Sabres over MiG Alley*, 129.

133 **the war "began to disappear from consciousness":** Bruce Cumings, *The Korean War* (New York: Modern Library, 2011), 63.

133 **When a Sabre downed a MiG, it was often front-page news:** Crane, *American Airpower Strategy in Korea*, 162.

134 **"If you shoot down five planes you join a group":** James Salter, *The Hunters* (1956; New York: Vintage Books, 1999), 134.

134 **"There were no other values. It was like money":** Ibid., 62–63.

134 **The "overriding philosophy was that if you weren't having accidents you weren't training realistically":** John Lowery, *Life in the Wild Blue Yonder* (North Charleston, S.C.: CreateSpace, 2013), 3.

134 **"Welcome to Nellis AFB, men":** Robert Holland, "Memories of Nellis," *Sabre Jet Classics* 13, no. 2 (Summer 2005), http://sabre-pilots.org/classics/ v132nellis.

135 **The Sabre was "the vehicle in which the new aces of the jet age were achieving stardom":** T. R. Milton, "Robinson Risner: The Indispensable Ingredient," in *Makers of the United States Air Force*, ed. John L. Frisbee (Washington, D.C.: Office of Air Force History, U.S. Air Force, 1987), 312–13.

135 **"The one thing that never left me was the intense, gripping anxiety and excitement":** Frederick C. Blesse, *Check Six: A Fighter Pilot Looks Back* (Mesa, Ariz.: Champlin Fighter Museum Press, 1987), 65, cited in Sherwood, *Officers in Flight Suits*, 91n95.

135 **Four out of five of the aces with thirteen or more "victories" died violently:** Werrell, *Sabres over MiG Alley*, 144–45. Werrell's book provides an excellent analysis of aces and their eagerness to risk everything and violate the Manchurian sanctuary.

135 **As many as twenty-five of the thirty-nine aces flew into Manchuria:** Ibid., 132–33.

136 **"I could pick, say, eighteen who could actually be depended upon":** Mahurin, *Honest John*, 31.

136 **"Over the past year of negotiations we have virtually curtailed military operations":** Kim Il Sung to Stalin via the Soviet embassy in Pyongyang, telegram, July 16, 1952, trans. in Kathryn Weathersby, "New Russian Documents," *CWIHP Bulletin*, no. 6/7 (Winter 1995/1996): 77.

137 **Characterized in an official U.S. Air Force history as "savage":** Futrell, *United States Air Force in Korea*, 517.

137 **So they launched Operation Pressure Pump:** Crane, *American Airpower Strategy in Korea*, 122–23; Futrell, *United States Air Force in Korea*, 517.

138 **Mao wanted the war to continue—and so did Stalin:** This argument and archival evidence for it are gathered in Kathryn Weathersby, "North Korea and the Armistice Negotiations," http://www.koreanwar.com/conference/conference_contents/contents/text/04_kathryn_weathersby.pdf.

138 **Stalin also found value in the war:** See Weathersby's analysis in "Stalin, Mao, and the End of the Korean War," in *Brothers in Arms: The Rise and Fall of the Sino-Soviet Alliance, 1945–1963*, ed. Odd Arne Westad (Washington, D.C.: Woodrow Wilson Center Press, 1998), 110.

138 **an end to the war "is highly disadvantageous to us":** Mao to Kim Il Sung, telegram, July 18, 1952, trans. in Weathersby, "New Russian Documents," 78.

138 **Mao said, the war "limits the mobility of the main forces of American imperialism":** Ibid.

138 **"This war is getting on America's nerves":** Conversation between Stalin and Zhou Enlai, Aug. 20, 1952, trans. Danny Rozas and Kathryn Weathersby, *CWIHP Bulletin*, no. 6/7 (Winter 1995/1996), 12.

139 **"Every American soldier is a speculator":** Ibid., 13.

139 **his third and final visit with Stalin** "Russian Documents on the Korean War: 1950–53," *CWIHP Bulletin*, no. 14/15 (Fall 2003–Spring 2004): 378.

140 **"It is necessary to send already trained air force bomber units":** Kim to Mao, telegram, July 16, 1952, History and Public Policy Program Digital Archive, 90–93, http://digitalarchive.wilsoncenter.org/document/113642.

Chapter 9: Attack Maps and Defection Bribes

145 **The North Koreans "should not be launching either strategic or tactical offensives":** Conversation between Stalin and Zhou Enlai, 13.

145 **"The Korean people look up to Marshal Stalin as to the sun":** Editorial, "The Boundless Gratitude of the Korean People Toward Marshal Stalin," *Rodong Sinmun*, May 22, 1952, 1, quoted in Scalapino and Lee, *Communism in North Korea*, 1:434.

146 **"In his revolutionary activities and entire career":** "The People's Love and Respect for the Leader," *Rodong Sinmun*, Apr. 1, 1952, 1, quoted in Scalapino and Lee, *Communism in Korea*, 1:428.

146 **"The focus on Kim became ever more conspicuous":** Ibid.

146 **"Kim's failure to unify Korea militarily gave rise to a conviction":** Dae-Sook Suh, *Kim Il Sung*, 127.

147 **The plot to overthrow Kim leaned heavily on the skills of officers from the institute:** See ibid., 128–30. This account is based on information that came out in 1953 at a trial. The facts might well have been invented by Kim's government, but Suh accepts the basic outline of the plot as real.

149 **Zhou Enlai "urgently proposed that the Soviet side assist the speeding up" of armistice talks:** Foreign Ministry of the U.S.S.R., "On the Korean War, 1950–53, and the Armistice Negotiations," trans. in "From the Russian Archive," *CWIHP Bulletin,* no. 3 (Fall 1993): 17.

150 **A meeting was proposed between the new Soviet premier:** See Jager, *Brothers at War,* 275.

150 **"The ardent heart of the great leader":** Kim Il Sung, "Stalin Is the Inspiration for the Peoples Struggling for Their Freedom and Independence," *Rodong Sinmun,* March 10, 1953, 1, repr. and trans. in Scalapino and Lee, *Communism in Korea,* 1:434.

151 **the fields that grew it could be classified as "war materiel":** Futrell, *United States Air Force in Korea,* 667.

151 **"Attacks on the irrigation dams":** Air University Quarterly Review staff, "The Attack on the Irrigation Dams in North Korea," *Air University Quarterly Review* 6, no. 4 (1953): 42.

151 **"The damage done by the deluge":** See Futrell, *United States Air Force in Korea,* 669; Crane, *American Airpower Strategy in Korea,* 163.

152 **"field after field of young rice":** See Futrell, *United States Air Force in Korea,* 669n78.

152 **Each MiG that the Americans shot down received more coverage:** Crane, *American Airpower Strategy in Korea,* 162.

152 **They called it Operation Moolah:** "Fat Offer," *Time,* May 11, 1953.

152 **General Mark W. Clark, commander of U.S. forces:** Mark W. Clark, *From the Danube to the Yalu* (New York: Harper & Brothers, 1954), 205–8.

153 **"He wouldn't have any worries the rest of his life":** Herbert A. Friedman, "Operation Moolah: The Plot to Steal a MiG-15," Psywarrior, http://www.psywarrior.com/Moolah.html.

153 **Russian pilots in Manchuria "felt they were not respected":** Alan K. Abner, *Psywarriors: Psychological Warfare During the Korean War* (Shippensburg, Pa.: Burd Street Press, 2001), 71.

153 **"disillusionment with the way [their] proposal had been distorted":** Ibid., 73.

153 **He told North Korean pilots to "strengthen their discipline and protect their equipment":** Futrell, *United States Air Force in Korea,* 653.

153 **"These pilots flew far fewer missions":** Mark W. Clark, *From the Danube to the Yalu*, 208.

154 **An air force analysis found "no positive information":** Crane, *American Airpower Strategy in Korea*, 194n22.

154 **What General Clark described as "our most spectacular psychological warfare exploit":** Clark, 205.

Chapter 10: Uncle Yoo

157 **"blaze of glory":** Futrell, *United States Air Force in Korea*, 683.

162 **"[He] believed his allies owed him":** Weathersby, "North Korea and the Armistice Negotiations," 93.

162 **North Korea vacuumed up more short- and long-term aid:** See Charles K. Armstrong, "'Fraternal Socialism': The International Reconstruction of North Korea, 1953–62," *Cold War History* 5, no. 2 (May 2005): 165; Erik van Ree, "The Limits of Juche: North Korea's Dependence on Soviet Industrial Aid, 1953–76," *Journal of Communist Studies* 5, no. 1 (March 1989): 57–58.

162 **China's no-strings aid to the North in 1954:** Shen Zhihua and Yafeng Xia, "China and the Postwar Reconstruction of North Korea, 1953–61" (working paper 4, North Korea International Documentation Project, Woodrow Wilson International Center for Scholars, May 2012), 7.

162 **"The Korean people are brave":** Ibid., 39–40.

163 **the "fundamental calculations are based not on the maximal use of domestic resources":** S. P. Suzdalev to the Soviet leadership, telegram, Aug. 7, 1953, cited and trans. in Weathersby, "North Korea and the Armistice Negotiations," 91n55.

Chapter 11: Flying Clear

169 **He needed to find, expose, and destroy a "wicked spy clique":** Baik, *Kim Il Sung Biography*, 2:388.

170 **Their confessions implicated Eisenhower in fantastic schemes "to topple the Party and the State":** Ibid., 393.

170 **"We must bear deeply in mind that if these factional elements are left alone":** Ibid., 389.

170 **Arrests of "anti-party traitors" had begun:** Dae-Sook Suh, *Kim Il Sung*, 130.

171 **He was on vacation in Tokyo:** Ibid., 132.

171 **"Any notion of plausibility seems to have deserted the scriptwriters":** Lankov, *From Stalin to Kim Il Sung*, 95–96.

171 **"I am a running dog of American imperialism":** Ibid., 96.

171 **He pleaded guilty to the absurd charge:** Dae-Sook Suh, *Kim Il Sung*, 132.

171 **"Although he called himself a Communist":** Lankov, *From Stalin to Kim Il Sung*, 96. The trial coverage quoted in Lankov comes from a detailed

account of the proceedings found in Kim Nam-sik, *Namnodang yongu* (Seoul: Tol Pegae, 1984), 480–506.

171 **"I am grateful for having been provided with an advocate":** Lankov, *From Stalin to Kim Il Sung,* 97.

172 **"To have successfully fought U.S. imperialism":** Baik, *Kim Il Sung Biography,* 2:393.

173 **Eighty MiGs in wooden crates had been smuggled:** J. L. Keiper, "Mig-15 Lands at Kimpo," *Friends Journal: The Air Force Museum Foundation Magazine,* Summer 2006, 12–14.

173 **One of these planes was later described as "ridden hard and put away wet":** Ibid., 13.

179 **It was so busy during daylight hours:** Wilfred M. Husted to Air Force Museum Foundation, Nov. 2, 2002. Husted worked in the control tower at Kimpo Air Force Base when No Kum Sok landed.

179 **"The perceived threat after the war had not changed":** Author interview with John Lowery (June 3, 2013), a combat pilot in Korea and Vietnam, as well as the author of *Life in the Wild Blue Yonder: Jet Fighter Pilot Stories from the Cold War* (North Charleston, S.C.: CreateSpace, 2013). Some details in this chapter draw on a chapter in that book titled "Escape to Freedom."

180 **"There is somebody landing the wrong way":** Author interview with Jim Sutton, a Sabre pilot who was on a landing approach to Kimpo at the moment when No Kum Sok landed. Sutton heard Williams shout over the radio. Dec. 15, 2013.

181 **American airmen were watching him with their fingers on the triggers:** Keiper, "Mig-15 Lands at Kimpo," 12.

181 **"I saw this jet coming in upwind":** "Former Red Airman, Yank Reunited," *Buffalo-Courier Express,* Feb. 25, 1956, 16.

182 **"The flier pulled out the picture of a girl":** Associated Press, "Red MiG Flies to U.S. Base; Pilot Quizzed," *Chicago Tribune,* Sept. 21, 1953, 1.

183 **The night before, at a sumptuous Kremlin dinner:** "Russia Will Provide Cash, Technical Aid to Rebuild North Korea," *Toronto Globe and Mail,* Sept. 21, 1953, 1.

183 **"The glorious Korean people have written a new and wonderful page":** "New Epoch in Far East; Mr. Malenkov on Korea Symbol," *Times* (London), Sept. 21, 1953, 8.

183 **In response, Kim thanked the Soviets:** "M. Malenkov Condemns U.S. Policy in Far East," *Times of India,* Sept. 21, 1953, 1.

184 **General Wang Yong, the top commander of the North Korean air force:** "Russ Heads Red Korea Air Force, Refugee Says," *Los Angeles Times,* June 23, 1955, 18. A United Press dispatch from Seoul reported that a newly arrived

defector, Captain Lee Un Yong, told American intelligence officers of the demotion of General Wang Yong and said it was due to No Kum Sok's defection.

184 **Soon after No shut down the engine on his MiG:** Associated Press, "Red MiG Flies to U.S. Base; Pilot Quizzed," 1.

184 **The Associated Press reported that an "Allied officer revealed":** Associated Press, "MiG Jet Flown to Allies May Be Reds' Latest Model," *Washington Post*, Sept. 22, 1953, 1.

184 **A MiG certainly would not approach the vital air base:** Associated Press, "Red MiG Flies to U.S. Base; Pilot Quizzed," 1.

185 **They did not realize what was in their midst:** Lowery, *Life in the Wild Blue Yonder*, 79; author interviews with Lowery and Sutton.

185 **Only then did the air base spring into action:** E-mail to the author from James K. Thompson, a Sabre pilot at Kimpo when the MiG landed. June 4, 2013.

185 **Dutifully, Husted said nothing:** Husted to Air Force Museum Foundation, Nov. 2, 2002.

186 **One of his commanders, General Earle E. Partridge, called him "a one-man war":** Michael E. Haas, *In the Devil's Shadow: U.N. Special Operations During the Korean War* (Annapolis, Md.: Naval Institute Press, 2186), 78.

186 **He had arrived in Korea in 1946:** Donald Nichols, *How Many Times Can I Die? Autobiography of Donald Nichols* (Brooksville, Fla.: Brooksville Printing, 1981).

186 **He controlled more than six hundred agents on both sides of the border:** Haas, *In the Devil's Shadow*, 78.

186 **Nichols lured—and later interrogated—the North Korean air force pilot:** Nichols, *How Many Times Can I Die?*, 124.

189 **Nichols personally wrote the report on No's initial interrogation:** Donald Nichols, Air Intelligence Information Report, Ro [*sic*] Kum Sok, North Korean People's Army Air Force, Sept. 24, 1953, 6. USAF Intl. Repts., 1942–64, AF 59786-597495, box 1793, 631/52/54/5; AF 592236, box 1758, 631/52/53/6, National Archives, College Park, Md.

189 **"Even after becoming full-fledged MiG-15 pilots":** Ibid., 4.

189 **No also explained the odd, erratic, and seemingly cowardly behavior:** Ibid., 46.

190 **No was asked why a lone MiG pilot:** Ibid.

Chapter 12: Squeezing the Moolah

194 **They authorized the air force to announce in Washington:** "Reward to Be Paid, Air Force Says," *New York Times*, Sept. 22, 1953, 3.

194 **Air force headquarters also sent a message to its Far East Command:** "U.S. Will Return MiG to 'Owner'; Withdraws Reward Offer in Korea," *New York Times*, Sept. 25, 1953, 1.

194 **"I realize that the recommendations sent to me:** Eisenhower to Smith, Sept. 21, 1953, Korea 1953 (1), International Series, Dwight D. Eisenhower: Papers as President, Eisenhower Presidential Library.

195 **The president wrote that if MIGs "start coming in to us by the hundreds":** Ibid.

195 **"We are not anxious to have this one":** Ibid.

195 **the United States could "stand before the world as very honorable people":** Ibid.

196 **transform his wrecked country into "a glorious socialist power":** Baik, *Kim Il Sung Biography*, 2:425.

196 **New factories . . . began churning out diesel motors:** Van Ree, "Limits of Juche," 57.

197 **"Comrade Kim Il Sung, with his unbounded love for the country and the people":** Baik, *Kim Il Sung Biography*, 2:435.

197 **He wanted it done fast, a blitzkrieg to industrial modernity:** Ibid., 426.

197 **"Reconstruction was, in a sense, war by other means":** Armstrong, "Fraternal Socialism," 168.

197 **His first three-year plan made no mention of building paved roads:** Balázs Szalontai, *Kim Il Sung in the Khrushchev Era: Soviet DPRK Relations and the Roots of North Korean Despotism, 1953–1964* (Washington, D.C.: Woodrow Wilson Center Press, 2005), 59.

198 **"It is a quite common scene that 6–8 women are dragging the plow":** Ibid., 63.

198 **In a foretaste of what would become North Korea's chronic "eating problem":** Ibid., 69.

200 **No replied, "Yes, they do, and they are preparing for it":** Greg MacGregor, "Pilot Says Reds Expect War," *New York Times*, Sept. 23, 1953, 3.

200 **He also said Kim Il Sung's government continued:** Reuters, "New Planes Flown into N. Korea, What Pilot Saw: Why He Came," *Manchester Guardian*, Sept. 23, 1953, 1.

200 **What "startled reporters" most at the press conference:** Victor Kendrick, "Runaway Pilot Says Reds Preparing to Resume War," United Press, *The Daily Notes* (Canonsburg, Pa.), Sept. 22, 1953, 1.

200 **"After a pause and alternately grinning and wetting his dry lips":** MacGregor, "Pilot Says Reds Expect War."

200 **"She is somewhere in South Korea":** Reuters, "New Planes Flown into N. Korea, What Pilot Saw."

201 **"He was most cooperative and in no way obnoxious":** Jack H. Bristow, Air Intelligence Information Report No. C-1717-G, 6004th Air Intelligence Service Squadron (n.d.), 1.

202 **Boyd's briefing covered these points:** Yeager and Janos, *Yeager*, 259–60; *Operation Moolah: A MiG-15 Reunion*, video with Tom Collins and No Kum Sok (a.k.a. Kenneth Rowe), Network Group, Sept. 1994.

202 **"I want Tom to be the first one to fly it":** *Operation Moolah: A MiG-15 Reunion.*

202 **Yeager, who hated to be second at anything, groaned:** Ibid., video remembrances of Collins. An alternate version of this story, found in Yeager and Janos, *Yeager*, 261, says that Collins and Yeager flipped a coin to see who would fly first and Collins won.

203 **Smith explained that he would "try to arrange to have the pilot reject the $100,000":** Smith to Eisenhower, memorandum, Sept. 23, 1953, Dulles-Herter Series, Eisenhower: Papers as President.

203 **Eisenhower scribbled at the bottom, "Now we're clicking":** Ibid.

204 **No's handler called himself Andy Brown:** This sketch of Arseny Yankovsky's life is drawn from interviews with Kenneth Rowe; David Wise, *Mole Hunt* (New York: Random House, 1992); Joseph J. Trento, *The Secret History of the CIA* (New York: Carroll & Graf, 2001), 110–16.

205 **After the polygraph, he settled into a grueling routine of interrogation:** "The Handling of North Korean Defector, No Kum Sok," History of 6002nd Intelligence Service Group, Jan.–June 1954, K-GP-Intel-6002-HI, 1.

206 **His control of the throttle "was very smooth":** Ben Thompson, "The Story of No Kum Sok," *Air Intelligence Digest*, Feb. 1955, 21.

Chapter 13: Right Stuff and Fake Stuff

210 **"No!" Yeager said. "Dr. Mach is very old and has a beard":** This encounter is described in detail by Collins in *Operation Moolah* and separately by Kenneth Rowe (a.k.a. No Kum Sok) in interviews.

211 **He had "been taken under the wing":** United Press, "MiG-15 Tested at Okinawa," *New York Times*, Oct. 3, 1953, 17.

211 **"The Koreans probably lost more pilots spinning than from American guns":** Yeager and Janos, *Yeager*, 260.

211 **"Frankly, we lost our guts and didn't spin it":** "These USAF Pilots Flew the MiG," *Air Intelligence Digest*, vol. 6, no. 12, Dec. 1953, 9.

211 **"The airplane was buffeting very bad":** Ibid., 10.

212 **Yeager could not see anything when the MiG "started pulling out":** Yeager and Janos, *Yeager*, 263; Collins, *Operation Moolah*.

212 **the plane's "handling qualities and Mach number limitations":** "These USAF Pilots Flew the MiG," 6.

213 **"We are not engaged in the revolution of another country":** Baik, *Kim Il Sung Biography*, 2:479.

213 **The Great Leader could be quite specific about what *juche* meant:** Yuk-Sa Li, ed., *Juche! The Speeches and Writings of Kim Il Sung* (New York: Grossman, 1972), 157.

213 *juche* **became an "assumption that Korea is the center of the world:** Cumings, *Korea's Place in the Sun*, 404.

213 **a "jumble of banalities" that is dull, evasive, and hard to understand:** B. R. Myers, *The Cleanest Race: How North Koreans See Themselves and Why It Matters* (Brooklyn: Melville House, 2010), 46–47.

214 **At that time, aid and loans from socialist countries financed more than 80 percent of the country's imports:** Van Ree, "Limits of Juche," 57–58.

214 **about half of the output from North Korean heavy industry was made possible by aid from Moscow:** Ibid., 69.

215 **Two days after No landed the MiG at Kimpo, Eisenhower told his secretary of state:** Memorandum of conversation with the president, Sept. 23, 1953; Meetings with the President 1953, White House Memoranda Series, John Foster Dulles Papers, Eisenhower Library.

215 **Then Dulles received a telephone call from Secretary of Defense Charles Wilson:** Memorandum of telephone conversations, prepared in the secretary of state's office, Oct. 9, 1953, Korean files, box 54, Dulles Papers, Eisenhower Library.

215 **"The press has displayed continued interest in the payment":** Ibid.

215 **Dulles conceded the point:** Ibid.

217 **"His reading and writing ability in English was good":** "Handling of North Korean Defector, No Kum Sok," 1.

218 **"I Flew My MiG to Freedom":** No Kum Sok, "I Flew My MiG to Freedom," with Martin L. Gross, *Saturday Evening Post*, Oct. 9, 1954, 19, Oct. 16, 1954, 36.

218 **No arrived in San Francisco on May 4, 1954:** Universal newsreel, vol. 27, no. 567, May 6, 1954, MCA/Universal Pictures Collection, 1929–1967, National Archives, College Park, Md.

218 **"Looking like an American Joe College in sports clothes":** Associated Press, "Pilot Who Stole MiG Will Aid South Korea," *Los Angeles Times*, May 5, 1954, 19.

Chapter 14: Learning and Purging

219 **Its luster was eventually lost to scandals:** Terence O'Hara, "Allbrittons, Riggs to Pay Victims of Pinochet," *Washington Post*, Feb. 26, 2005, A1; Timothy L. O'Brien, "At Riggs Bank, a Tangled Path Led to Scandal," *New York Times*, July 19, 2004.

220 **Kim told reporters that No had "asked for a lawyer":** Associated Press, "Ex-MiG Pilot Arrives in Washington," *Washington Post*, May 6, 1954, 3.

221 **Kim also told the press that whatever money remained:** Ibid.

222 **"He lived up well to the 'No' part of his name":** Associated Press, "Korean Who Delivered MiG for $100,000 Starts as Delaware University Freshman," *New York Times*, Sept. 18, 1954, 3.

223 **"Little Stalins" were being elbowed out of power:** See Andrei Lankov, *Crisis in North Korea: The Failure of De-Stalinization* (Honolulu: University of Hawaii Press, 2005). This book is a detailed, well-sourced account of Kim's defeat of reform in the 1950s and establishment of what Lankov calls "national Stalinism."

223 **In every Eastern bloc country except Albania:** Szalontai, *Kim Il Sung in the Khrushchev Era*, 80.

223 **"Everything is decided by Kim Il Sung alone":** "Report by N. T. Fedorenko on a Meeting with DPRK Ambassador to the U.S.S.R. Li Sang Jo, 29 May 1956," cited in James F. Person, "New Evidence on North Korea in 1956," *CWIHP Bulletin*, no. 16 (Spring 2008): 471.

223 **Reality was indeed grim:** Szalontai, *Kim Il Sung in the Khrushchev Era*, 65.

223 **"When the participants of the revolutionary movement in Korea":** "Report by N. T. Fedorenko on a Meeting with DPRK Ambassador to the U.S.S.R. Li Sang Jo, 29 May 1956," Cited in Person, "New Evidence on North Korea," 477.

224 **The party's Central Committee scolded Kim:** Lankov, *Crisis in North Korea*, 77–78.

224 **He conceded the "correctness of the comradely advice":** Person, "New Evidence on North Korea in 1956," 448.

224 **Yi said that he and other disgruntled cadre members would use "sharp and decisive criticism within the party":** Yi Pil Gyu, "Memorandum of Conversation with the Head of the Department of Construction Materials Under the Cabinet of Ministers," July 20, 1956, cited in Person, "New Evidence on North Korea in 1956," 479.

224 **The Soviet diplomat had told a Hungarian colleague:** Szalontai, *Kim Il Sung in the Khrushchev Era*, 72.

225 **As Kim's official biographer explained:** Baik, *Kim Il Sung Biography*, 2:550–551.

225 **Mao "began to complain about Kim Il Sung":** Lankov, *Crisis in North Korea*, 138. Lankov quotes from his interview with V. V. Kovyzhenko, a Korea specialist for the Soviet Union who traveled to Pyongyang in 1956 with the joint delegation that criticized Kim. Lankov cautions that Kovyzhenko did not attend the meeting with Mao when the Chinese leader supposedly said these words.

226 **As he later told an Albanian diplomat, "Mikoyan and Peng Dehuai":** Husan Alimerko (Albanian ambassador to North Korea), "Memorandum of Conversation Between Kim and Myftiu Manush," Oct. 4, 1961, trans. Enkel Daljani, cited in James F. Person, "'We Need Help from Outside': The North Korean Opposition Movement of 1956" (working paper 52, CWIHP, Washington, D.C., Aug. 2006), 2.

226 **But Kim reneged on a promise:** "Memorandum of Conversation Between Soviet Chargé d'Affaires V. I. Ivanov and Chinese Charge d'Affaires Chao Ke Xian," Oct. 26, 1956, cited in Person, "'We Need Help from Outside,'" 82.

227 **The North Korean People's Army had made sure of that:** Person, "New Evidence on North Korea in 1956," 460.

227 **The Great Leader could not have been more pleased:** Ibid.

227 **"Those who [had] the intention":** Person, "'We Need Help from Outside,'" 2.

Epilogue

232 **suspected of being "hostile and reactionary elements":** Lankov, *Crisis in North Korea,* citing Soviet archival record of a 1959 conversation between the diplomat V. I. Pelishenko and Pang Hak Se, minister of interior under Kim, 182.

233 **Hundreds of thousands of "wrong thinkers" and their families:** David Hawk, *The Hidden Gulag,* 2nd ed. (Washington, D.C.: Committee for Human Rights in North Korea, 2012), 25.

233 **Guards have license to murder, rape, starve, and torture prisoners:** See ibid.; Blaine Harden, *Escape from Camp 14* (New York: Viking, 2012); Kang Chol-hwan and Pierre Rigoulot, *The Aquariums of Pyongyang* (New York: Basic Books, 2001); Kim Yong, *Long Road Home* (New York: Columbia University Press, 2009).

233 **Kim also created a caste system:** Robert Collins, "Marked for Life: Sungbun, North Korea's Social Classification System" (Committee for Human Rights in North Korea, Washington, D.C., 2012), http://www.hrnk.org/uploads/pdfs/HRNK_Songbun_Web.pdf.

233 **This forced labor was tacked on:** Szalontai, *Kim Il Sung in the Khrushchev Era,* 121.

233 **Cartoonish histories of Kim and his partisans in Manchuria became required texts:** Lankov, *Crisis in North Korea,* 205.

234 **An estimated thirty-four thousand monuments:** Don Oberdorfer, *The Two Koreas* (New York: Basic Books, 2001), 20.

234 **He had at least five palaces:** Ibid.

234 **When he traveled, his aides brought along a special toilet:** Ibid.

234 **emotional and intellectual lives around "burning loyalty to the Leader":** Lankov, *From Stalin to Kim Il Sung,* 70–71.

234 **The growth, called a *hok* in Korean:** Bruce Cumings, *North Korea: Another Country* (New York: New Press, 2003), xii.

235 **"I have never seen a public figure so fat":** Sidney Rittenberg and Amanda Bennett, *The Man Who Stayed Behind* (New York: Simon & Schuster, 1993), 245–46.

235 **He ordered the killing of his uncle Jang Song Thaek for "dreaming different dreams":** "Report on Enlarged Meeting of Political Bureau of Central Committee of WPK," Korean Central News Agency, Dec. 8, 2013.

235 **calling for "absolute trust, single-minded unity, and monolithic leadership":** Ruediger Frank, "Some Thoughts on the North Korean Parliamentary Election of 2014," *38 North* (blog), March 14, 2014, http://38north.org/2014/03/rfrank031414/.

235 **"The United States and other hostile forces, ignoring our magnanimity and goodwill":** "North Korea Leader Warns of 'Very Grave' Situation," Agence France-Presse, Apr. 2, 2014.

236 **the U.S. Air Force responded by flying nuclear-capable B-2 stealth bombers:** Jethro Mullen, "U.S. Says It Sent B-2 Stealth Bombers over South Korea," CNN, March 28, 2013, http://www.cnn.com/2013/03/28/world/asia/korea-us-b2-flights/.

240 **"I thought everything was going well":** Gene Rector, "Father of Man in Apparent Murder-Suicide Defected with MiG After Korean War," *Macon Telegraph*, Sept. 24, 2008, 1.

BIBLIOGRAPHY

Abner, Alan K. *Psywarriors: Psychological Warfare During the Korean War.* Shippensburg, Pa.: Burd Street Press, 2001.

Armstrong, Charles K. "The Destruction and Reconstruction of North Korea, 1950–1960." *Asia-Pacific Journal* 8, issue 51, no. 2 (Dec. 20, 2010). http://www.japanfocus.org/-charles_k_-armstrong/3460#sthash.wp9QFc1Z.dpuf.

———. "'Fraternal Socialism': The International Reconstruction of North Korea, 1953–62." *Cold War History* 5, no. 2 (May 2005): 165.

———. *The North Korean Revolution, 1945–1950.* Ithaca, N.Y.: Cornell University Press, 2003.

Baik Bong. *Kim Il Sung Biography.* Vols. 1–2. Tokyo: Miraisha, 1969.

Bajanov, Evgeniy P., and Natalia Bajanova. "The Korean Conflict, 1950–1953: The Most Mysterious War of the 20th Century—Based on Secret Soviet Archives." Unpublished manuscript.

Blair, Clay. *The Forgotten War.* New York: Doubleday, 1987.

Buzo, Adrian. *The Guerilla Dynasty: Politics and Leadership in North Korea.* Boulder, Colo.: Westview Press, 1999.

Cathcart, Adam, and Charles Kraus. "Peripheral Influence: The Sinuiju Student Incident of 1945 and the Impact of Soviet Occupation in North Korea." *Journal of Korean Studies* 13, no. 1 (Fall 2008): 1–28.

Clark, Donald N. *Living Dangerously in Korea: The Western Experience, 1900–1950.* Norwalk, Conn.: EastBridge, 2003.

Clark, Mark W. *From the Danube to the Yalu.* New York: Harper & Brothers, 1954.

Collins, Robert. "Marked for Life: Sungbun, North Korea's Social Classification System." Washington, D.C.: Committee for Human Rights in North Korea, 2012. http://www.hrnk.org/uploads/pdfs/HRNK_Songbun_Web.pdf.

Crane, Conrad C. *American Airpower Strategy in Korea, 1950–1953.* Lawrence: University Press of Kansas, 2000.

Cumings, Bruce. *The Korean War.* New York: Modern Library, 2011.

———. *Korea's Place in the Sun.* New York: W. W. Norton, 1997.

———. *North Korea, Another Country.* New York: New Press, 2003.

———. *Origins of the Korean War.* 2 vols. Princeton, N.J.: Princeton University Press, 1981.

Davis, Larry. *Air War over Korea.* Carrollton, Tex.: Squadron/Signal Publications, 1982.

Dean, William F. *General Dean's Story.* New York: Viking, 1954.

Dildy, Douglas C., and Warren E. Thompson. *F-86 Sabre vs. MiG-15: Korea, 1950–53.* Oxford: Osprey, 2013.

Eberstadt, Nicholas, and Judith Banister. *The Population of North Korea.* Berkeley: Institute of East Asian Studies, University of California, 1992.

Everest, Frank K. *The Fastest Man Alive.* New York: Pyramid Books, 1959.

Futrell, Robert Frank. *The United States Air Force in Korea, 1950–1953.* Washington, D.C.: U.S. Air Force, 1983.

Gellately, Robert. *Stalin's Curse: Battling for Communism in War and Cold War.* New York: Knopf, 2013.

Goncharov, Sergei N., John W. Lewis, and Xue Litai. *Uncertain Partners: Stalin, Mao, and the Korean War.* Palo Alto, Calif.: Stanford University Press, 1993.

Haas, Michael E. *In the Devil's Shadow: U.N. Special Operations During the Korean War.* Annapolis, Md.: Naval Institute Press, 2000.

Haggard, Stephan, and Marcus Noland. *Famine in North Korea: Markets, Aid, and Reform.* New York: Columbia University Press, 2007.

Halberstam, David. *The Coldest Winter.* New York: Hyperion, 2007.

Han, Hongkoo. "Wounded Nationalism: The Minsaengdan Incident and Kim Il Sung in Eastern Manchuria." Ph.D. diss., University of Washington, 1999.

———. "The Handling of North Korean Defector, No Kum Sok." History of 6002nd Intelligence Service Group, Jan.–June 1954, K-GP-Intel-6002-HI, 1.

Harden, Blaine. *Escape from Camp 14: One Man's Extraordinary Odyssey from North Korea to Freedom in the West.* New York: Viking, 2012.

Hastings, Max. *The Korean War.* New York: Touchstone, 1987.

Hawk, David. *The Hidden Gulag.* 2nd ed. Washington, D.C.: Committee for Human Rights in North Korea, 2012.

Jager, Sheila Miyoshi. *Brothers at War: The Unending Conflict in Korea.* New York: W. W. Norton, 2013.

Kang Chol-hwan and Pierre Rigoulot. *The Aquariums of Pyongyang.* New York: Basic Books, 2001.

Kim Il Sung. *With the Century.* Vols. 1–7. Pyongyang: Foreign Languages Publishing House, 1996.

———. *Works.* Vols. 1–46. Pyongyang: Foreign Languages Publishing House, 1984.

Kim Yong. *Long Road Home.* New York: Columbia University Press, 2009.

Korean Bar Association. *2008 White Paper on Human Rights in North Korea.* Seoul: Korean Bar Association, 2008.

Lankov, Andrei. *Crisis in North Korea: The Failure of De-Stalinization.* Honolulu: University of Hawaii Press, 2005.

———. *From Stalin to Kim Il Sung: The Formation of North Korea, 1945–1960.* New Brunswick, N.J.: Rutgers University Press, 2002.

———. *The Real North Korea: Life and Politics in the Failed Stalinist Utopia.* New York: Oxford University Press, 2013.

Lim Un. *The Founding of a Dynasty in North Korea: An Authentic Biography of Kim Il-song.* Tokyo: Jiyu-sha, 1982.

Lowery, John. *Life in the Wild Blue Yonder.* North Charleston, S.C.: CreateSpace, 2013.

Mahurin, Walker M. *Honest John: The Autobiography of Walker M. Mahurin.* New York: Putnam, 1962.

Manchester, William. *American Caesar: Douglas MacArthur, 1880–1964.* Boston: Little, Brown, 1978.

Mansourov, Alexandre Y. "Stalin, Mao, Kim, and China's Decision to Enter the Korean War." *CWIHP Bulletin,* no. 6/7 (Winter 1995–96). http://www.wilson center.org/sites/default/files/CWIHP_Bulletin_6-7.pdf.

Martin, Bradley K. *Under the Loving Care of the Fatherly Leader.* New York: Thomas Dunne Books, 2004.

Millett, Allan R. *The War for Korea, 1945–1950: A House Burning.* Lawrence: University Press of Kansas, 2005.

Molony, Barbara. *Technology and Investment: The Prewar Japanese Chemical Industry.* Cambridge, Mass.: Council on East Asian Studies, Harvard University, 1990.

Myers, B. R. *The Cleanest Race: How North Koreans See Themselves and Why It Matters.* Brooklyn: Melville House, 2010.

Myers, Ramon H., and Mark R. Peattie, eds. *The Japanese Colonial Empire, 1895–1945.* Princeton, N.J.: Princeton University Press, 1984.

Neer, Robert M. *Napalm: An American Biography.* Cambridge, Mass.: Belknap Press of Harvard University Press, 2013.

Nichols, Donald. *How Many Times Can I Die? Autobiography of Donald Nichols.* Brooksville, Fla.: Brooksville Printing, 1981.

No Kum Sok. "I Flew My MiG to Freedom." With Martin L. Gross. *Saturday Evening Post,* Oct. 9, 1954; Oct. 16, 1954.

——. *A MiG-15 to Freedom.* With J. Roger Osterholm. Jefferson, N.C.: McFarland, 1996.

Oberdorfer, Don. *The Two Koreas.* New York: Basic Books, 2001.

Pantsov, Alexander V. *Mao: The Real Story.* With Steven I. Levine. New York: Simon & Schuster, 2012.

Person, James F. "New Evidence on North Korea in 1956." *CWIHP Bulletin,* no. 16 (Spring 2008). http://www.wilsoncenter.org/sites/default/files/CWIHPBulletin16_p51.pdf.

Reaves, Joseph A. *Taking in a Game: A History of Baseball in Asia.* Lincoln: University of Nebraska Press, 2002.

Ree, Erik van. "The Limits of Juche: North Korea's Dependence on Soviet Industrial Aid, 1953–76." *Journal of Communist Studies* 5, no. 1 (March 1989): 57–58.

Rittenberg, Sidney, and Amanda Bennett. *The Man Who Stayed Behind.* New York: Simon & Schuster, 1993.

Salter, James. *The Hunters.* New York: Vintage Books, 1999.

Scalapino, Robert, and Chong-Sik Lee. *Communism in Korea.* 2 vols. Berkeley: University of California Press, 1972.

Seidov, Igor. *Red Devils over the Yalu: A Chronicle of Soviet Aerial Operations in the Korean War, 1950–53.* West Midlands: Helion, 2014.

Seiler, Sydney A. *Kim Il Song, 1941–1948: The Creation of a Legend, the Building of a Regime.* Lanham, Md.: University Press of America, 1994.

Service, Robert. *Stalin: A Biography.* Cambridge, Mass.: Belknap Press of Harvard University Press, 2005.

Shen Zhihua. *Mao, Stalin, and the Korean War: Trilateral Communist Relations in the 1950s.* Translated by Neil Silver. London: Routledge, 2012.

——. "Sino–North Korean Conflict and Its Resolution During the Korean War." *CWIHP Bulletin,* no. 14/15 (Fall 2003–Spring 2004). http://www.wilsoncenter.org/sites/default/files/CWIHPBulletin14-15_tableofcontents_0.pdf.

Shen Zhihua and Yafeng Xia. "China and the Postwar Reconstruction of North Korea, 1953–61." Working paper 4, North Korea International Documentation Project, Woodrow Wilson International Center for Scholars, May 2012. http://www.wilsoncenter.org/sites/default/files/NKIDP_Working_Paper_4_China_and_the_Postwar_Reconstruction_of_North_Korea.pdf.

Sherwood, John Darrell. *Officers in Flight Suits.* New York: New York University Press, 1996.

Short, Philip. *Mao: A Life.* New York: Henry Holt, 2000.

Stueck, William. *The Korean War: An International History.* Princeton, N.J.: Princeton University Press, 1995.

——. *Rethinking the Korean War.* Princeton, N.J.: Princeton University Press, 2004.

Suh, Dae-Sook. *Documents of Korean Communism, 1918–1948.* Princeton, N.J.: Princeton University Press, 1970.

——. *Kim Il Sung: The North Korean Leader.* New York: Columbia University Press, 1988.

Suh, Jae-Jung, ed. *Origins of North Korea's Juche.* Lanham, Md.: Lexington Books, 2013.

Szalontai, Balázs. *Kim Il Sung in the Khrushchev Era: Soviet-DPRK Relations and the Roots of North Korean Despotism, 1953–1964.* Washington, D.C.: Woodrow Wilson Center Press, 2005.

"These USAF Pilots Flew the MiG." *Air Intelligence Digest,* Dec. 1953, 6–11.

Thompson, Ben, "The Story of No Kum Sok." *Air Intelligence Digest,* Sept. 1954, 28–34; Oct. 1954, 36–41; Jan. 1955, 32–36; Feb. 1955, 20–22.

Trento, Joseph J. *The Secret History of the CIA.* New York: Carroll & Graf, 2001.

"12 Minutes to Freedom: The Story Told by the North Korean Pilot Who Flew from Sunan to Seoul." *Air Intelligence Digest,* Nov. 1953, 32–37.

Uchida, Jun. *Brokers of Empire: Japanese Settler Colonialism in Korea, 1876–1945.* Cambridge, Mass.: Harvard University Asia Center, 2011.

United Nations. *Report of the Commission of Inquiry on Human Rights in the Democratic People's Republic of Korea,* Feb. 7, 2014. http://www.ohchr.org/EN/HR Bodies/HRC/CoIDPRK/Pages/ReportoftheCommissionofInquiryDPRK.aspx.

U.S. Air Force. Declassified Air Intelligence Information Report on Ro Kum Sok and Other Interrogation Documents, 1953–54. RG 341 USAF Intl. Repts., 1942–64, AF 59786-597495, box 1793, 631/52/54/5; AF 592236, box 1758, 631/52/53/6, National Archives, College Park, Md.

U.S. Air Force Directorate of Intelligence. "Maintenance of Falcon." *Air Intelligence Digest,* Feb. 1955, 6–15.

Weathersby, Kathryn. "Dependence and Mistrust: North Korea's Relations with Moscow and the Evolution of Juche." Working paper 08-08, Dec. 2008. U.S.-Korean Institute at the Johns Hopkins School of Advanced International Studies. http://uskoreainstitute.org/wp-content/uploads/2010/09/USKI-WP08-8.pdf.

——. "Ending the Korean War: Considerations on the Role of History." Working paper 08-07, Dec. 2008. U.S.-Korean Institute at the Johns Hopkins School of Advanced International Studies. http://uskoreainstitute.org/wp-content/uploads/2010/02/USKI-WP08-07.pdf.

——. "The Impact of the Wartime Alliance on Postwar North Korean Foreign Relations." Unpublished paper courtesy of author.

——. "New Findings on the Korean War." *CWIHP Bulletin,* no. 3 (Fall 1993). http://www.wilsoncenter.org/sites/default/files/ACF1BD.pdf.

——. "North Korea and the Armistice Negotiations." http://www.koreanwar.com/conference/conference_contents/contents/text/04_kathryn_weathersby.pdf.

———. "Should We Fear This? Stalin and the Danger of War with America." Working paper 39, July 2002. Cold War International History Project, Woodrow Wilson International Center for Scholars, Washington, D.C. http://www.wilsoncenter.org/sites/default/files/ACFAEF.pdf.

Werrell, Kenneth P. *Sabres over MiG Alley*. Annapolis, Md.: Naval Institute Press, 2013.

Williams, William J., ed. *A Revolutionary War: Korea and the Transformation of the Postwar World*. Chicago: Imprint Publications, 1993.

Wise, David. *Mole Hunt*. New York: Random House, 1992.

Yang Jisheng. *Tombstone: The Great Chinese Famine, 1958–1962*. New York: Farrar, Straus and Giroux, 2012.

Yeager, Chuck, and Leo Janos. *Yeager: An Autobiography*. New York: Bantam, 1985.

Zhang, Xiaoming. *Red Wings over the Yalu: China, the Soviet Union, and the Air War in Korea*. College Station: Texas A&M University Press, 2002.

INDEX

INDEX